YOUR PERFECT RIGHT

NINTH EDITION

YOUR PERFECT RIGHT

NINTH EDITION

Assertiveness and Equality
In Your Life and Relationships

Robert Alberti, Ph.D.
Michael Emmons, Ph.D.

Impact Publishers®

ATASCADERO, CALIFORNIA

158.2
ALB

Editions
First Edition, October, 1970; Second Edition, January, 1974;
Third Edition, May, 1978; Fourth Edition, April 1982;
Fifth Edition, July 1986; Sixth Edition, October, 1990; Seventh Edition, October
1995; Eighth Edition, April 2001; Ninth Edition, February 2008
Copyright © 1970, 1974, 1978, 1982, 1986, 1990, 1995, 2001, 2008
by Robert E. Alberti and Michael L. Emmons

ATTENTION ORGANIZATIONS AND CORPORATIONS:
This book is available at quantity discounts on bulk purchases for educational,
business, or sales promotional use. For further information, please contact Impact
Publishers, P.O. Box 6016, Atascadero, CA 93423-6016, Phone: 1-800-246-7228,
e-mail: sales@impactpublishers.com

Library of Congress Cataloging-in-Publication Data

Alberti, Robert E.
  Your perfect right : assertiveness and equality in your life and relationships /
Robert E. Alberti and Michael L. Emmons. — 9th ed.
    p. cm.
  Includes bibliographical references and index.
  ISBN-13: 978-1-886230-86-6 (cloth : alk. paper)
  ISBN-13: 978-1-886230-85-9 (pbk. : alk. paper)
1. Assertiveness (Psychology) 2. Interpersonal communication. I. Emmons,
Michael L. II. Title.
BF575.A85A43 2008
158.2—dc 22

                                                        2007046897

Mixed Sources

Product group from well-managed
forests and other controlled sources
www.fsc.org Cert no. SW-COC-002283
© 1996 Forest Stewardship Council

FSC

Impact Publishers and colophon are registered trademarks of Impact Publishers, Inc.

Cover design by Gayle Downs, Gayle Force Design, Atascadero, California
Typesetting by UB Communications, Parsippany, New Jersey
Printed in the United States of America on acid-free, recycled paper
Published by *Impact ✇ Publishers*®
            POST OFFICE BOX 6016
    ATASCADERO, CALIFORNIA 93423-6016
        www.impactpublishers.com

Contents

Acknowledgements   vii

PART I: YOU AND YOUR PERFECT RIGHT

1. Assertiveness and You   1

2. Are You Assertive Now?   11

3. Keep Track of Your Growth   17

PART II: DISCOVERING ASSERTIVENESS

4. Whose Perfect Right?   23

5. What It Means to Be Assertive   37

6. "Can You Give Me an Example?"   52

PART III: BECOMING ASSERTIVE

7. Set Goals for Yourself   59

8. It's Not What You Say, It's How You Say It!   69

9. Assertive Messages — Twenty-First Century Style   89

10. Thinking Assertively   100

11. There's Nothing to Be Afraid Of   113

12. It's a Skill You Can Learn   130

13. Take It One Step at a Time   137

PART IV: BUILDING ASSERTIVE RELATIONSHIPS

14. Assertiveness Builds Equal Relationships   145

15. All in the Family: Assertiveness for Parents,
    Children, and Seniors   159

16. Assertiveness, Intimacy, and Sexuality   167

PART V: APPLYING YOUR ASSERTIVENESS

17. Anger Is Not a Four-Letter Word   185

18. Must We Put Up with Put-Downs?   207

19. Assertiveness Works at Work Too   214

20. Dealing with Difficult People   229

PART VI: LIVING AN ASSERTIVE LIFE

21. Deciding When to Be Assertive — or Not   237

22. When Assertiveness Doesn't Work   244

23. Helping Others Deal with the New Assertive You   251

24. Beyond Assertiveness   259

Appendix: Assertiveness Practice Situations   273

References and Further Reading   283

Online Resources of Interest   289

Index   291

Acknowledgements

Nine editions, nearly a million-and-a-half copies in print, editions in more than twenty languages, lots of glowing feedback . . . it's very rewarding to know our work may have touched so many lives. We're as humbled as we are honored that so many readers, reviewers, therapists, and others have found value in these pages over the last four decades.

And, of course, we didn't accomplish this alone. Hundreds — perhaps thousands — of colleagues, known and unknown, in psychology and the other human service professions have contributed to this book with their honest critiques, support, praise, and recommendation to clients. We are very grateful to know that you consider this the best of the many books on the subject of assertiveness, and one of the best of all self-help books. (Blush.) We hope this ninth edition will continue to serve as a valuable resource to your clients.

Many, many people have contributed to our knowledge and to the success of *Your Perfect Right* over the last four decades. As we attempt to thank those who have made direct contributions, we're bound to miss a few. Please accept our apologies if you're not mentioned here. It's not because we don't appreciate your help; it's because we're not perfect. Special thanks go to Nancy Austin, Albert Ellis (deceased), Kay Emmons, Cyril Franks, Carol

Geer, W. Harold Grant, Chuck Hillinger, Arnold Lazarus, Lachlan MacDonald, Carita and Charles Merker (deceased), Stanlee Phelps, all our friends at Research Press (in part because they didn't publish it), Mike Serber (deceased), Janet Wolfe, Joseph Wolpe (deceased), and the dedicated staff at Impact Publishers over the years.

Finally, Bob wants to add a very special recognition to Deborah Alberti, for five decades of support and loving partnership. Michael would like to acknowledge his wife, Janet, for her role in helping him translate the lessons of assertiveness into their everyday encounters while parenting, working, and loving.

R.E.A.
M.L.E.

Atascadero and San Luis Obispo, California
February 2008

1

Assertiveness and You

Be fair with others,
but then keep after them
until they're fair with you.
— ALAN ALDA

D O YOU LIKE BEN & JERRY'S ICE CREAM? Maybe "Chunky Monkey" or "Chubby Hubby" or "Cherry Garcia" or "White Russian"? (Hey, B&J, whatever happened to White Russian, anyway?)

OK, it's a trick question. Who *doesn't* like rich, premium ice cream? (Except, of course, for those unlucky folks who are lactose intolerant.) We ask because there's an interesting story behind Ben & Jerry's success in becoming a national — now international — brand.

In 1984, after Ben and Jerry had built up an enviable reputation in the New England states for their rich "homemade" product, featuring Vermont cows on the label, they came close to extinction. It was about that time that Ben & Jerry's ice cream really began to get noticed. So much so, in fact, that Pillsbury, the parent company of Häagen-Dazs ice cream, began to tell its resellers they could not carry Ben & Jerry's if they wanted to sell Häagen-Dazs. And, as you might guess, Pillsbury's clout scared Ben & Jerry's grocery outlets; most of them were ready to give up "Vermont's finest."

Fortunately for ice cream lovers everywhere, however, Ben & Jerry's was not intimidated. In addition to antitrust legal action, they began a publicity campaign, under the slogan "What's the Doughboy Afraid Of?" With leaflets, t-shirts, and bumper stickers, the Ben & Jerry's team kept up the PR pressure, while the top-flight Boston legal counsel they engaged kept the antitrust negotiations on the front burner. After a year of lawsuits, countersuits, and priceless national publicity, the dispute was settled out of court, and Ben & Jerry's became a premium ice cream brand to be reckoned with. (If you'd like to follow up the Ben & Jerry's story, get a copy of *Ben & Jerry's: The Inside Scoop* by Fred "Chico" Lager.)

Now, let's be clear: this is not a book about ice cream, or about antitrust law suits, or even about David vs. Goliath. (Well, maybe a *little* about David and Goliath.) We're not offering a "Charles Atlas" approach to punching out the guy who kicks sand in your face. Nor will you learn techniques for pushing to the front of the line or even winning a lawsuit. If you're looking for lessons in how to manipulate others, you're reading the wrong book. We believe there's too much of that in the world already.

Our purpose here is to encourage people — like you — to stand up for themselves — just as Ben Cohen and Jerry Greenfield did with Pillsbury back in the 1980s. And the straightforward process we've developed over four decades will help you do just that. We advise *assertiveness* as a tool for making your relationships more *equal* — for avoiding the one-down feeling that often comes when you fail to express what you really want. This approach to human relationships *honors everyone*, helping underdogs to level the playing field and express themselves *while respecting the rights of others*. What's more, it works as well for conveying your positive feelings as it does for standing your ground.

So, How Does It Work?

The process itself is pretty straightforward. We'll teach you some basic principles, give you some examples, and present a series of specific procedures for you to follow. Your job — if you decide to try this approach — is to read carefully and carry out the steps we've outlined.

Sound like a lot of work? It's not really. It just takes persistence and a determination to make your life better!

Here's another example of what we're talking about:

> Caitlin looked at her watch — 7:15. Sean would be furious, or worried sick, she knew. Her boss had appeared at Caitlin's desk at 4:55 and asked her to get this report ready for the board meeting at 8:15 in the morning. It wasn't the first time . . .

Feelings of anger, confusion, and helplessness can result from situations like these. What can you do? How can you express your feelings when such frustrations come up? There are no *easy* answers, but there are answers, if you are willing to make the effort. It may require that you make some changes in your life.

Changing yourself is challenging, but you can do it, and we'll show you how. This book offers you a proven step-by-step method — generally called *assertiveness training* — for improving your relationships with others. If you follow it, we're confident it can work for you. Millions of folks have learned to express themselves more effectively and achieve more of their life goals using these procedures.

Incidentally, you may be amazed to learn — as we were when the research was published — that our brains contain a remarkable system of neural networks that have a major influence on our social behavior. It's only in the last decade or so that neuroscientists have discovered some of the key patterns. They're important to our ability to express our social emotions effectively.

ASSERTIVENESS AND YOUR BRAIN

A ton of research on brain development and function has appeared in the last eight or ten years. It turns out, researchers tell us, that one's capacity for effective social relationships develops very early in life and becomes virtually "hardwired" via neural pathways in the brain. Psychologists these days refer to those characteristics that we're more or less born with as "temperament" — very close to what used to be loosely referred to as "personality."

These "social intelligence" brain patterns focus mostly on two themes:

❖ *sensitivity to the feelings of others* (e.g., the ability to detect and empathize with the feelings of others), and

❖ *behavioral skills for responding appropriately* to those feelings (e.g., social skills)

Those response patterns established early on in the brain are hard to change, but they *can* be changed. That means everyone can learn more effective personal expressiveness. It also means you'll need to take into consideration your own temperament and learning style.

Those for whom *sensitivity to the feelings of others* is central will need to develop their ability to recognize signals (social cues) from others and to discover how to *detect* and *understand* the needs, feelings, and behavior of other people. (Interestingly, psychologists did a great deal of work in that area even before the brain patterns were measurable; back in the 1960s and 1970s, we called it "sensitivity training.")

Those who need to learn *behavioral skills for responding appropriately* to others' feelings will find that assertiveness — the skill you'll be learning about in this book — is central to one's repertoire of social skills.

The brain research on social relationships is new, very exciting, ongoing, and very complex. We'll have more to say about this work throughout the book.

WHO NEEDS IT?

Jeanette was really upset when her neighbor came over and talked nonstop for forty-five minutes about neighborhood gossip. Mostly, she was upset with herself for letting it happen . . . again.

Is this stuff mainly for those — like Jeanette — who aren't able to stand up for themselves? Only partly. We wrote the first edition of this book (in 1970) for folks who have that trouble, but we've learned a lot over the years, and one thing we now know is that *everyone* needs a hand at times in getting along better with others.

If you're like most of us, your personal power is diminished every day — at home, on the job, at school, in stores and restaurants, in club meetings — in ways both trivial and important. Many people find themselves at a loss for just the right action.

How do you handle it when:

❖ you want to cut short a telephone sales pitch?

❖ a co-worker puts you down?

❖ your spouse gives you a dirty look?

❖ a neighbor blasts his stereo until 3 a.m.?

❖ one of your children snaps at you?

Are you able to express warm, positive feelings to another person? Are you comfortable starting a conversation with strangers at a party? Do you sometimes feel ineffective in making your desires clear to others? Do you have difficulty saying no to persuasive people? Are you often at the bottom of the "pecking order," pushed around by others? Or maybe you're the one who pushes others around to get your way?

At times like these we all need "survival tactics" — ways to respond that let others know something's wrong. Some folks swallow their feelings, say nothing, and remain upset. Others blast the offender with a punishing, put-down response.

> *Assertiveness is a tool for making your relationships more equal.*

We think there's a better way. We endorse *equality* as a style. Not "getting your way." Not "getting back at" the other person. And not "turning the other cheek." We think the important thing is to *affirm self-worth* — both yours and the other person's.

Although there's no one "right way" to handle such events, there are some basic principles that will help you to gain confidence and effectiveness in your relationships with others. You're going to learn those principles as you read this book. You'll discover how to develop and use tactics that are fair, leaving both parties with their self-respect intact.

You don't have to intimidate others in order to avoid being intimidated. And you don't have to allow anybody to push you around. By learning to be effectively *assertive*, you can deal with such upsets directly and honestly and keep everyone on an equal footing — most of the time, anyway.

The sidebar on the next page identifies more of the kinds of everyday situations we're talking about.

The Assertive Alternative

> *Travis and Linda were not sure if the waiter had forgotten them, was ignoring them, or was simply very busy. He had not been at their table for at least fifteen minutes. And they had theater tickets...*

Assertiveness is an alternative to personal powerlessness or manipulation. You'll find in this book a program that will help you develop effective ways to express yourself, maintain your self-respect, *and* show respect for others. We firmly believe in the equal worth of every human being, and this book celebrates that belief and encourages positive relationships between persons who respect and value each other.

There are lots of popular ideas you may have heard about what it means to be assertive. We don't agree with most of them!

Common Situations Calling for Assertiveness

❖ You'd like your partner to initiate intimacy more often.

❖ You're tired of family arguments at the dinner table.

❖ You want your adult children to visit more often.

❖ You object to the way your doctor's office patronizes older patients.

❖ Your roommate has guests in too often and too late for your comfort.

❖ You've received an email that sounds like a put-down, but you're not sure.

❖ A co-worker is too nosy about your personal life.

❖ Your boss makes unreasonable demands on your time.

❖ You know about illegal practices in your workplace.

❖ Your professional association takes political stands you don't agree with.

❖ You are very upset about a recent decision of your local school board.

❖ Your employer doesn't pay equal wages to men and women for the same work.

❖ Your auto mechanic has done work you did not authorize.

❖ Your landlord refuses to make needed repairs to your apartment.

❖ Your neighbors have loud parties lasting until the wee hours.

❖ Patrons in your local movie theater often talk loudly during films.

❖ You know a neighbor's child has been bullying your youngster.

❖ You've seen others cheating in your college courses.

❖ As a teacher, you want your students to improve classroom discipline.

❖ You'd like to be able to express praise and affection openly.

❖ Your child is being bullied after school.

❖ You have a hard time refusing to do favors and accept invitations.

❖ When asked for a personal opinion, you usually say, "I don't care."

❖ On the highway, you find yourself frequently cursing at other drivers.

❖ You're afraid to show your anger.

❖ You have trouble asking for service in restaurants.

❖ Salespeople intimidate you into buying things you don't want.

An old Ziggy cartoon, for example, illustrates the unfortunate image that many hold. We find our hero walking up to a door labeled "Assertiveness Training Class." Below that sign is another: "Don't bother to knock, barge right in!" (You can probably guess our view: *barging in is not being assertive!*)

Over the years there have been other popular books that talk about "assertiveness" as a technique for getting your way. That's *not* our goal. As we've said, you won't find gimmicks on how to manipulate others in this book. We advocate a less aggressive view of self-expression and have tried to correct that false concept of assertiveness. We'll help you to clarify your personal goals in relationships, and we'll show you how to retain a sense of control, a sense of power in your own life, without trying to control others in the process.

Aggression and assertiveness are commonly confused, but they are distinctly different. Aggressiveness means "me first," pushing others around, denying their rights. As you'll learn in the pages to come, assertiveness reflects genuine concern for *everybody's* rights.

Here's our definition of healthy assertiveness:

> *Assertive self-expression is direct, firm, positive — and when necessary persistent — action intended to promote equality in person-to-person relationships. Assertiveness enables us to act in our own best interests, to stand up for ourselves without undue anxiety, to exercise personal rights without denying the rights of others, and to express our feelings (e.g., affection, love, friendship, disappointment, annoyance, anger, regret, sorrow) honestly and comfortably.*

Confronted with a difficult situation, lots of folks tend to respond nonassertively, thinking of an appropriate comeback long after the opportunity has passed. Others react aggressively and make a deep and negative impression that they often regret later. By developing a more adequate repertoire of assertive behavior, you'll be able to choose appropriate and self-fulfilling responses in a variety of situations.

WHAT GETS IN THE WAY OF SELF-EXPRESSION?

In helping thousands of persons learn to value themselves and to express themselves directly and honestly, we have found three particularly difficult barriers to self-assertion:

❖ Many people don't *believe they have the right* to be assertive.

❖ Many people are highly *anxious or fearful* about being assertive.

❖ Many people lack the *skills* to express themselves effectively.

In addition, some of that exciting recent research in neuroscience sheds new light on our subject. For example, brain scientists now tell us that some people are born with a genetic predisposition to shyness or social inhibition. Yet even that obstacle can be overcome to a large extent with diligent application of the procedures we describe. We've addressed these barriers to personal power and healthy relationships and offered proven, effective tools to overcome them.

In later chapters, you'll learn about the concepts of *nonassertive*, *aggressive*, and *assertive* behavior, and lots of examples and specific instructions will show you how they may apply in your life.

Incidentally, on the plus side, brain studies also show that we're all equipped with something scientists call "mirror neurons" in the brain, which lead us to mimic the behavior of others and help us to learn socially appropriate behavior and to respond effectively. As we learn more about our human strengths and weaknesses, the methods of self-expression we'll teach you in this book offer a powerful source of personal effectiveness.

How Can You Benefit from This Book?
Learning to respond more effectively will reduce the anxiety you may feel in dealing with others. You may even begin to feel better in other ways as well. Headaches, general fatigue, stomach disturbances, rashes, even asthma are sometimes related to a failure to express feelings directly. Assertiveness can help you avoid such symptoms.

Hundreds of research studies have shown that by developing the ability to stand up for yourself, overcome your anxiety in social situations, and take the initiative to do what's important to you,

You won't find gimmicks on how to manipulate others in this book.

you can cut down your stress and increase your sense of worth as a person. Countless thousands of individuals who had trouble expressing their feelings have achieved greater self-fulfillment by learning to assert themselves effectively.

You can be healthier, more in charge of yourself in relationships, more confident, more capable, and more spontaneous in expressing your feelings. And you'll likely find yourself more admired by others as well.

Whether your goals are personal, social, job related, or world changing, you will find a careful reading-and-practice approach to these ideas and procedures will help you to develop more effective self-expression and healthier relationships.

We are especially pleased that thousands of therapists have recommended this book as helpful reading for their clients. Indeed, maybe that's why you're reading it now. And we've been gratified to note that, in three separate surveys of practicing professionals, this book has consistently received the highest rating among assertiveness books and has been among the most often recommended of all self-help books.

Before you go on to the next chapter, think a bit about why you picked up this book. Are you looking for help in specific areas of your life — on the job perhaps, or with your family relationships? Do you have some ideas about how you'd like your life to be different? Chapter 7 goes into specifics about setting goals for your growth, but give a few moments of thought now to what you'd like to gain from reading *Your Perfect Right*. Then, when you're ready, push ahead and let's find out what this "assertiveness" stuff is all about.

2

Are You Assertive Now?

There is no greatness where there is
not simplicity, goodness, and truth.
— LEO TOLSTOY

BEFORE WE CONTINUE OUR EXPLORATION of what assertive behavior is and how it can help you create a more satisfying life for yourself, we think you'll find it helpful to explore your own style of self-expression. In this chapter, we've provided a short questionnaire that will tell you more about your own effectiveness in responding to everyday social situations.

What do you know about your own assertiveness? Others' reactions give you clues: Aunt Maria says, "You're sassy!" The boss tells you to be more forceful with customers. Or perhaps the children believe you need to "tell off" the mechanic. Maybe you tried to speak up to a clerk, who responded with a scornful look.

While everyday comments and reactions such as these are helpful indications of your progress in assertiveness, we hope you'll be more thorough and systematic in observing yourself.

We should first point out to you that *measuring* assertiveness is one of the toughest problems trainers and trainees have faced since assertiveness training got started. Many, many tests have been developed. None really does the job thoroughly and accurately.

Our *Assertiveness Inventory* on the following two pages is not perfect either, but we think you'll find it a helpful tool as you improve your understanding and awareness of yourself.

ASSERTIVENESS INVENTORY
Robert E. Alberti and Michael L. Emmons

The following questions will be helpful in assessing your assertiveness. Be honest in your responses. All you have to do is draw a circle around the number that describes you best. For some questions the assertive end of the scale is at 0, for others at 3. Key: 0 means **no** or **never**; 1 means **somewhat** or **sometimes**; 2 means **usually** or a **good deal**; and 3 means **practically always** or **entirely**.

1. When a person is highly unfair, do you call it to attention?	0 1 2 3
2. Do you find it difficult to make decisions?	0 1 2 3
3. Are you openly critical of others' ideas, opinions, and behavior?	0 1 2 3
4. Do you speak out in protest when someone takes your place in line?	0 1 2 3
5. Do you often avoid people or situations for fear of embarrassment?	0 1 2 3
6. Do you usually have confidence in your own judgment?	0 1 2 3
7. Do you insist that your spouse or roommate take on a fair share of household chores?	0 1 2 3
8. Are you prone to "fly off the handle"?	0 1 2 3
9. When a salesperson makes an effort, do you find it hard to say no even though the merchandise is not really what you want?	0 1 2 3
10. When a latecomer is waited on before you are, do you call attention to the situation?	0 1 2 3
11. Are you reluctant to speak up in a discussion or debate?	0 1 2 3
12. If a person has borrowed money (or a book, garment, or thing of value) and is overdue in returning it, do you mention it?	0 1 2 3
13. Do you continue to pursue an argument after the other person has had enough?	0 1 2 3
14. Do you generally express what you feel?	0 1 2 3
15. Are you disturbed if someone watches you at work?	0 1 2 3

16. If someone keeps kicking or bumping your chair in a movie or a lecture, do you ask the person to stop? 0 1 2 3

17. Do you find it difficult to keep eye contact when talking to another person? 0 1 2 3

18. In a good restaurant when your meal is improperly prepared or served, do you ask the server to correct the situation? 0 1 2 3

19. When you discover merchandise is faulty, do you return it for an adjustment? 0 1 2 3

20. Do you show your anger by name-calling or obscenities? 0 1 2 3

21. Do you try to be a wallflower or a piece of the furniture in social situations? 0 1 2 3

22. Do you insist that your property manager (mechanic, repair person, etc.) make repairs, adjustments, or replacements that are her or his responsibility? 0 1 2 3

23. Do you often step in and make decisions for others? 0 1 2 3

24. Are you able to express love and affection openly? 0 1 2 3

25. Are you able to ask your friends for small favors or help? 0 1 2 3

26. Do you think you always have the right answer? 0 1 2 3

27. When you differ with a person you respect, are you able to speak up for your own viewpoint? 0 1 2 3

28. Are you able to refuse unreasonable requests friends make? 0 1 2 3

29. Do you have difficulty complimenting or praising others? 0 1 2 3

30. If someone smoking nearby disturbs you, can you say so? 0 1 2 3

31. Do you shout or use bullying tactics to get others to do as you wish? 0 1 2 3

32. Do you finish other people's sentences for them? 0 1 2 3

33. Do you get into physical fights with others, especially with strangers? 0 1 2 3

34. At family meals, do you control the conversation? 0 1 2 3

35. When you meet a stranger, are you the first to introduce yourself and begin a conversation? 0 1 2 3

The real problem in measuring assertiveness, of course, is that it is such an elusive concept. There is no one single human characteristic you can put a finger on and say, *"That's assertiveness!"* It is a complex phenomenon that depends on both the persons involved and the particular situation.

A thorough assessment of assertiveness would be based on a better definition of the concept than currently exists. And it would take into account the four dimensions we are discussing: situations, attitudes, behaviors, and obstacles. A simple paper-and-pencil test can hardly do it justice!

That doesn't mean that we ought to quit trying to figure out how we're doing in assertive self-expression. It can be very valuable to take a close look at your life and identify your strengths and weaknesses. Just don't try to lump those all together and say, "I scored 73. I must be pretty assertive!"

Take a few minutes right now to respond to the *Assertiveness Inventory*. This is just for you, so be honest with yourself. After you complete the *Inventory*, read on for the discussion of results and for specific steps you can take to make the results practical in your life. The *Inventory* is not a "psychological test," so just relax and enjoy this brief exploration of when and how you express yourself.

As we've said, you'll find the *Inventory* less than perfect. Some items won't apply to your life. And you may want to respond, *"What does that mean?"* or, *"It depends on the situation."* Don't let your criticism of the questions get in the way. If you take the time to answer honestly, the *Inventory* can be a helpful tool in your growth in assertiveness.

"WHADJAGET?"
When you complete the *Inventory*, you'll probably be tempted to add up your total score. *Don't!* A "total score" really has no meaning, since no general trait of "assertiveness" has been found to exist. As you have no doubt experienced in your own

life, "what is assertive" must be answered in terms of the *person* and the *situation*.

As we noted above, the *Inventory* is not a standardized psychological test; the studies required to thoroughly evaluate and approve a test have not been conducted. Thus, a "total score" approach is not appropriate.

ANALYZING YOUR RESULTS

We suggest the following steps for analysis of your responses to the *Assertiveness Inventory:*

❖ Look at individual events in your life involving particular people or groups and consider your strengths and shortcomings accordingly.

❖ Look at your responses to questions 1, 2, 4, 5, 6, 7, 9, 10, 11, 12, 14, 15, 16, 17, 18, 19, 21, 22, 24, 25, 27, 28, 30, and 35. These questions are oriented toward nonassertive behavior. Do your answers to these items tell you that you are rarely speaking up for yourself? Or are there perhaps some specific situations that give you trouble?

❖ Look at your responses to questions 3, 8, 13, 20, 23, 26, 29, 31, 32, 33, and 34. These questions are oriented toward aggressive behavior. Do your answers to these questions suggest you are pushing others around more than you realized?

Most people confirm from completing these three steps that assertiveness is *situational* in their lives. No one is nonassertive all the time, aggressive all the time, assertive all the time! Each person behaves in each of the three ways at various times, depending upon the situation. It is possible that you have a *characteristic style* that leans heavily in one direction. You may discover your own weak spot and thereby begin the process of change.

❖ Reread the *Inventory* and write in your journal a discussion of your feelings about each item. (Oops. We haven't talked about a "journal" yet, have we? Stay tuned. It's the subject of the next chapter.) An example:

> **Question 1:** When a person is highly unfair, do you call it to attention?
> **Response:** O
> **Discussion:** I'm afraid that if I said anything, the other person would become very angry. Perhaps I'd lose a friend, or maybe the person would yell at me. That would upset me a lot.

❖ Go over all of the information you have generated from the preceding steps, and begin drawing some general conclusions. Look specifically at four aspects of the information:

> . . . What *situations* give you trouble? Which can you handle easily?
>
> . . . What are your *attitudes* about expressing yourself? Does it generally feel "right" to you?
>
> . . . What *obstacles* are in the way of your assertions? Are you afraid of the consequences? Do other people in your life make it especially difficult to be assertive?
>
> . . . Are your *behavior skills* up to the job? Can you be expressive when you need to be?

Examine these four areas carefully. Write comments in your journal, summarizing your observations of yourself.

Spending some time now to think about these aspects of your own style of self-expression will help you to see your own needs more clearly, to set goals for yourself (more about goal setting in chapter 7), and to determine where to go from here in your efforts to become more assertive.

The following chapter will help you set up a personal journal so you can keep track of "how it's going" as you work through this process of personal growth.

3

Keep Track of
Your Growth

*Where I was born and where and how I have
lived is unimportant. It is what I have done with
where I have been that should be of interest.*
— GEORGIA O'KEEFFE

W E'D LIKE TO ENCOURAGE YOU TO GET STARTED NOW on
your own process of growth toward more effective
self-expression by starting a "personal growth
journal." Nothing fancy, just a simple device for jotting down
notes about how things are going in your life as you take this
journey toward greater assertiveness.

A daily record of your assertiveness will help you judge your
progress over time. After a few weeks, you'll find it provides a
wealth of information about your ongoing assertiveness. We urge
you to get a special notebook, pad, or folder, whatever, so you
can record your thoughts, observations, feelings, and progress.

Your journal entries can include self-examination, notes on
your reading, goals, . . . anything you'd like to keep track of.
Give at least some space to five dimensions of your life that
relate to assertiveness: *situations* that come up; *people* in your
life; your own *attitudes, thoughts,* and *beliefs*; your *behaviors*; and
obstacles to expressing yourself.

A sample page of your journal might look like this:

PERSONAL GROWTH JOURNAL FOR _____ (date)

Situations

People

Attitudes/Thoughts/Beliefs

Behaviors

Obstacles

Notes (Progress/Problems/Comments/Goals)

If you keep it up regularly, your journal can become a very important tool for your growth program — both to record your progress and to serve as a "motivator" to continue working on your personal development.

As you undertake specific changes in your life, you might decide to become more thorough in your journal-keeping. The ideas that follow may be of some help.

❖ You may wish to refer to the *Assertiveness Inventory* (chapter 2). Which *situations* and *people* can you handle effectively and which are troublesome? Write down the results in your journal. Pay particular attention to any patterns in your life. Are you more assertive with strangers than with intimates, for example, or perhaps vice versa? Can you readily stand up for your rights but fall down on expressing affection? Do such factors as age, sex, or roles (e.g., authority) of the other person make a difference?

❖ It is very difficult to accurately measure *attitudes*, and it is particularly difficult to be objective about your own. Nevertheless, we encourage you to write down in your journal your feelings about your right to behave assertively. Look at the various situations and people in the definition of assertive behavior (chapter 1) and in the situations described in the *Assertiveness Inventory* (chapter 2). For example, do you feel that it's OK to respond when a boss or teacher has criticized you?

❖ Evaluating your *behavior* is not as difficult, but may take longer. In chapter 6, we'll describe in detail several components of behavior that are part of any assertive act. If you watch your own behavior carefully for a time (a week or more is a good idea) and record your observations regularly in your journal, you will have a good idea of your own effectiveness with eye contact, facial expression, body posture, and the other components. It may help to watch some other people you consider effectively assertive and to note in your journal some of their behavioral qualities as well.

❖ *Obstacles* may be the easiest area for you to keep track of. Most people want to act assertively, but there are many barriers that seem to make assertion difficult. Common obstacles within you fall into two categories:

- *anxiety* — fear of the possible consequences (Maybe the other person won't like me, or will hit me, or will think I'm crazy; or maybe I'll make a fool of myself; or maybe I'll fail to get what I want; or maybe I just feel anxious!)
- *lack of skills* (I don't know how to meet girls. What do I do to express a political opinion? I never learned how to show affection.).

Perhaps the most difficult external obstacles are the other people in your life. (Parents, friends, lovers, roommates, and others have an interest in making it difficult for you to change, even if they believe they want you to be more assertive.)

Record in your journal those obstacles that you think are making assertiveness more difficult for you.

MAKING YOUR JOURNAL WORK FOR YOU

If you take the time and effort to keep a journal and, as you learn more about assertiveness, proceed carefully and thoroughly with your self-assessment, you'll find that the results will help to pinpoint specifically what you need to do to increase your assertiveness. At every point, of course, you may choose whether to carry this personal growth program further and what direction you will take. And *choice* is the key element in your assertiveness anyway!

Every week or so, carefully examine your journal entries: situations, attitudes, behaviors, obstacles, and notes. Look for patterns. Remember to evaluate your strengths as well as your weaknesses.

The first week or two of entries in your journal should give you a good picture of how you are doing now and provide a basis for setting goals for yourself. While we have not yet presented a systematic process for setting goals (that comes in chapter 7), we encourage you to continue to think about your own hopes for improved assertiveness and to make notes in your journal about them.

Your journal might show you that you have difficulty with people in authority — that you don't believe you have a right to speak up to them, that you can't maintain good eye contact with them and that you're very anxious around such people. You can work on these items individually through the step-by-step procedures described in this book.

Changing long-standing aggressive, nonassertive, or other behaviors is difficult. Your journal is a crucial asset in the process of change. As you become aware of your behavior patterns, you can begin to choose deliberately and act in ways that will move you toward your goals. As your initial awkward attempts at assertion are rewarded — "Hey, it worked!" — you'll find the assertive choice will become easier and easier.

Start your journal today with notes about your reading thus far in the book. Keep using your journal throughout your reading of *Your Perfect Right* and beyond to keep a careful record of how you're doing as you apply these concepts in your own life. Your journal will provide a series of "benchmarks" so you can watch yourself grow. It will help motivate you to work at your progress. It will remind you how far you really have come — especially valuable at those times when you begin to think you aren't getting anywhere! Reading your journal will reassure you that you are making progress, even if it is slow.

Your journal will help you to be more systematic about your work on assertiveness. And that can make all the difference!

As you learn new things about yourself, you may find complex and severe shortcomings in some of the behavioral areas we've discussed. In that case, you may want some professional assistance in reaching your goal. Particularly if you experience very high levels of anxiety about being assertive, we suggest contact with a qualified counselor, psychologist, psychiatrist, or other therapist. Your local community mental health center or college/university counseling center can assist you in finding someone to help.

4

Whose Perfect Right?

Between people, as among nations, respect
of each other's rights insures the peace.
— BENITO JUAREZ

It seems that we have — as a society — reached
a point of much greater openness and freedom
of expression. That may not be all to the good . . .
Some folks have used "assertiveness" as a pretext
for all sorts of uncivil behavior — misinterpreting
the concept as if it gave them license for rudeness,
road rage, and boorishness. Fortunately that's
not the rule, but I sometimes think we may have
"created a monster," despite our best efforts to teach
a self-expressive style that is respectful of others.
— ROBERT E. ALBERTI

I N AN INTERVIEW for his 2006 book, *Therapy's Best*, therapist-author Howard Rosenthal asked Bob Alberti this question: *Are people more assertive now than when you first published the original edition of [Your Perfect Right]?* Bob's comment — the statement quoted above — offers a good point to begin this chapter's discussion of how we treat each other in an assertive society. Have we succeeded in teaching "a self-expressive style that is respectful of others"?

Up to now, you've been exploring what it might mean to you to become more effective in expressing yourself. Now let's take a look at some of the ways assertive actions fit — or don't fit — into a larger view of society.

We believe and have long taught the concept that *every individual has the same fundamental human rights as every other, regardless of gender, age, ethnicity, role, or title.* That's an idea worth some thought. And if the notion of equality of human rights is not idealistic enough for you, here's another: *Equality is fundamental to assertive living.* We'd like to see all persons exercise their rights without infringing on the rights of others.

The *Universal Declaration of Human Rights*, adopted by the United Nations General Assembly in 1948, is an excellent statement of goals for human relationships. A few key clauses from that document appear on the next page. Should you wish to examine the entire *Declaration*, it's available at www.un.org/Overview/rights.html.

The Declaration is idealistic, to be sure, and we doubt that any country in the world lives up to its ideals entirely. Still, we urge you to let those principles encourage you to support the rights of every individual — including yourself!

The twenty-first century is seeing progress around the globe toward the development of societies based upon these values. Individuals and groups have spoken out, and some intolerable conditions have changed. It appears that relationships, from the most intimate of love partners to the most distant of neighbors and co-workers, have begun to reflect a more equal valuing of both persons. Assertiveness training has had something to do with some of those needed changes, and we're proud to acknowledge that this book, first published in 1970 and now available in sixteen languages, has been a contributor to that process.

Keeping a broad view of individual human rights can help us to counteract the forces that pit us against one another. We are

Excerpts from the Universal Declaration of Human Rights

Article 1

All human beings are born free and equal in dignity and rights. They are endowed with reason and conscience and should act towards one another in a spirit of brotherhood.

Article 2

Everyone is entitled to all the rights and freedoms set forth in this Declaration, without distinction of any kind, such as race, colour, sex, language, religion, political or other opinion, national or social origin, property, birth or other status.

Article 7

All are equal before the law and are entitled without any discrimination to equal protection of the law.

Article 12

No one shall be subjected to arbitrary interference with his privacy, family, home or correspondence, nor to attacks upon his honour and reputation.

Article 18

Everyone has the right to freedom of thought, conscience and religion...

Article 19

Everyone has the right to freedom of opinion and expression...

all human beings after all, citizens of a very small planet, and dependent upon each other in many ways. We need mutual support and understanding for our very survival.

ARE SOME MORE EQUAL THAN OTHERS?

Unfortunately, society often evaluates human beings on scales that rank some people as more important than others. Here are a few popular notions about the value of persons. Which ones do you agree with?

More Valuable	Less Valuable
Adults	Children
Bosses	Employees
Men	Women
White People	People of Color
Physicians	Plumbers
Teachers	Students
Politicians	Voters
Generals	Privates
Winners	Losers
Americans	"Foreigners"
Wealthy people	Poor people

The list could go on and on. Many of our society's organizations tend to perpetuate these myths and to allow individuals in these roles to be treated as if they were of lesser value as human beings. The good news, however, is that lots of folks are finding ways to express themselves as equals.

ASSERTIVE WOMEN IN THE TWENTY-FIRST CENTURY

Through the first few editions of this book, the movement popularly known as "women's liberation" was gaining momentum. We don't hear the term so much any more, but the concept of liberated individuals — free to be themselves — has not gone away.

An assertive, independent, and self-expressive woman has come to be valued by society, by men, and by other women. She is capable of choosing her own lifestyle, free of dictates of tradition, government, husband, children, social groups, and bosses. She may elect to be a homemaker and not fear intimidation by those who work outside the home. Or she may elect to pursue a male-dominated profession and enjoy confidence in her rights and abilities.

In their excellent book *The Assertive Woman*, Stanlee Phelps and Nancy Austin present the behavioral styles of four "women we all know." Their characterizations of *Doris Doormat, Agatha Aggressive, Iris Indirect,* and *April Assertive* are self-explanatory by the names alone. Yet, in describing the patterns of each, Phelps and Austin help us to gain a clearer picture of the social mores that have in the past devalued assertiveness in women. Agatha gets her way, though she hasn't many friends. Iris, the sly one, also gains most of what she wants, and sometimes her "victims" never even know it. Doris, although denied her own wishes much of the time, was once highly praised by men and by the power structure as "a good woman." April's honesty and forthrightness may have created trouble for her at home, at school, on the job, and even with other women.

In her sexual relationships, an assertive woman can be comfortable taking initiative and asking for what she wants (and thereby freeing her partner from the expected role of making the first move). She and her partner can share equally in the expression of intimacy.

She can say no with firmness — and can make it stick — to requests for favors, to unwanted sexual advances, to her family's expectations that she "do it all."

As a consumer, she can make the marketplace respond to her needs by refusing to accept shoddy merchandise, service, or marketing techniques.

A number of factors have combined to help women achieve long overdue gains in recognition of their individual rights. The popularity of assertiveness training for women, including specialized workshops in management and other fields, has been a contributing factor. Women of all social viewpoints, ethnic and socioeconomic backgrounds, and educational and professional involvements — homemakers, hard hats, and high-ranking executives — have made phenomenal gains in assertive expression. As a result, the old "ideal," which identified women as "passive, sweet, and submissive," is no more.

By developing the ability to stand up for yourself and do things on your own initiative, you can cut down your stress and increase your sense of worth as a person.

Today's assertive *woman* is an assertive *person* who exhibits the qualities we espouse throughout this book; and she likes herself — and is liked — better for it!

What's more, many of these changes are recognized around the world. This book and *The Assertive Woman* have been translated and published in China, Germany, India, Israel, Japan, Poland, and many other countries. In Japan, a survey reported in 1990 by a major bank showed that 28 percent of employees would welcome a female boss; the figure a decade earlier had been 12 percent. And local governments in Japan have offered classes in business expertise for women entrepreneurs. Even in Muslim societies, although women continue to be subject to severe cultural and legal restrictions, women in some regions are making gains in personal and political equality, according to press reports.

Men Can Be Assertive Too!

Imagine the following scene: John's day has been exhausting; he has washed windows, mopped floors, completed three loads of wash, and continuously picked up and cleaned up after the children. He is now working hurriedly in the kitchen preparing dinner. The children are running in and out of the house, banging the door, screaming, and throwing toys.

In the midst of this chaos, Mary arrives home from an equally trying day at her office. She offers a cursory "I'm home!" as she passes the kitchen on her way to the family room. Dropping her briefcase and kicking off her shoes, she flops in her favorite chair in front of the television set, calling out, "John, bring me a beer! I've had a helluva day!"

This scene is humorous partly because it counters cultural stereotypes. After all, shouldn't John also have a career, working for a salary instead of at home? Isn't a man's place to go out and conquer the world on behalf of his family? To demonstrate his manhood, his macho, his strength, and his courage?

For too long we accepted as proper the stereotype of the male as "mighty hunter," who must protect and provide for his family. Indeed, from earliest childhood, the accepted male roles of earlier days encouraged assertive — and often aggressive — behavior in pursuit of this "ideal." Competitiveness, achievement, and striving to be the best were integral components of male child-rearing and formal schooling — much more so than for their sisters. Men have been treated as if they were by nature strong, active, decisive, dominant, cool, and rational.

Late in the twentieth century, a growing number of men began to acknowledge a great gap in their preparation for interpersonal relationships. Limited in the past to only two options — the powerful, dominating aggressor or the wimp with sand in his face — most found neither to be particularly satisfying. Assertiveness offered them an effective alternative, and a new generation of men has rejected the aggressive, climbing, "success" stereotype in favor of a more balanced role and lifestyle.

Psychological concepts of "masculinity" have changed to acknowledge the caring, nurturing side of men as well. Men have recognized that they can accomplish their own life goals in assertive — not aggressive — ways. Professional advancement is available for the competent, confident, assertive man.

We have witnessed remarkable changes in our society's definition of what it means to be a man. The emerging definition looks remarkably like the *assertive man* we have been encouraging for over four decades: firm but not pushy, self-confident but not arrogant, self-assertive but committed to equality in relationships, open and direct but not dominant.

"Traditional" male activities continue to reflect the old ways, of course, but a growing number of men are moving beyond sports teams, adult "fraternities," and community service clubs to form personal growth and consciousness-raising groups (not unlike those their wives, sisters, and mothers formed decades before). "Male bonding," although still material for stand-up comic routines and sit-com segments, is no longer a joke for tens of thousands of men who are seeking something more meaningful than a weekly backslapping lunch with the Old Boys Club.

We admire those men who are beginning to acknowledge to themselves and to each other (if not yet to women) their needs and desires, their strengths and their vulnerabilities, their anxieties and their guilt, and the internal and external pressures that drive their lives.

Assertive men are held in high esteem in relationships with the important others in their lives. Family and friends are closer to and have greater respect for the man who is comfortable enough with himself that he needn't put others down in order to put himself up. The honesty of assertiveness is an incalculable asset in close personal relationships, and assertive men are coming to value such closeness right along with the traditional rewards of economic success.

Researchers who have studied large groups of men over long time periods have noted that many men who lived the aggressive style in their twenties and thirties found that the achievements thus gained meant little in their later years. The values of personal intimacy, family closeness, and trusted friendships — all fostered by assertiveness, openness, and honesty — are the lasting and important ones.

The assertive man is finding himself too!

Living in a Multicultural, Pluralistic World

The essence of our approach to assertiveness training has always been *equality*. The goal of this book is to foster better communication between equals, not to help one to be superior to another or to step on others to get her way. Open and honest communication — mutual, cooperative, affirming — is the process that can achieve the desired outcome of equality: a place for everyone.

These days, however, that goal may be more challenging than ever before, as the world grows smaller. Global economic, political, and personal changes have led to more awareness of and direct contact with people of different cultural backgrounds. Every day, right here at home, most of us can see that the world is becoming a multicultural "mixing pot" to a greater degree than ever before. It's exciting and refreshing to see different faces, hear different languages, and encounter different lifestyles.

At times, it can also be uncomfortable.

No other nation has the cultural diversity of the United States. Our home state of California is in the forefront of the interface of cultures but is by no means alone. In fact, Anglos are now a minority in California, Hawaii, New Mexico, and Texas. More than half of the population of each of these states are people of color, including Hispanic/Latino, African American, Asian, Native American, and other ethnic groups. In the public schools — a microcosm of the larger society — teachers of English as a second language face a sea of faces from dozens of diverse cultures. In one Los Angeles school, a reported twenty-two different languages are spoken!

As California's multiethnic population has grown, similar population changes are occurring throughout the United States.

Can we all live together? Do we respect and value one another? Or are we threatened by the entry of each newcomer, each "foreigner," each person who is "different"?

Protection of human rights, equality of treatment, and respect for persons regardless of ethnic or personal traits: the more we can become aware of and understand and accept each other —

including those who are "different" — the stronger we will be as individuals (and as a nation and world).

How Different Is "Different"?

When people think about other cultures, they commonly assume that "all people from a culture behave in the same way." For too long, argues UCLA professor Steven Lopez, "understanding" people of other backgrounds has meant lumping cultural groups together and ignoring individuals. Such stereotyping *creates* barriers, it doesn't erase them.

You hear, as we hear, stereotypes about other cultures all the time. Here are a few: in some cultures if a woman smiles at a stranger it has sexual implications; African American males do not like to maintain eye contact in conversations; the male rules the household in the Mexican American culture; Saudi Arabians stand very close and seldom use their right hand when communicating; in some cultures the death of a loved one is a joyous occasion.

Can it be that all people from a certain culture (or all women, or all teenagers) have the same beliefs? Or act the same way? Of course not. And such stereotypic assumptions are as dangerous as they are false. We get into trouble when we assume that all people from any group behave in the same way or share the same beliefs.

The catch is that it's equally false — and dangerous — to assume that "people are people" and deep down we're all alike as human beings, regardless of our groups. Culture, gender, and age are important, and to understand an individual requires that you acknowledge these vital characteristics — and treat her or him individually.

What Does Background Have to Do with Assertiveness?

As you begin to develop growing assertive skills, how can you use them in dealing with people from different backgrounds?

First, *treat each person with respect*; second, *educate yourself* about the backgrounds of people you encounter; and third, if something seems unusual in an individual's style — standing too close, avoiding eye contact, being overly shy or pushy — *check it out.* You might say something such as, "I find it a little uncomfortable when you stand so close to me. I guess I'm not used to that."

Keep in mind that each human being is unique, a complex blend of age, gender, genes, culture, beliefs, and personal life experiences. All Italians, or Irish, or Vietnamese, or Mexicans are not alike, but members of each group have much in common. All teenagers, or senior citizens, or preschoolers are not the same, but it helps to know something about the needs and characteristics of one's group as you deal with an individual. All working women, or midlife men, or "thirtysomethings" are not identical, but they have similarities that *may* be important to know if you want to get to know someone who fits one of those labels.

In sum, as you seek to understand people of other cultures or backgrounds, *begin first with the individual*. Don't underestimate cultural or group-specific behavior or overestimate the universality of human behavior. When in doubt, show respect, ask questions, and listen, listen, listen.

SOCIETY OFTEN DISCOURAGES ASSERTIVENESS
Despite important improvements in some areas, society's rewards for appropriate assertive behavior are still limited. The assertions of each individual, the right of self-expression without fear or guilt, the right to a dissenting opinion, and the unique contribution of each person all need greater recognition. We can't overemphasize the importance of the difference between appropriate *assertion* and the destructive *aggression* with which it is often confused. (More on that in the next chapter.)

Assertion is often actively discouraged in subtle — or not so subtle — ways in the family, at school, at work, in church, in our political institutions, and elsewhere.

Each of us has the right to be and to express ourselves, and to feel good (not powerless or guilty) about doing so, as long as we do not hurt others in the process

In the *family*, the child who decides to speak up for his or her rights is often promptly censored: "Don't talk to your mother (father) that way!" "Children are to be seen, not heard." "Don't be disrespectful!" "Never let me hear you talk like that again!" Obviously, these common parental commands are not conducive to a child's assertion of self!

At *school*, teachers are frequently inhibitors of assertion. Quiet, well-behaved children who do not question authority are rewarded, whereas those who "buck the system" in some way are dealt with sternly. Educators acknowledge that the child's natural spontaneity in learning is conditioned out no later than the fourth or fifth grade, replaced by conformity to the school's approach.

The results of such upbringing affect functioning on the job, and the *workplace* itself often is no help. At work, employees usually assume that it's best not to do or say anything that will rock the boat. The boss is in charge, and everyone else is expected to "go along with the program" — even if they consider the expectations completely inappropriate. Early work experiences taught that those who speak up are not likely to obtain raises or recognition and may even lose their jobs. You quickly learn not to make waves, to keep things running smoothly, to have few ideas of your own, and to be careful how you act lest it get back to the boss.

Fortunately, things have changed somewhat in recent years, with more employee rights and a greater balance emerging. A collegial atmosphere now pervades high-tech firms. Low unemployment has required employers to accommodate a variety of individuals with talent. Many people work at home, as independent contractors or telecommuting, for virtually all of their working lives. In many work environments, employees no longer fear speaking out on the job, but "whistleblowers" — those who openly report unfair, unethical, or illegal activities in the workplace — are often shunned and rebuked, in spite of laws allegedly protecting them. There are still many influences that suggest it's best to be nonassertive at work!

The teachings of many *churches* suggest that assertive behavior is somehow at odds with religious commitment. Such qualities as humility, self-denial, and self-sacrifice may be encouraged to the exclusion of standing up for oneself. There is a mistaken notion that religious ideals must, in some mystical way, be incompatible with feeling good about oneself and with being calm and confident in relationships with others. Quite the contrary; assertiveness is not only compatible with the teachings of major religions, it frees you of self-defeating behavior, allowing you to be of greater service to others as well as to yourself!

Political institutions may not be as likely as the home, school, workplace, and church to influence the early development of assertive behavior, but they do little to encourage its expression. Political decision making still remains largely inaccessible to the average citizen. Nevertheless, it is still true that the "squeaky wheel gets the grease," and when individuals — especially when they get together in groups — become expressive enough, governments usually respond. Of course, since September 11, 2001, restrictions on civil liberties (e.g., the USA PATRIOT Act) have made it more hazardous for individuals — and even groups — to express dissent from government policies, even in the "free speech" United States.

We have been gratified to see the growth and successes of assertive citizen lobbies. Minority/homeless/children's/gay and other rights movements, MoveOn.org, Public Citizen, Common Cause (for political reform), AARP and Gray Panthers (for older Americans), and the various tax reform movements

are powerful evidence that *assertion does work!* And there may
be no more important arena for its application than overcoming
the sense of "What's the use? I can't make a difference," that
tends to pervade the realm of personal political action.

Sadly, of course, social institutions change slowly. Colleges
and universities, governments, political institutions, and
international conglomerate corporations often resist change until
conditions become so oppressive that some people consider it
necessary to become aggressive in pursuit of their goals. They
may take to the streets in violent protest, vandalize property, or
even hurt other people in order to make a point.

Yet such institutions tend to dig in and resist violent change;
they are most likely to respond favorably to persistent *assertive*
action.

Those who have been carefully taught by family, school,
and society not to speak up or demand their reasonable rights
may feel powerless to express themselves or highly anxious
when they do stand up to be counted. We look forward to the
day when most families, schools, businesses, churches, and
governments encourage individual self-assertion and stop
limiting self-fulfilling actions. We love it when frustrated
individuals and groups seeking change develop assertive
alternatives in pursuit of their goals.

After all, *each of us has the right to be and to express ourselves and
to feel good (not powerless or guilty) about doing so, as long as we do
not hurt others in the process.*

5

What It Means to Be Assertive

There are three possible broad approaches to the conduct of interpersonal relations. The first is to consider one's self only and ride roughshod over others . . . The second . . . is always to put others before one's self . . . The third approach is the golden mean . . . The individual places himself first, but takes others into account.

— JOSEPH WOLPE

THEY HARVEST FRUITS AND VEGETABLES that nobody else wants and distribute them to people who would otherwise be without. They're the "Senior Gleaners" of Northern California, an all-volunteer assembly of some 1,100 people of retirement age, loosely affiliated with groups in other areas around the country through "Second Harvest" — the National Food Bank Network. The Gleaners was started in 1976 by a retired engineer, Homer Fahrner, who gathered the first thirty volunteers in his Sacramento garage. In an interview with psychologist-author Bill Berkowitz for a feature story in the book, *Local Heroes*, Fahrner was asked for the key to the group's early success. He responded enthusiastically: "I'm saying first, right out, when the crops grow, go out and see those people and persist. Because one turns you down, maybe he's got a good reason. Go on, go on, go on."

Homer Fahrner's admonition could be the mantra of this book: "go on, go on, go on." *Persistence* may just be the single most important thing you learn from this process.

But wait! Yes, persistence is important, and we encourage you to make it a part of your "assertiveness toolkit," but it's not *all* there is to being assertive. Stay with us as we take another look at the concept of assertiveness as we defined it in chapter 1:

> *Assertive self-expression is direct, firm, positive — and when necessary persistent — action intended to promote equality in person-to-person relationships. Assertiveness enables us to act in our own best interests, to stand up for ourselves without undue anxiety, to exercise personal rights without denying the rights of others, and to express our feelings honestly and comfortably (e.g., affection, love, friendship, disappointment, annoyance, anger, regret, sorrow).*

Let's examine those elements in greater detail:

To be direct, firm, positive, and persistent means to express your thoughts and feelings spontaneously, directly to the person(s) involved, firmly enough to make your point clear and persistently enough so the other(s) recognize you're serious about it.

To promote equality in person-to-person relationships means to put both parties on an equal footing, to restore the balance of power by giving personal power to the "underdog," to make it possible for everyone to gain and no one to lose.

To act in your own best interests refers to the ability to make your own decisions about career, relationships, lifestyle, and time schedule, to take initiative starting conversations and organizing activities, to trust your own judgement, to set goals and work to achieve them, to ask for help from others, and to participate socially.

To stand up for yourself includes such behaviors as saying no, setting limits on time and energy, responding to criticism or put-downs or anger, and expressing or supporting or defending an opinion.

To exercise personal rights relates to competency, as a citizen, as a consumer, as a member of an organization or school or work group, and as a participant in public events, to express opinions, to work for change, and to respond to violations of one's own rights or those of others.

To not deny the rights of others is to accomplish the above personal expressions without unfair criticism of others, without hurtful behavior toward others, without name-calling, without intimidation, without manipulation, and without controlling others.

To express feelings honestly and comfortably means to be able to disagree, to show anger, to show affection or friendship, to admit fear or anxiety, to express agreement or support, and to be spontaneous — all with little or no painful anxiety.

Putting those elements of the definition back together, you can see that assertive behavior is a positive self-affirmation that also values the other people in your life. It contributes both to your personal life satisfaction and to the quality of your relationships with others.

Studies show that, as a direct result of gains in self-expressiveness, individuals have improved their self-esteem, reduced their anxiety, overcome depression, gained greater respect from others, accomplished more in terms of their life goals, increased their level of self-understanding, and improved their capacity to communicate more effectively with others. We can't promise any specific results for you, of course, but the evidence is impressive!

Assertive, Nonassertive, and Aggressive Behavior

We get a lot of mixed messages about appropriate behavior these days. Conflict between what's *recommended* and what's *rewarded* is evident in many areas of life. Ideally each of us should respect the rights of others. And the public comments of political leaders frequently repeat that ideal. But what about the real world? All too often parents, teachers, and business, government, and other institutions say one thing and do another, contradicting these values in their own actions. Tact, diplomacy, politeness, refined manners, modesty, civility, and self-denial are generally praised; yet, realistically, to get ahead it seems to be pretty much acceptable to step on others.

Athletes, for example, are encouraged to be aggressive in competitive sports, perhaps even to bend the rules a little. That's winked at because "winning is the only thing," right? "It's not important how you play the game; it's just important that you win."

So, how to deal with these mixed messages? We believe you should be able to *choose for yourself* how to act. If your "polite restraint" response is too strong, you may be unable to express yourself as you would like. If your aggressive response is overdeveloped, you may achieve your goals by hurting others. Freedom of choice and self-control are possible when you develop assertive responses for situations you have previously handled nonassertively or aggressively.

Throughout the nine editions and four decades of this book's history, one of the most popular (and frequently reproduced) sections has been our simple chart, contrasting assertive, nonassertive, and aggressive actions. The chart (on the next page) helps to clarify the concepts by displaying several feelings and consequences typical for the person (*sender*) whose actions are nonassertive, assertive, or aggressive. Also shown for each of these actions are the likely consequences for the person toward whom the action is directed (*receiver*).

As the chart shows, a *nonassertive* response means that the sender is denying self-expression and is inhibited from letting feelings show. People who behave nonassertively often feel hurt and anxious since they allow others to choose for them. They seldom achieve their own desired goals.

NON-ASSERTIVE BEHAVIOR	AGGRESSIVE BEHAVIOR	ASSERTIVE BEHAVIOR
Sender	**Sender**	**Sender**
Self-denying	Self-enhancing at expense of another	Self-enhancing
Inhibited	Expressive	Expressive
Hurt, anxious	Controlling	Feels good about self
Allows others to choose	Chooses for others	Chooses for self
Does not achieve desired goal	Achieves desired goal by hurting others	May achieve desired goal
Receiver	**Receiver**	**Receiver**
Guilty or angry	Self-denying	Self-enhancing
Depreciates sender	Hurt, defensive, humiliated	Expressive
Achieves desired goal at sender's expense	Does not achieve desired goal	May achieve desired goal

The person who carries a desire for self-expression to the extreme of *aggressive* behavior accomplishes goals at the expense of others. Although frequently self-enhancing and expressive of feelings in the situation, aggressive behavior hurts other people in the process by making choices for them and by minimizing their worth.

Aggressive behavior commonly results in a *put-down* of the receiver. Rights denied, the receiver feels hurt, defensive, and humiliated. His or her goals in the situation, of course, are not achieved. Aggressive behavior may achieve the sender's goals but may also generate bitterness and frustration that may later return as vengeance.

Some professionals who work with assertiveness training prefer to add a fourth category — *indirect aggression* — to this model. They note that much aggressive behavior takes the form of passive, nonoppositional action. Sometimes such actions are sneaky or sly; other times they may simply be *double entendres*. This is the smiling, friendly, agreeable behavior that hides a backstabbing or undermining action. We consider this category to be a form of aggression and have simplified our model by not dealing with it separately. We do acknowledge its importance, however, and will have more to say about it in chapter 18.

Appropriately *assertive* behavior in the same situation would be self-enhancing for the sender, an honest expression of feelings, and will usually achieve the goal. When you choose for yourself how to act, a good feeling typically accompanies the assertive response, even when you do not achieve your goals.

When the consequences of these three contrasting behaviors are seen from the viewpoint of the receiver of the action, we see a parallel pattern. Nonassertive behavior may produce sympathy, confusion, or outright contempt for the sender. Also, the receiver may feel guilt or anger at having achieved goals at the sender's expense. The receiver of aggressive actions often feels hurt, defensive, put down, or perhaps aggressive in return.

In contrast, assertion tends to enhance the feeling of self-worth of both parties and permits both full self-expression and achievement of goals.

In summary, it is clear that self-denial in nonassertive behavior hurts the sender; aggressive behavior may hurt the receiver (or even both parties). In the case of assertion, neither person

> *Assertive behavior is a positive self-affirmation which also values the other people in your life.*

is hurt, and it is likely that both will succeed. The series of example situations that appears in chapter 6 will help to make these distinctions more clear.

It is important to note that *assertive behavior is person and situation specific*, not universal. What may be considered assertive depends upon the persons involved and the circumstances of the situation. Although we believe the definitions and examples presented in this book are realistic and appropriate for most people and circumstances, individual differences must be considered. Cultural or ethnic background, for example, may create a different set of personal circumstances that would change the nature of "appropriateness" in assertive behavior.

ASSERTIVENESS AND PERSONAL BOUNDARIES

There's lots of talk these days about "boundaries." The concept of personal boundaries is a graphic way of describing how close you allow others to come to you — physically, emotionally, sexually, intellectually, and spiritually.

Your sense of yourself provides the foundation for your creation of boundaries. It might appear that someone who has a strong self-concept would have solid boundaries: a virtual bubble in which one can walk at a safe distance from other people. We don't see it that way. In our view, a strong self-concept will enable you to allow others to get close to you because you're secure in yourself. Personal insecurity — a weak self-concept —

may lead you to keep others at a distance, lest their closeness become a threat.

The relationship between personal boundaries and assertiveness is strong but not necessarily simple. Assertive self-expression allows you to communicate your boundaries to others: "That's as close as I'll allow you to get to me." "Don't touch me." "You're in my space now; please back off." But assertiveness is not all about setting limits or maintaining control in relationships. The equal-relationship assertiveness we urge is about closeness as well. We want you to be able to act assertively in drawing people closer to you as well as in keeping them away, *as you choose*.

Romantic relationships provide classic examples of how personal boundaries work. If Jill finds Jack attractive, she may approach him with an invitation to get together socially, expanding her personal boundaries in an effort to draw him closer. Jack may misinterpret Jill's invitation and conclude that he is at liberty to make sexual advances. Jill may consider such actions a boundary violation and push Jack away. How close is "close enough"?

Effective personal boundaries are not set in stone. They're flexible, they vary with each person with whom you have a relationship, and they vary with time. Jill might have welcomed Jack's sexual advances at a later time. By invading her boundary too early, however, he has probably lost the opportunity to develop a longer-term relationship.

Once again, *choice* is the bottom line here. Our goal in facilitating your growth in assertive self-expression is to free you to make those choices: to be close when you want and to maintain distance when you prefer that; to nurture your ties with friends and loved ones and to set firm limits with those you don't want close; to speak up when it's necessary to defend your personal space and to reach out when you want to expand your personal space; and to recognize that the other person has rights too. As Justice Oliver Wendell Holmes, Jr. put it, "Your right to swing your fist ends where my nose begins."

CULTURAL DIFFERENCES IN SELF-ASSERTION

While the desire for self-expression may be a basic human need, assertive behavior in interpersonal relationships is primarily characteristic of Western cultures. (For purposes of illustration, please permit us a few cultural generalizations and a stereotype or two. We discussed this topic in the previous chapter, but it's important enough to take another look.)

In many Asian cultures, group membership (family, clan, workgroup) and "face" are highly valued. How others see one tends to be more important to an individual than is self-concept. Politeness is a key virtue, and communication is often indirect so as to avoid confrontation or offending one another. Those who value tradition generally do not consider assertiveness, in the Western sense of direct self-expression, appropriate. Many young people, however, and those whose business activities include considerable contact with the United States and Europe have developed more direct, informal, and assertive styles.

Many individuals and subcommunities in Latino and Hispanic societies have emphasized the notion of "machismo" to the point that assertiveness — as we have defined it— seems rather tame, at least for men. In those cases, a greater display of strength is the norm for male self-expression.

Yet, people from cultures where self-assertion traditionally has not been valued may be just those who most need its benefits. As our world shrinks, it may be that current and future international relations require more open and direct communication and a greater sense of equality — expressed on both sides of the table.

"BUT ISN'T AGGRESSION JUST HUMAN NATURE?"

Aggression and violence are often excused on the grounds that they are innate in the human organism and cannot be avoided.

Not so, say the most distinguished scholars who have researched the subject. The "Seville Statement" — written in 1986 by twenty distinguished social and behavioral scientists from twelve nations and endorsed by the American Psychological and American Anthropological Associations — says:

> "It is *scientifically incorrect* to say...
>
> ❖ "... that we have inherited a tendency to make war from our animal ancestors.... Warfare is a peculiarly human phenomenon and does not occur in other animals.... War is biologically possible, but it is not inevitable....
> ❖ "... that war or any other violent behavior is genetically programmed into our human nature.... Except for rare pathologies, the genes do not produce individuals necessarily predisposed to violence. Neither do they determine the opposite....
> ❖ "... that in the course of human evolution there has been a selection for aggressive behaviour.... Violence is neither in our evolutionary legacy nor in our genes.
> ❖ "... that humans have a 'violent brain'. While we do have the neural apparatus to act violently... there is nothing in our neurophysiology that compels [such behavior]....
> ❖ "... that war is caused by 'instinct' or any single motivation....
>
> "We conclude that biology does not condemn humanity to war, and that humanity can be freed from the bondage of biological pessimism.... The same species (that) invented war is capable of inventing peace...."

CLASSIFYING BEHAVIOR: "A ROSE, BY ANY OTHER NAME..."

"I told my father-in-law not to smoke his cigar in my house. Was that assertive or aggressive?"

Members of assertiveness training groups and workshops have often asked us to classify a particular act as "assertive" or "aggressive." What makes the important difference? We have suggested that assertive and aggressive behavior differ principally in that the latter involves hurting, manipulating, or denying others in the course of expressing oneself. Practitioners and writers with a psychoanalytic orientation have proposed that *intent* must be considered. That is, if you intended to hurt your father-in-law, that's aggressive; if you simply wanted to inform him of your wishes, you were acting assertively.

Many psychologists insist that behavior must be measurable according to its *effects*. Thus, if your father-in-law gets the assertive message and responds accordingly — by agreeing not to smoke — your behavior may be classified as assertive. If he pouts in a corner or shouts, "Who do you think you are?" your statement may have been aggressive.

As we have noted, the *sociocultural context* must be taken into account in classifying behavior as assertive or aggressive or nonassertive. A culture that highly values honoring one's elders may view the request as clearly out of line and aggressive, regardless of the behavior, response, or intent.

There are no absolutes in this area, and some criteria may be in conflict. A particular act may be at once assertive in *behavior* and *intent* (you wanted to and did express your feelings), aggressive in response (the other person could not handle your assertion), and nonassertive in the social *context* (your culture expects a powerful, put-down style). It's not always easy to classify human behavior!

A specific situation may vary considerably from the examples we discuss here. In any event, the question "Is it assertive or aggressive?" is not one that may be answered simply! Each situation ultimately must be evaluated on its own. The labels "nonassertive," "assertive," and "aggressive" themselves carry no magic, but they may be useful in assessing the appropriateness of a particular action.

Bottom line: Don't sweat the labels. We want you to be able to *choose for yourself* how you will act and to know that you have the tools you need to succeed.

Social Consequences of Assertion

While you're learning skills to improve your ability to express yourself appropriately and responsibly, keep in mind that self-expression must be modulated by its *context*. Just as freedom of speech does not convey the right to yell "fire" in a crowded theater, so the form of self-expression we advise is one that considers its consequences. Once again we commend Justice Holmes's comment: "Your right to swing your fist ends where my nose begins."

The perfect right you have to say no exists alongside the other person's right to say yes. And your desire to accomplish your goals through self-assertion must be weighed against the needs of the larger society. Speak out or write about any idea you choose to support, but recognize the other person's right to do the same. And be prepared to pay some dues — perhaps in jail — if your expression goes beyond words and includes civil disobedience. Just as there are taxes for those who accumulate wealth, there is a price to pay for freedom of expression.

While you have a perfect right to maintain a viewpoint, everyone else has the same right — and your views may conflict. Keep this in mind on your journey toward greater personal assertiveness.

Assertiveness in the Twenty-First Century

In early editions of *Your Perfect Right*, we used the following example of a situation calling for assertive action: *"Has anyone ever cut in front of you in a line?"* Our advice, of course, was to speak up for yourself, to call attention to the situation, to ask that the line-jumper respect the rights of those who have already been waiting. Today, frankly, we're not so sure.

New York Times columnist and author Thomas Friedman (*The World Is Flat*) tells of an incident in an airport bookshop a few years back that illustrates this point. Thinking he was next, he put his money on the counter and heard the woman next to him say, "Excuse me, I was here first" — obviously this was someone in a hurry to make her purchase. Friedman said he was very sorry, but he was clearly there first. Today, he says, he would have responded very differently: "I would have said, 'Miss, I'm so sorry. I am entirely in the wrong. Please go ahead. And can I buy your magazines for you?'" These days, Friedman muses, you never know how people will react. "I'd be thinking there is some chance this woman has a blog, or a camera in her mobile phone, and could, if she so chose, tell the whole world about our encounter — entirely from her perspective — and my utterly rude, boorish, arrogant, thinks-he-can-butt-in-line behavior. Yikes!"

And if the other person in such an encounter were inclined to be directly aggressive, Friedman might have wound up with a bloody nose!

For nearly forty years, through eight editions and nearly one and a half million copies of this book, we have emphasized the importance of individual self-expression, and our commitment to the value of each individual human being has not wavered. But we would like to comment on a few of the realities in which we find ourselves in the United States in the twenty-first century.

We have long considered appropriate assertiveness to be "person and situation specific." The cutting-in-line situation must be assessed more carefully today than forty years ago. Our "perfect rights" haven't changed, of course, but we must exercise our right to *express* them with greater caution. It has always been true that you risk being punched in the nose when you speak up for yourself. Today, however, the probability of a violent reaction seems greater than ever before. A punch in the nose, an obscene gesture, even a knife or gun are seen as the quick answer to many disagreements.

Cut me off on the freeway? The least you'll get is my horn and the extended digit of my free hand. You may get bumped the next time traffic slows down. Or I may just decide to run you off the road.

Reprimand or fire me at work? I may return with a gun to "pay you back," if I'm emotionally unstable or wigged out on drugs. (Law enforcement officials tell us that a huge percentage of convicted criminals are chronic drug users.)

There are, of course, no easy answers to such dilemmas of life in a violence-prone, post-9/11 society. We cannot recommend that you take the risks of asserting yourself under all circumstances, nor will we advise you to duck inside your shell and avoid any situation in which your safety may be at stake. What we do advise is that you exercise appropriate caution in risky situations. Take time to consider the possible consequences of your actions, how well you know the person(s) you're dealing with, how well you know the territory in which you find yourself, how important it is to have your say, whether you're likely to accomplish anything by speaking up, etc.

In chapter 21, we elaborate on those thoughts and put together a checklist of criteria to aid you in deciding "Is this a situation in which I want to be assertive?"

Don't misunderstand our caveat here. We do not want you to avoid reasonable assertions because there may be risk. There is risk in getting out of bed in the morning. There is risk in driving your car (even without the "crazies"). There is risk in most jobs (ask your employer about the cost of workers' compensation insurance, even for "nonhazardous" jobs!). There is risk in living in the city — or in the country. There is risk in involving yourself in a relationship.

To avoid risk is to avoid life — and we want you to live as fully as you can. As psychologist and philosopher William James said, "Live all you can; it's a mistake not to." Just consider taking risks that count for something!

Our society needs all the help it can get in creating harmony. Let's focus our assertiveness where it's meaningful: working toward equality and cooperation in relationships with others.

Eleven Key Points about Assertive Behavior

To summarize this chapter, here is a list of eleven key qualities of assertive behavior:

1. *Self-expressive*
2. *Respectful* of the rights of others
3. *Honest*
4. *Direct and firm*
5. *Equalizing*, benefiting both parties in a relationship
6. Both *verbal* (including the content of the message) and *nonverbal* (including the style of the message)
7. *Positive* at times (expressing affection, praise, appreciation) and *negative* at times (expressing limits, anger, criticism)
8. *Appropriate for the person and situation,* not universal
9. *Socially responsible*
10. *Learned*, not inborn, although early brain development can present a challenging obstacle to new learning
11. As *persistent* as is necessary to achieve one's goals without violating the ten points above.

Now you have a better idea of what it means to be assertive, and you are probably ready to begin taking steps toward increasing your own effectiveness in self-expression.

The following chapter provides many examples of life situations calling for assertive action. It's likely you'll find yourself nodding in recognition as you read them!

6

"Can You Give Me an Example?"

*We are all controlled by the world
in which we live. . . . The question is this:
are we to be controlled by accidents,
by tyrants, or by ourselves?*
— B. F. SKINNER

A LOOK AT SOME EVERYDAY SITUATIONS will improve your understanding of the behavioral styles we've discussed. As you read the examples in this chapter, you may wish to pause and think about your own response before reading the alternative responses we have presented. These examples are oversimplified, of course, so we can demonstrate the ideas more clearly.

SOMETHING BORROWED

Yolanda is a flight attendant, bright, outgoing, a good worker, and liked by customers and peers. She lives in a condo with two roommates and is looking forward to a quiet evening at home one Friday when her roommate Marcy asks a favor. Marcy says that she is going out with a special man and wants to borrow Yolanda's new and quite expensive necklace. The necklace was a gift from her brother, with whom Yolanda is very close, and it means a great deal to her. Her response is:

Nonassertive: She swallows her anxiety about loss or damage to the necklace. Although she feels that its special meaning makes it too personal to lend, she says "Sure!" She denies herself, rewards Marcy for making an unreasonable request, and worries all evening.

Aggressive: Yolanda is outraged at her friend's request, tells her "Absolutely not!" and rebukes her severely for even daring to ask "such a stupid question." She humiliates Marcy and makes a fool of herself too. Later she feels uncomfortable and guilty. Marcy's hurt feelings show all evening, and she has a miserable time, which puzzles and dismays her date. Thereafter, the relationship between Yolanda and Marcy is very strained.

Assertive: Yolanda explains the significance of the necklace to her roommate. Politely but firmly, she observes that the request is an unreasonable one since this piece of jewelry is particularly personal. Marcy is disappointed but understanding, and Yolanda feels good for having been honest. Marcy impresses her date just by being herself.

DINING OUT

Akim and Letitia are at dinner in a moderately expensive restaurant. Akim has ordered grilled chicken breast; but when the entree is served, he finds it overcooked and dry. His action is:

Nonassertive: Akim grumbles to Letitia about the "burned meat" and vows that he won't patronize this restaurant in the future. He says nothing to the server, responding "Fine!" to her inquiry, "Is everything all right?" His dinner and evening are spoiled, and he feels angry with himself for taking no action. Akim's estimate of himself and Letitia's estimate of him are both deflated by the experience.

Aggressive: Akim angrily summons the server to his table. He criticizes her loudly and unfairly for not complying with his order. His actions ridicule the server and embarrass Letitia. He demands and receives another chicken breast, this one more to his liking. He feels in control of the situation, but Letitia's embarrassment creates friction between them and spoils their night out. The server is humiliated and angry for the rest of the evening.

Assertive: Akim motions the server to his table. He shows her the overcooked meat, and asks politely but firmly that it be returned to the kitchen and replaced. The server apologizes for the error and shortly returns with a properly cooked order of chicken. Akim and Letitia enjoy dinner, and Akim feels satisfaction with himself. The server is pleased with a satisfied customer and a generous tip.

HAVE A SNORT!

Lindsay is a friendly, socially active graduate student who has been going out with Paulo and has come to care a lot for him. One evening, he invites her to attend a small get-together with two other couples. As everyone gets acquainted at the party, Lindsay is enjoying herself. After an hour or so, one of the new friends brings out a small bag of cocaine. Everyone responds eagerly except Lindsay. She has not tried coke and does not wish to experiment. She is in real conflict because Paulo offers her a snort. She decides to be:

Nonassertive: She accepts the cocaine and pretends to have used it before. She carefully watches the others to see how they inhale the drug. She dreads the possibility they may ask her to take more. Lindsay is worried about what her friend is thinking about her. She has denied her feelings, been dishonest with Paulo, and feels remorseful for giving in to something she did not wish to do.

Aggressive: Lindsay is visibly upset when offered the cocaine and blasts Paulo for bringing her to a party of this type. She demands he take her home right away. When the others at the party say that she does not have to use if she doesn't wish to, she yells at them. As she continues to behave indignantly, Paulo is humiliated, embarrassed before his friends, and disappointed in her. Although he remains cordial toward Lindsay as he takes her home, he bad-mouths her to his friends the next day.

Assertive: Lindsay does not accept the cocaine, replying simply, "No, I don't want it." She asks Paulo to take her home. On the way, she makes clear to him her concern that he didn't tell her in advance that cocaine would be offered at the party. She emphasizes that he also had exposed her to possible arrest, had the party been discovered by the police. Lindsay tells Paulo she'll break off the relationship if he continues to use drugs.

THE HEAVYWEIGHT

Dominic and Gina, married nine years, have been having marital problems recently because he insists that she is overweight and needs to reduce. He brings the subject up continually, pointing out that she is no longer the woman he married (she was twenty-five pounds lighter then). He keeps telling her that such overweight is bad for her health, that she is a bad example for the children, and so on.

Dominic teases Gina about being "chunky," looks longingly at thin women, while commenting how attractive they look, and makes reference to her figure in front of their friends. Dominic has been acting this way for several months and Gina is highly upset. She has been attempting to lose weight for months, with little success. Following Dominic's most recent rash of criticism, Gina is:

Nonassertive: She apologizes for her overweight, makes feeble excuses, or simply doesn't reply to some of Dominic's comments. Internally, she feels both hostile toward her husband for his nagging and guilty about being overweight. Her feelings of anxiety make it even more difficult for her to lose weight and the battle continues.

Aggressive: Gina goes into a long tirade about how her husband isn't any great bargain anymore, either. She brings up the fact that at night he falls asleep on the couch half the time, is a lousy sex partner, and doesn't pay enough attention to her. She complains that he humiliates her in front of the children and their close friends and that he acts like a "lecherous old man" by the way he eyes other women.

In her anger, she succeeds only in wounding Dominic and driving a wedge between them by her counterattack.

Assertive: Approaching her husband when they are alone and will not be interrupted, Gina says that she feels that Dominic is right about her need to lose weight, but she does not like the way he keeps after her about the problem. She points out that she is doing her best and is having a difficult time losing the weight and maintaining the loss. He admits that his harping is ineffective, and together they work out a plan to exercise together. Dominic also resolves to reinforce her systematically for her efforts to lose weight.

VOLUME UNCONTROLLED

Edmond and Virginia have a two-year-old boy and a baby girl. Over the last several nights, their neighbor's son, seventeen, has been sitting in his car in his own driveway with his car stereo blaring loudly. He begins just about the time their two young children go to bed on the side of the house closest to the music. They've found it virtually impossible to get the children to sleep until the music stops. Edmond and Virginia are both disturbed and decide to be:

Nonassertive: They move the children into their own bedroom on the other side of the house, wait until the noise stops (around midnight), and then transfer the children back to their own rooms. Then they go to bed much past their own usual bedtime. They quietly curse the teenager, and soon become alienated from their neighbors.

Aggressive: They call the police and protest that "one of those wild teenagers next door is creating a disturbance." They demand that the police put a stop to the noise at once. The police do talk with the boy and his parents, who get very angry as a result of their embarrassment about the police visit. They denounce Edmond and Virginia for reporting to the police without speaking to them first and resolve to have nothing further to do with them.

Assertive: Edmond goes over to the boy's house early one evening and tells him that his stereo is keeping the children awake at night. Edmond suggests they try to work out an arrangement that allows the boy his music but does not disturb the children's sleep. The boy reluctantly agrees to set a lower volume during the late hours, but he appreciates Edmond's cooperative attitude. Both parties feel good about the outcome and agree to follow up a week later to be sure it is working as agreed.

THE LOSER

Chang is a twenty-two-year-old college dropout who works as a software developer. He lives alone in a converted loft not far from his workplace. Chang has had no dates for the past fourteen months. He left college after a series of depressing events — academic failures, a "Dear John" letter, and some painful harassment by other students in his residence hall. He has been in jail overnight for drunkenness on two recent occasions.

Yesterday, Chang received a letter from his mother inquiring about his well-being but primarily devoted to a discussion of his brother's recent successes. Today, his supervisor criticized him harshly for a mistake that was actually the supervisor's own fault. A co-worker he admires turned down his invitation to dinner.

When he arrived at his apartment that evening, feeling particularly depressed, his landlord met him at the door with a tirade about "drunken bums" and a demand that he pay this month's rent on time. Chang's response is:

Nonassertive: He takes on himself the burden of the landlord's attack, feeling added guilt and even greater depression. A sense of helplessness overcomes him. He wonders how his brother can be so successful while he considers himself so worthless. The co-worker's rejection and the boss's criticism strengthen his opinion that he is worthless. He decides he really has nothing to live for and begins to think about how he will commit suicide.

Aggressive: The landlord has added the final straw to Chang's burden. He becomes extremely angry and pushes the landlord out of the way in order to get into his room. Once alone, he resolves to "get" the people who have been making his life so miserable recently: the supervisor, the co-worker, the landlord, whoever. He remembers the guns he saw in the pawn shop window yesterday...

Assertive: Chang responds firmly to the landlord, noting that he has paid his rent regularly and that it is not due for another week. He reminds the landlord of a broken rail on the stairway and the plumbing repairs that were to have been accomplished weeks earlier. The following morning, after giving his life situation a great deal of thought, Chang calls the local mental health clinic to ask for help. At work, he approaches the supervisor calmly and explains the circumstances surrounding the mistake. Though somewhat defensive, the supervisor acknowledges her error and apologizes for her aggressive behavior.

RECOGNIZING YOUR OWN NONASSERTIVE AND AGGRESSIVE BEHAVIOR

The examples given in this chapter help to point out what assertiveness means in everyday events. Perhaps one or more of the situations rang a bell in your own life. Take a few minutes to listen honestly to yourself describe your relationships with others who are important to you. Carefully examine your contacts with parents, peers, co-workers, classmates, spouse, children, bosses, teachers, salespeople, neighbors, and relatives. Who is dominant in these relationships? Are you easily taken advantage of in dealings with others? Do you usually express your feelings and ideas openly? Do you take advantage of or hurt others frequently?

Your responses to such questions provide hints that may lead you to explore in greater depth your assertive, nonassertive, or aggressive behavior. If you did not complete the *Assertiveness Inventory* in chapter 2, we urge you to do so now. We think you'll find such a self-examination rewarding and a very important step toward increasing your interpersonal effectiveness.

7

Set Goals for Yourself

Never play another
person's game.
Play your own.
— ANDREW SALTER

A PROFESSOR WE ADMIRED used to tell his graduate students that changing yourself is like planning a trip: you have to find out where you are now, decide where you want to go, then figure out how to get *there* from *here*.

Much of the material in this book so far has been devoted to helping you find out where you are now in relation to assertiveness. In the following chapters we'll be focusing on ways to "get there." This chapter is the bridge — to help you decide where you're headed. Setting your goals may be the most important and most difficult step of all.

"HOW DO I KNOW WHAT I WANT?"

Assertiveness training evolved out of the idea that people live better lives if they can express what they want, if they can let others know how they would like to be treated. Some folks, however, find it hard to know what they really want from life. If you have spent most of your life doing for others and believing that what you want is not important, it can be quite a chore to get a handle on just what is important to you!

59

Some people do seem to know exactly how they feel and what they want. If the neighbor's dog is barking loudly, the feeling may be annoyance or anger or fear, but such people are able to translate the feeling, get to the key issue at hand, and make the needed assertions, if any.

Others find it difficult to know what their feelings are and what they want to accomplish in an encounter. They often hesitate to be assertive, lamenting, "Assert *what?* I don't know what I want!" If you have such trouble you may find it valuable to try to *label* your feelings. Anger, anxiety, boredom, discomfort, and fear are common feelings. Among others you will experience are happiness, irritation, love, relaxation, and sadness.

Some people will require only a few moments reflection to reveal what they are feeling inside. Others may need a more active first step. It often helps to say *something* to the people involved: "I'm upset, but I'm not sure why." Or perhaps, "I'm feeling depressed." "Something feels wrong, but I can't put my finger on it." Such a statement will start you on an active search for the feeling you're sensing and will help you begin to clarify your goals.

Perhaps it is a fear of some sort that is preventing you from recognizing your feelings — a type of protective mechanism. Or you may just be so far out of touch with your feelings that you have virtually forgotten what they mean. Don't get bogged down at this stage. Go ahead and try to express yourself. You will probably become aware of your goal even as you proceed. Indeed, maybe all you wanted was to say something! If you do begin to recognize the underlying feeling and decide to change directions in mid-stream ("I started out angry, but realized that what I really wanted was attention!"), that is a constructive step.

You can go a long way toward clarifying your feelings in a specific situation by identifying your general life goals. Assertiveness does need direction; while it seems to be a good idea in general, it is of little value for its own sake!

You'll find at times that goals will be in conflict. You may wish, for example, to keep a friendly relationship with your next-door neighbor but *also* wish to quiet his noisy dog. If you confront him about the dog, you may risk the good relationship. At such a point, clarification of your own goals will be invaluable in deciding what to do and how to do it.

A Behavioral Model for Personal Growth

Dr. Carl Rogers is recognized as the most influential psychological thinker of the second half of the twentieth century. His ideas were the major influence in the development of the "Human Potential Movement." Dr. Alberti prepared the list on the following two pages in the early 1970s in an attempt to translate Dr. Rogers's ideas into specific behaviors that could be carried out. We think you'll find it helpful, as you consider this matter of goals for your own growth, to read and ponder the *Behavioral Model for Personal Growth*.

Structuring Your Goals

OK, let's get specific. You want to write in your journal (you are keeping a journal, right?) a few goals that will help guide your work on assertiveness in the weeks to come. Start by thinking creatively about what you want to get out of this program of personal growth. Brainstorm about your assertiveness, writing down anything that comes to mind. Write quickly. Don't ignore or criticize any idea, no matter how silly it may seem. Be as open-minded as you can.

After you have compiled a list of possibilities, you'll need to pare it down into a short list of specific goals. What should go into that list? Consider six key criteria as you decide: *personal factors, ideals, feasibility, flexibility, time,* and *priorities.* Make each of your own goals "qualify" in terms of those six criteria.

Personal Factors

As you evaluate your specific goals for assertive growth, use your discoveries about yourself from the *Assertiveness Inventory* in chapter 2 and your journal entries.

A BEHAVIORAL MODEL FOR PERSONAL GROWTH
Robert E. Alberti, Ph.D.

Dr. Carl Rogers, in his book *On Becoming a Person*, identified three major characteristics of healthy personal growth. The following "behavioral model" is based on the three qualities identified by Rogers.

"An Increasing Openness to Experience"
How recently have you

❖ participated in a new sport or game?

❖ changed your views on an important (political, personal, professional) issue?

❖ tried a new hobby or craft?

❖ taken a course in a new field?

❖ studied a new language or culture?

❖ spent fifteen minutes or more paying attention to your bodily feelings, senses (relaxation, tension, sensuality)?

❖ listened for fifteen minutes or more to a religious, political, professional, or personal viewpoint with which you disagreed?

❖ tasted a new food, smelled a new odor, listened to a new sound?

❖ allowed yourself to cry? or to say "I care about you"? or to laugh until you cried? or to scream at the top of your lung capacity? or to admit you were afraid?

❖ watched the sun (or moon) rise or set? or a bird soar on the wind's currents? or a flower open to the sun?

❖ traveled to a place you had never been before?

❖ made a new friend? or cultivated an old friendship?

❖ spent an hour or more really communicating (actively listening and responding honestly) with a person of a different cultural or racial background?

❖ taken a "fantasy trip" — allowing your imagination to run freely for ten minutes to an hour or more?

"Increasingly Existential Living"

How recently have you

❖ done something you felt like doing at that moment, without regard for the consequences?

❖ stopped to "listen" to what was going on inside you?

❖ spontaneously expressed a feeling — anger, joy, fear, sadness, caring — without thinking about it?

❖ done what you wanted to, instead of what you thought you "should" do?

❖ allowed yourself to spend time or money on an immediate payoff rather than saving for tomorrow?

❖ bought something you wanted on impulse?

❖ done something no one (including you) expected you to do?

"An Increasing Trust in One's Organism"

How recently have you

❖ done what felt right to you, against the advice of others?

❖ allowed yourself to experiment creatively with new approaches to old problems?

❖ expressed an unpopular opinion assertively in the face of majority opposition?

❖ used your own intellectual reasoning ability to work out a solution to a difficult problem?

❖ made a decision and acted upon it right away?

❖ acknowledged by your actions that you can direct your own life?

❖ cared enough about yourself to get a physical exam (within two years)?

❖ told others of your religious faith or philosophy of life?

❖ assumed a position of leadership in your profession, an organization, or your community?

❖ asserted your feelings when you were treated unfairly?

❖ risked sharing your personal feelings with another person?

❖ designed and/or built something on your own?

❖ admitted you were wrong?

In chapter 3, "Keep Track of Your Growth," we suggested that you keep track of your assertive behavior using five categories:

❖ *Situations* that are difficult or easy for you

❖ Key *people* in your life

❖ Your *attitudes*, *thoughts*, and *beliefs* about expressing yourself

❖ *Obstacles* to your assertiveness, such as certain people or fears

❖ The *skills* you possess relating to assertive behavior, such as eye contact, voice volume, and gestures

Spend some time now reviewing your journal, looking for ideas that will help you to define goals for yourself.

You may, for example, find a pattern of difficulty dealing with a co-worker who is pushy. Maybe she insists on doing things her way, doesn't listen to your ideas, and ignores your good suggestions. Your response may be to withdraw, avoiding confrontation by swallowing your disagreement and keeping quiet. You may also be wasting time and energy as you look for ways to stay clear of her and work on your own. Could an assertive approach help you here?

Ideals

There are probably many people you admire. If you select the qualities of one or more "models" of assertiveness as ideals toward which you can strive, you'll have some specific behavioral goals already in mind. A well-chosen ideal will inspire you to stick to your goals.

A good model may be a best friend, a beloved teacher, a public figure, a community leader, an entertainer or actor, a family member, a clergyperson, a business executive, or someone of historical importance. This person's behavior can be one basis for your goals.

Focus on the qualities that you want to attain. Key in on such areas as self-confidence, courage, persistence, and honesty. Measure your behavior against the model you choose.

Think often about the person. Let your reflection on your model's behavior give you energy to keep at your own process of improvement in assertiveness.

> *You can go a long way toward clarifying your feelings in a situation by identifying your general life goals.*

Feasibility

As we have suggested at various points in *Your Perfect Right*, go after your changes in assertive behavior slowly and in small steps to increase your chances of success. Don't set your goals too high and risk early failure. Instead, do a little each day, advancing step by step.

Author/philosopher Morton Hunt illustrates this advice in a poignant way. He tells the story of how he learned to cope with major life stresses by remembering a harrowing experience at age eight. Hunt and several friends climbed a cliff near his home. Half way up, he got very scared and could go no farther. He was caught: to think of going either up or down overwhelmed him. The others left him behind as darkness approached.

Eventually his father came to the rescue, but Morton had to do the work! His father talked him down, and the pattern was established to overcome future fearfulness. The advice was timeless... "take one step at a time," "go inch by inch," "don't worry about what comes next," "don't look way ahead."

Later in life, when faced with major fearful events, Morton Hunt remembered that simple lesson: don't look at the dire consequences; start with the first small step and let that small success provide the courage to take another and another. The small-step goals will add up until the major goal is accomplished.

The suggestions Hunt's father gave are an excellent approach to growth in assertiveness.

❖ Continually remind yourself to break your major goals into small, manageable steps. Take your time.

❖ Soon the end will be in sight; you will notice changes in yourself; and you will reach your goals, one step at a time.

Flexibility

Deciding whether and how you'd like to change can be a complex and never-ending process. Goals are never "set"; they constantly change as you and your life circumstances change.

Maybe at one time you wanted to finish school, and when you did, suddenly a whole new range of possibilities opened up. Or perhaps you sought to make $40,000 a year; by the time you reached that level you needed $60,000! Then there was that promotion; when you got it, you found you didn't like your new responsibilities as well as your old.

So *change* itself is the constant factor. Keep your goals flexible enough that you can adapt to the inevitable changes that will come in your life.

Time

How about listing your goals according to how long it will take to accomplish them? Here are some examples of assertiveness goals:

Long-Range Goals
- Behave more assertively with my spouse.
- Take more risks in my life.
- Reduce my anxiety about behaving assertively.
- Overcome my fear of conflict and anger.
- Gain a good understanding of how my childhood experiences influenced my assertiveness.

One-Year Goals
- Compliment those close to me more frequently.
- Speak out in front of groups more often.
- Say no and stick to it!
- Improve my eye contact in conversation.
- Not say "I'm sorry" or "I hate to bother you" so much.

One-Month Goals
- Return the faulty vacuum cleaner to the store.
- Say no to the finder of committee members at work.
- Get firmer in disciplining my children.
- Invite my new neighbor over for coffee.
- Start listening to CDs, tapes, or downloads on assertiveness.

These lists are only ideas from hundreds — or thousands — of possibilities! Develop your own unique, personal lists. Be assertive! No one knows your needs better than you.

Priorities

After identifying your short-range, mid-range, and long-range lists of goals, sort each group according to your own priorities.

Identify "top, middle, and bottom drawer" goals.

	One month	One year	Long range
Top drawer	• Return faulty vacuum • Invite new neighbor over	• Speak out more • Say no & stick to it! And don't say I'm sorry!	• Overcome my fear of conflict & anger • Take more risks
Middle drawer	• Start assertiveness tapes • Get firmer with kids	• Compliment John more often	• Behave more assertively with John
Bottom drawer	• Say no to fund drive	• Improve eye contact	• Think about how childhood experience influenced me

Top Drawer — goals that are most important

Middle Drawer — goals that are important but don't need to be accomplished right away

Bottom Drawer — goals that can be put off indefinitely without causing great stress

If you select two top-drawer goals from each of the three time lists, you'll have six top-priority items to work on during a period of one month. Each month you can select a new list. Some goals will stay top drawer, others won't.

GOAL FOR IT!

You have identified some possible goals for your growth, evaluated them, and begun to sort them according to their importance and feasibility.

Select — and write in your journal — a few goals to work on over the next weeks and months.

Throw out the ideas that are too far-fetched or out of reach for you at this time. Be practical at this point. Narrow down exactly what your next steps will be in your assertiveness journey.

As you proceed in your choice-making process, keep in mind your model/ideal person. See if your choices generally agree with those qualities you want to develop. Your assertive behavior won't exactly match that of your ideal — in fact, you don't want it to. You are trying to be the person *you* really are, not someone else.

Remember that your choices are always tentative and subject to change with new circumstances and information. Stay on your course, but remain flexible, making adjustments as needed. Setting goals for your own life can be an exciting process. As you take steps toward each goal, you'll find a genuine sense of accomplishment in your progress. Pat yourself on the back as you achieve each step. Use your journal regularly to keep track. And most important: *let this be for you.* Your goals needn't please anybody else. Pay careful attention to your own desires and needs; *play your own game.*

8

It's Not What You Say,
It's How You Say It!

It takes two to speak truth —
one to speak and another to hear.
— HENRY DAVID THOREAU

SELF-EXPRESSION IS A UNIVERSAL HUMAN NEED. The form it takes is unique to each of us, of course. In this chapter, we'll take a look at the several components of behavior that go together to make up our individual styles. While individual differences "make the world go 'round," each of us can learn the skills necessary for good communication.

(The chapter may seem a little long, but we think you'll agree it's worth it as you learn how the components fit together to create an assertive message.)

"I NEVER KNOW WHAT TO SAY!"

Many people view assertiveness as a verbal behavior, believing that they must have "just the right words" to handle a situation effectively. On the contrary, we've found that *how* you express an assertive message is a good deal more important than *what* you say. Although scripts of "what to say when..." are popular with many assertiveness trainers, those have never been our style. We're primarily concerned with encouraging honesty and directness, and much of that message is communicated *nonverbally.*

Participants in our groups and workshops have enjoyed watching us role-play a scene that makes this point clear: Bob acts as a dissatisfied customer who wishes to return a defective copy of *Everything You Always Wanted to Know about Assertiveness, but Were Too Timid to Ask* to the bookstore; Mike is the clerk. Using essentially the same words, "I bought this book here last week and discovered that twenty pages are missing. I'd like a good copy or my money back," Bob approaches Mike in three different ways:

1. Bob walks slowly and hesitantly to the counter. His eyes are downcast at the floor, he speaks just above a whisper, his face looks as though it belongs on the cover of the book. He has a tight grip on the book, and a "please don't hurt me" posture.

2. Bob swaggers toward the counter, glares at Mike, addresses him in a voice heard all over the store. Bob's posture and fist-like gesture are an obvious attempt to intimidate the clerk.

3. Bob walks up to the counter facing Mike. He stands relaxed and erect, smiles, and looks directly at Mike with a friendly expression. In a conversational volume and tone of voice, he states the message, gesturing to point out the flaw in the book.

The three styles are overexaggerated in our demonstration, of course, but the point is clear. The nonassertive, self-defeating style says to Mike that this customer is a pushover, and the slightest resistance will cause him to give up and go away. The second approach may achieve the goal of refund or exchange, but the aggressive Bob will leave with Mike's hostility directed at his back! With the assertive approach, Bob gets what he came for, and Mike feels good about solving a problem for an appreciative customer.

THE COMPONENTS OF ASSERTIVE BEHAVIOR

Systematic observations of assertive behavior have led behavioral scientists to conclude that there are several important components that contribute to an assertive act. The late Michael Serber, M.D., a California psychiatrist who did extensive work with assertiveness training in the 1960s and 1970s significantly influenced our thinking in this area.

More recently, the work of psychologist Paul Ekman and his colleagues at the University of California, Berkeley, has confirmed much of what Serber and others posited long ago: the words may be even *less important* than the nonverbal components.

It should be noted that most of the research in this field has been done with North Americans of European ancestry. Ethnic and cultural considerations are very important influences on the components described in this chapter. We urge you to reread the discussion of cultural factors in chapter 4 and to be aware of cultural dimensions as you study these aspects of behavior.

With that caveat in mind, then, let's examine the key components of assertive behavior in detail.

Eye Contact. One of the most obvious aspects of behavior when talking to another person is where you look. In general, if you look directly at the person as you speak, it helps to communicate your sincerity and to increase the directness of your message. If you look down or away much of the time, you present a lack of confidence or a quality of deference to the other person. If you stare too intently, the other person may feel an uncomfortable invasion.

We do not suggest that you *maximize* eye contact. Continuously looking at someone can make the other person uncomfortable, is inappropriate and unnecessary, and may appear to be a game.

> *There are several important components which contribute to an assertive act.*

Moreover, eye contact is a cultural variable; many cultural groups limit the amount of eye contact that is acceptable, particularly between age groups or members of the opposite sex.

Nevertheless, the importance of eye contact is obvious. A relaxed and steady gaze at the other, looking away occasionally as is comfortable, helps to make conversation more personal, to show interest in and respect for the other person, and to enhance the directness of your message.

As is true with other behaviors, conscious effort may improve eye contact in small steps. Be aware of your eyes as you talk with others, and attempt to gradually optimize your eye attention in conversation.

Body Posture. As you watch other people talking with each other, carefully observe how each is standing or sitting. You may be as amazed as we have been by the number of people who talk with someone while their bodies are turned away from that person. People sitting side by side often turn only their heads toward one another while talking. Next time you are in that situation, notice how much more personal the conversation becomes with a slight turn of the shoulders and torso — say 30 degrees — toward the other person.

Standing or sitting may emphasize relative "power" in an encounter. A particularly evident power imbalance may be seen in the relationship between a tall adult and a small child; the adult who is thoughtful enough to bend or crouch to the child's height will find an observable difference in the quality of communication and usually a much more responsive child!

In a situation in which you are called upon to stand up for yourself, it may be useful to do just that — stand up. An active and erect posture, while facing the other person directly, lends additional assertiveness to your message. A slumped, passive stance gives the other person an immediate advantage, as does any tendency on your part to lean back or move away. Remember Bob's first approach to the "bookstore clerk" at the beginning of this chapter?

Distance/Physical Contact. An interesting aspect of cross-cultural research into nonverbal communication is that of distance vs. closeness between people in conversation. As a very broad generalization, it has been said that, among European peoples, the farther North one goes, the farther apart individuals stand when engaged in conversation. In the United States, as in Europe, closeness seems to increase in warmer climates; but there are important exceptions, notably among ethnic subcultures that value closeness and contact differently. Closeness is, of course, not necessarily related to temperature. Cultural and social customs are products of very complex historical factors. In the Arab world, for example, it is customary for men to greet one another with a hug and kiss and to stand very close to each other. Interestingly, however, it would be considered very inappropriate for an Arab man to behave toward a woman in this way, yet that is quite common in the United States and Southern Europe.

Distance from another person does have a considerable effect upon communication. Standing or sitting very close, or touching, suggests intimacy in a relationship, unless the people happen to be in a crowd or very cramped quarters. The typical discomfort of elevator passengers is a classic example of the difficulty we have in dealing with closeness! Coming too close may offend the other person, make her or him defensive, or open the door to greater intimacy. It can be worthwhile to check out verbally how the other person feels about your closeness.

Gestures. Accentuating your message with appropriate gestures can add emphasis, openness, and warmth. Bob Alberti traces his enthusiastic use of gestures in conversation to his Italian heritage. While gesturing is indeed a somewhat culturally related behavior, a relaxed use of gestures can add depth or power to your messages. Uninhibited movement can also suggest openness, self-confidence (unless the gesturing is erratic and nervous), and spontaneity on the part of the speaker.

Facial Expression. Ever see someone trying to express anger while smiling or laughing? It just doesn't come across. Effective assertions require an expression that agrees with the message. An angry message is clearest when delivered with a straight, nonsmiling countenance. A friendly communication should not be delivered with a dark frown. Let your face say the same thing your words are saying!

Dr. Paul Ekman of the University of California has published extensively on the subject of how important facial expression is to interpersonal communication. Ekman and his colleagues developed the "Facial Action Coding System," a tool for actually measuring muscular movements in the face and relating those movements to emotions. Ekman's research shows that people can easily learn to read the subtle facial movements of others and thus to be more sensitive to the emotions they're expressing. Moreover, you may be able to begin to control your own facial expressions to more accurately reflect your feelings or, if you prefer, to hide them.

If you look at yourself in the mirror, you can learn a great deal about what your face says on your behalf. First, relax all the muscles of your face as much as you can. Let go of your expression, relax the muscles around your mouth, let your jaw go loose, let your cheeks soften along with the wrinkles of your forehead and around your eyes. Pay careful attention to the relaxed, soft feelings. Now smile, bringing your mouth up as widely as you can. Feel the tightness in your cheeks, around your eyes, all the way up to your ears. Hold that smile, look at the expression in the mirror, and concentrate on the feelings of tightness. Now relax your face completely again. Notice the difference between the relaxed feelings and those of the tight smile, and the difference between the expressions you see in the mirror.

With greater awareness of how your facial muscles feel in various expressions and of how you look when you smile and when you are relaxed, you can begin to control your facial expression more consciously and to make it congruent with what you are thinking, feeling, or saying. And you may develop a more natural, less "plastic" smile for those times when you really want your happiness to show!

(For more on this topic, you may enjoy reading Ekman's book, *Emotions Revealed*, cited in the References.)

Voice Tone, Inflection, and Volume. The way we use our voices is a vital element in our communications. The same words spoken through clenched teeth in anger offer an entirely different message than when they are shouted with joy or whispered in fear.

A level, well-modulated, conversational statement is convincing without being intimidating; a whispered monotone will seldom convince another person that you mean business; while a shouted epithet will bring defenses into the path of communication.

Voice is one of the easiest of the components of behavior on which to gain accurate feedback these days. Most everyone has easy access to a small voice recorder that can be used to "try out" different styles of your voice. You may wish to experiment with a conversational tone, an angry shouted blast, a caring message, and a persuasive argument. You may be surprised at how quiet your "shouts" are or at how loud your "conversational tone" is.

Consider at least three dimensions of your voice:

❖ *tone* (Is it raspy, whiny, seductively soft, angry?)

❖ *inflection* (Do you raise the pitch at the end of sentences, as in a question, or speak in a monotone, or with "sing-song" effect?)

❖ *volume* (Do you try to gain attention with a whisper or to overpower others with loudness, or is it very difficult for you to shout even when you want to?)

If you can control and use your voice effectively, you have acquired a powerful tool in your self-expression. Practice with a recorder, trying out different styles until you achieve a style you like. Allow time for changes to come, and use the recorder regularly to check your progress.

Fluency. Psychiatrist Mike Serber employed an exercise he called "sell me something," in which he asked the client to talk persuasively about an object, such as a watch, for thirty seconds. For many people, it is very difficult to put together a string of words lasting thirty seconds.

A smooth flow of speech is a valuable asset to get your point across in any type of conversation. It is not necessary to talk rapidly for a long period; but if your speech is interrupted with long periods of hesitation, your listeners may get bored and will probably recognize you are very unsure of yourself. Clear and slow comments are more easily understood and more powerful than rapid speech that is erratic and filled with long pauses and stammering.

Once again, a digital or tape recorder is a valuable tool. Use the device to practice by talking on a familiar subject for thirty seconds. Then listen to yourself, noticing pauses of three seconds or more and space fillers such as "uhhh" and "you know." Repeat the same exercise, more slowly if necessary, trying to eliminate any significant pauses. Gradually increase the difficulty of the task by dealing with less familiar topics, trying to be persuasive, pretending to respond in an argument, or working with a friend to keep a genuine dialogue going.

The program of the Toastmasters (International Trainers in Communication) organization offers a unique opportunity for practice with feedback from a supportive audience. You may want to check out a branch in your community.

Timing. In general, we urge spontaneity of expression as a goal. Nevertheless, while hesitation may diminish the effectiveness of your assertions, it is never "too late" to be assertive! Even though the ideal moment has passed, you will often find it worthwhile to go to the person at a later time and express your feelings. Indeed, psychologists have even developed special techniques to help individuals express strong emotions toward those who may have died (e.g., parents) before the feelings could be expressed.

Spontaneous assertion will help keep your life clear, and will help you to focus accurately on the feelings you have at the time. At times, however, it is necessary to choose an occasion to discuss a strong feeling. It is not a good idea to confront someone in front of others, for example, because extra defenses are sure to be present under those conditions. If you must "let it all hang out," find a private place and time to do so!

Listening. This component is perhaps the most difficult both to describe and to change, yet it may well be the most important. Assertive listening involves an active commitment to the other person. It requires your full attention, yet calls for no overt act on your part, although eye contact and certain gestures — such as nodding — are often appropriate. Listening demonstrates your respect for the other person. It requires that you avoid expressing *yourself* for a time, perhaps even putting your own needs on hold as you listen, yet is not a nonassertive act.

Listening is not simply the physical response of hearing sounds — indeed, hearing-impaired persons may be excellent "listeners." Effective listening may involve giving feedback to the other person, so that it is clear that you understood what was said. Assertive listening requires at least these elements:

❖ *tuning in* to the other person by stopping other activities — turning off the TV, computer, or iPod — ignoring other distractions, and focusing your energy in his or her direction

❖ *paying attention* to the message by making eye contact if possible, nodding to show that you hear, and perhaps touching her or him

❖ actively *attempting to understand* before responding by thinking about the underlying message — the feelings behind the words — rather than trying to interpret or to come up with an answer.

Assertiveness includes respect for the rights and feelings of others. That means assertive *receiving* — sensitivity to others — as well as assertive *sending*.

As with other components of assertive behavior, listening is a skill that can be learned. It is hard work, takes patience, and requires other people willing to work with you. Try to hook up with a "practice partner," and take turns listening to each other and sharpening each other's listening skills. Practice accurate *paraphrasing* of each other's communications, refining your paraphrases until the partner agrees you've got it right. It will strengthen your capacity to listen.

Good listening will make all of your assertions more effective and will contribute much to the quality of your relationships.

Thoughts. Another component of assertiveness that escapes direct observation is the thinking process. Although it has long been understood intuitively that attitudes influence behavior, only recently has psychological research been sophisticated enough to deal directly with the link. The late psychologist Albert Ellis of New York City, psychologist Donald Meichenbaum of Ontario, Canada, and psychiatrists Aaron Beck of Philadelphia and David Burns of the University of Pennsylvania have been particularly influential in focusing attention on the *cognitive* dimensions of behavior.

Ellis, for example, reduced the process to a simple A-B-C: (A) an event takes place, (B) a person sees and interprets it internally,

(C) the person reacts in some way. Part B — the perception and thought process — often was ignored in the past.

The work of Meichenbaum, Beck, and Burns, together with that of others in the field of "cognitive behavior therapy" — much of it built upon Ellis's work — has produced a variety of specific procedures for developing assertive thinking. Thus you can now work on your thoughts as well as your eye contact, posture, and gestures.

Thinking, of course, is probably the most complex thing we humans do. As you might imagine, procedures for changing our thoughts and attitudes are very complex also. We will discuss this area more in chapter 10, but for now, consider two aspects of your assertive thinking: your attitudes about *whether it is a good idea in general* for people to be assertive, and your *thoughts about yourself* when you are in a situation that calls for assertive action. Some people, for instance, think it is not a good idea for *anybody* to express himself or herself. And some say it's OK for *others*, but not for *me*. If either of these beliefs rings a bell with you, we want you to pay particular attention to chapter 10 and work on thinking assertively!

Persistence. As you may recall, we opened chapter 5 with a brief story about the "Senior Gleaners" of Northern California and their founder, Homer Fahrner. Remember Fahrner's comment about being persistent in the face of rejection? "I'm saying first, right out, when the crops grow, go out and see those people and *persist*. Because one turns you down, maybe he's got a good reason. Go on, go on, go on."

Indeed, persistence — going on — is a key element in assertive self-expression. Not giving up. Not saying, "Oh well, there's nothing I can do about it." Not concluding that you're not worth it. Because you are worth it, and there very likely is something you can do about it.

Many of the procedures we've described in *Your Perfect Right* may be effective immediately. Speaking up clearly with good eye contact and posture appropriate to your message may get you what you're asking for: a raise, prompt service, a refund, less noise from the neighbors . . . But some situations require a longer-term effort. You may need to, as Mr. Fahrner put it, "go on, go on, go on."

That doesn't mean, incidentally, using some variation of the once-popular "broken record" approach, in which you're advised simply to repeat the language of your request over and over. We don't consider that to be effective or appropriate. In fact, it's likely to get doors slammed in your face. When we encourage "persistence," we mean something more akin to Alan Alda's advice to his daughter: "Be fair with others, and keep after them until they're fair with you."

Strangely enough, we've not talked much about this key component in previous editions of this book. Perhaps we've taken it for granted. Don't make our mistake and ignore it in your life. Keep on keeping on.

To get the city to fix that major pothole on your street may require repeated visits to the public works office, perhaps visits to the city manager, and maybe even an appearance before the city council. *Persistence.*

To get your boss to address an issue of harassment or discriminatory compensation or an unsafe working environment may mean repeated visits to the HR department, speaking up at company meetings, private conversations in his office, or a complaint to your union representatives. *Persistence.*

To get your "lemon" repaired properly — or replaced — may mean speaking with the dealership service manager, the general manager, the owner, the manufacturer's district representative, the manufacturer's public relations department, a vice president or the president of the company, or a public consumer advocate (e.g., a state official or a TV, magazine, or newspaper personality). *Persistence.*

To get the attention of the VA or Congress to improve the mental health care available to returning war veterans who suffer from post-traumatic stress disorder may mean letters, petitions, visits to the district office, visits to Washington, even marches in the streets. *Persistence.*

All of the components of assertive behavior we have described in this book — direct language, eye contact, posture, gestures, voice qualities, etc. — apply to such situations, of course. The element of persistence simply means applying them again, and again, and again, as needed.

Content. We save this obvious dimension of assertiveness for last to emphasize that although what you say is clearly important, it is often less important than most people generally believe. Many people hesitate because they don't know *what* to say. Others have found the practice of saying *something* about their feelings at the time to be a valuable step. We encourage honest and spontaneous expression. That means saying forcefully, "I'm really upset about what you just did!" rather than, "You're an S.O.B.!"

Let's take a closer look at some effective ways to "slice and dice" the content of an assertive message.

❖ *"I-messages."* We encourage you to express yourself — and to take responsibility for your feelings; don't blame the other person for how you feel. Note the difference in the above example between *"I'm* upset" and *"You're* an S.O.B." It is not necessary to put the other person down (aggressive) in order to express your feeling (assertive). Use "I-messages" to express your own feelings, rather than passing responsibility for how you feel to someone else. Your feelings are yours, and it's OK to say so.

Expressing your feeling in the form of an "I-message" was the brainchild of Dr. Thomas Gordon, a California psychologist and author of the bestseller *Parent Effectiveness Training.* Dr. Gordon offered the idea in the context of parent-child communication, but it quickly found a home in all venues of interpersonal contact. The idea is simply to let the other person know how *you* are feeling about his or her behavior. The other interprets an I-message as a statement of how you are feeling, not as an accusation or evaluation of her or him. Thus, once again, "I'm upset" is a clearer and more effective message than "You're an S.O.B." Likewise, "I'm hurt" is more honest than "You're unfair."

Dr. Gordon, incidentally, didn't like the idea of expressing anger as an "I-message," believing that it contained a hidden "you-message": implicitly blaming the other person for your anger. We don't agree, but we do recognize the potential value of clarifying your statement by spelling it out more fully: "I'm upset about what you just did because I feel disrespected when I'm criticized in front of others."

(Incidentally, *Parent Effectiveness Training* was first published in the same year as the first edition of *Your Perfect Right:* 1970.)

❖ *Categories.* Psychologists Myles Cooley and James Hollandsworth developed another model for assertive statements. They grouped seven elements into three general categories:

Saying no or taking a stand includes stating your position, explaining your reason, and expressing understanding.

Asking favors or asserting rights may be expressed by stating the problem, making a request, and getting clarification.

Expressing feelings is accomplished by a statement of your emotions in a situation.

(You may find it valuable to practice each of these categories of statements with your practice partner or into a recorder.)

❖ *Syntonics.* You can best achieve your goals in communication by being in harmony — "syntony" — with the other person linguistically. Linguist Dr. Suzette Haden Elgin wrote a popular series of books on "syntonics" — *The Gentle Art of Verbal Self-Defense* and its sequels — in which she compares effective interpersonal communication to tuning a musical instrument. You have a standard to work toward (an electronic tuner, for instance), and you must gradually adjust your pitch to equal that of the standard. Likewise in communicating, your words and your nonverbal style can be fine-tuned until they match well with those of your listener.

One of the techniques of syntonics involves adjusting to the other person's *sensory preference:* seeing, hearing, touching, smelling, and tasting. Thus, one person may say, "I *see* what you mean." while another means exactly the same thing when she says, "I *hear* you."

(You'll recognize the parallels here to our earlier discussion of so-called "mirror neurons" in the human brain. We are hardwired to mimic the feelings expressed by others as we interact.)

The idea is to help us learn to "read" our audiences and to communicate verbally and nonverbally in ways that will encourage them to respond positively to our messages. Used carefully and ethically, such procedures can be valuable tools in improved communication. (Needless to say, there is plenty of room for abuse here!)

❖ *Target audience.* One further word about content. Psychologist Donald Cheek, a neighbor and former university faculty colleague of ours, writing about assertiveness from an African American perspective, pointed out the need to adapt assertiveness to your cultural setting. Particularly for minorities who may find themselves in "survival" situations, Cheek emphasized that *what* you say must take into consideration *to whom* you are saying it! Language that would be interpreted as assertive within one's own subculture, for example, could easily be interpreted as aggressive by "outsiders." The issue is remarkably complex, however.

For example, cross-cultural research on facial expression (recall the work of Paul Ekman, discussed earlier in the chapter) suggests that different aspects of expression are both universal and culture specific. Individual differences may be greater than differences between cultural groups!

We do not advise that you change yourself to adapt to whatever any situation seems to invite. Nevertheless, all of us do deal with individuals differently, depending upon our respective roles and the perceived "power" of others over us. We hope you can be yourself; honesty remains the best overall guide.

Assertiveness doesn't depend upon being highly verbal, but some folks do seem to have difficulty finding the "right words." We don't recommend particular formulas or scripts for assertive expression because we'd rather see you use your own language. We hope it's clear by now that the *style* of your delivery is more important than the *words* anyway. It's surprising how often clients tell us *very clearly* how they feel about a particular situation and then ask, "What shall I say to the person?" Our answer is usually: "Say the same thing you just said to me!" You very likely have the "right words" without knowing it.

Don't misunderstand us here; *content is not unimportant*. It's just not usually the content that hangs people up. It is anxiety, lack of skills, or the belief that "I have no right . . ."

(Chapter 10, "Thinking Assertively," has more ideas you may find helpful as you consider the content of your assertive messages.)

You can imagine a wide variety of situations that show the importance of how you make yourself heard. The time you spend thinking about "just the right words" would be better spent making those assertions! The ultimate goal is to express yourself — honestly and as spontaneously as the situation allows — in a manner right for you.

CHECK OUT YOUR "COMPONENT COMPETENCE"

We hope this chapter has caused you to think more systematically about your own self-expression and to formulate some goals for your own work in assertiveness. To improve your familiarity with the components and to relate each one more directly to yourself, we suggest you take a few minutes right now to assess your own strengths with a short exercise:

On a blank sheet in your journal, draw fourteen lines across the page, a half-inch or so apart (if your journal is too small, use a couple of pages).

What you say must take into consideration to whom you are saying it

Label each line with one of the components described in this chapter (eye contact, facial expression, etc.).

Divide each line into six segments (place a small mark in the middle, then use similar marks to divide each half into thirds).

At the top of the page, near the left end of the lines, write "I Need Work." At the top of the page, near the center of the lines, write "I'm OK." At the top of the page, near the right end of the lines, write "I'm Excellent."

Or, if you prefer, you may simply copy our chart on the next two pages!

Now rate yourself on each component by placing marks on the lines in accordance with how well satisfied you are with your skills in each area. You may, for example, feel "OK" about your level of eye contact and the appropriateness of your facial expression in most situations but feel your use of gestures and your voice need some work. If you really have a "way with words," you may consider your content to be "excellent." Take enough time to reread the descriptions of the components in this chapter and to give yourself a thorough evaluation. Be sure to record this effort in your journal, as we have suggested above.

Such a brief self-assessment is necessarily imprecise and requires you to make a "global" evaluation of your skills. (Remember that assertiveness varies with situations and persons.) Nevertheless, we believe you will benefit by giving yourself this "benchmark," then referring back to it in the weeks ahead — perhaps repeating the exercise and recording it in your journal from time to time — as you progress in developing greater skills in assertiveness.

SELF-RATING ON COMPONENTS OF ASSERTIVE BEHAVIOR

Eye Contact

I need work   I'm OK   I'm excellent

|___|___|___|___|___|

Body Posture

I need work   I'm OK   I'm excellent

|___|___|___|___|___|

Distance/Physical Contact

I need work   I'm OK   I'm excellent

|___|___|___|___|___|

Gestures

I need work   I'm OK   I'm excellent

|___|___|___|___|___|

Facial Expression

I need work   I'm OK   I'm excellent

|___|___|___|___|___|

Voice Tone

I need work   I'm OK   I'm excellent

|___|___|___|___|___|

Voice Inflection

I need work   I'm OK   I'm excellent

|___|___|___|___|___|

(Cont'd.)

SELF-RATING ON COMPONENTS
OF ASSERTIVE BEHAVIOR (Continued)

Voice Volume

I need work   I'm OK   I'm excellent

Fluency

I need work   I'm OK   I'm excellent

Timing

I need work   I'm OK   I'm excellent

Listening

I need work   I'm OK   I'm excellent

Thoughts

I need work   I'm OK   I'm excellent

Persistence

I need work   I'm OK   I'm excellent

Content

I need work   I'm OK   I'm excellent

The Components of Assertive Behavior

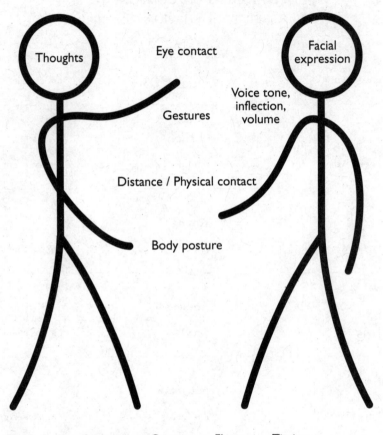

Thoughts

Eye contact

Facial expression

Voice tone, inflection, volume

Gestures

Distance / Physical contact

Body posture

Listening ... Content ... Fluency ... Timing

9

Assertive Messages — Twenty-First Century Style

The effect on language of the electronic age is obvious to us all, even though the process has only just begun, and its ultimate impact is as yet unimaginable.

— LYNNE TRUSS

ALMOST ALL OF THE IDEAS in the previous chapter pretty much assume that you're face-to-face with the other person — spouses, family members, bosses, co-workers, neighbors, strangers, teachers, or sales clerks. We've emphasized the importance of nonverbal components of behavior (e.g., eye contact, posture, gestures, and facial expression) in getting your message across.

Yet, the reality of interpersonal communication in the twenty-first century is that much of our contact with others is at a distance, not face to face. We talk on the telephone, send emails and instant messages, interact by posting notes to online blogs or listservs, and — on rare occasions — even *write* to each other. Much of this communication is private or anonymous, but a great deal is very open, telling the world about ourselves on MySpace, Facebook, or YouTube.

Indeed, the list of new communications technologies is long and includes such techie hardware as cell phones, computers, PDAs, iPods, BlackBerrys, and Bluetooth, and such online applications as email, web pages, blogs, text messaging, instant messaging, YouTube, MySpace, Facebook, Twitter, and who knows what else by the time you're reading this? Youngsters tell us that "email is for old people; we use IM." *(We suggest you search online — e.g., on Google or Wikipedia — for detailed descriptions of any of these terms that are not familiar to you.)*

And, even when we are face to face, many of us *avoid* contact. Stroll downtown or through a shopping mall; walk across a contemporary college campus; sit for a while in a restaurant or in the library. Doesn't it seem that every other person is talking to someone somewhere else via cell phone? Seems hardly anyone actually looks at the people around them or makes eye contact any more.

A colleague recently told us of observing his daughter and her friends — three twelve-year-olds — *in the same room* "talking" to each other via Instant Messaging.

What are the implications of assertiveness for the many ways people connect today?

How Will You Send It?

Actually, there seems to be no end to the variety of methods for delivering your assertive messages. The means you choose will depend upon your target audience, the nature of your message, your time frame, and other variables.

❖ Are you addressing a loved one or friend, someone you see regularly, someone you see rarely or never, an online friend or colleague, or an organization or institution? The closer your connection, the more important your method will be.

❖ What's the nature of your message? Are you reaching out to a loved one, friend, or family member? Are you expressing your anger at mistreatment as a customer? Do you have a political viewpoint to deliver? Saying "I miss you" demands a much more personal method than saying, "We object to the way you treat employees!"

❖ Immediacy matters also. Are you face to face right now? Will you see the person later today? Is the target of your assertive message far away, reachable only by a long-distance method?

The number of possibilities for contact at a distance is mind-boggling, and they're not all high-tech or even new. Let's not ignore the "old-time" systems such as letters, notes, letters to the editor, newspaper ads, speeches or lectures, call-in radio shows, landline phone calls, billboards, public events, radio ads, public service announcements, picket signs, protest marches, press releases, and sky writing (don't laugh; marriages have been proposed in the sky!).

Some of these approaches are more obvious than others, and it's not our purpose in this book to give you a detailed guide to all the possibilities. It's evident that many of the components of behavior we've discussed are not available to us when we're talking on the phone, typing an email, or "thumbing" a text message. Eye contact, posture, and gestures are no longer relevant. Facial expression matters on YouTube, but not in a letter.

This chapter offers a few comments on using the newer technologies to deliver your assertive message. First, however, let's review the fundamentals of assertiveness.

ASSERTIVENESS COUNTS

Let's start with the assumption that assertiveness has a place in all forms of self-expression. *How* we express ourselves remains the key, so we can address ways one might apply the principles you're learning in this book to your communication with others via one or more of the many venues — including the newer technological systems — for connecting.

Regardless of the system of communication you're using — face-to-face, digital, written, telephone — there are some pretty basic guidelines for dealing assertively in your interaction with others. You may not be able to express yourself via eye contact, posture, facial expression, or gestures, but you can "make yourself heard" effectively via whatever means may be available to you. Our take on assertive communication at a distance begins with the eleven key qualities of assertive behavior we listed in chapter 5.

Assertiveness is:

1. *Self-expressive*
2. *Respectful* of the rights of others
3. *Honest*
4. *Direct and firm*
5. *Equalizing*, benefiting both parties in a relationship
6. Both verbal (including the content of the message) and *nonverbal* (including the style of the message)
7. *Positive* at times (expressing affection, praise, or appreciation), and *negative* at times (expressing limits, anger, or criticism)
8. *Appropriate for the person and situation*, not universal
9. *Socially responsible*
10. *Learned*, not inborn, although early brain development can present a challenging obstacle to new learning
11. As *persistent* as is necessary to achieve one's goals without violating the ten points above.

That said, what are the qualities of assertive communication that apply to contact at a distance?

Remember the Basics
- Review the material on *timing* in chapter 8. Before you respond emotionally (e.g., in anger), wait overnight if possible.
- Review the material on *listening* in chapter 8.

- Review the material on *thoughts* in chapter 8.
- Review the material on *content* in chapter 8.

Telephone Messages

- Review the material on *voice tone, inflection,* and *volume* in chapter 8. Remember that a smile — or a scowl — on your face will be heard in your voice.
- Review the material on *fluency* in chapter 8.
- Don't say it on the phone if you would not say it in person.
- Start and continue very personal cell phone conversations in private. Avoid public places where others can't help overhearing you.
- Consider very carefully the messages you leave on voice mail and answering machines. Keep your tone friendly — even if you're calling to complain or argue — especially if you want the other person to call you back!

Written Messages — Online or Snail Mail

- Think hard about how your message will come across to the other person before you write. If you're misunderstood, you won't be present to explain.
- Ask questions and invite responses to engage the other person in dialogue.
- Remember that what you write down will always be available for others to read. Exercise some judgement.
- If you are unsure how your written message might come across and it's not too private to share, having a friend or co-worker read it first to judge the tone before you send it can be a helpful yardstick.
- Don't say it online or in a letter if you would not say it in person.
- If you must criticize or disagree with another's messages or posts, do so privately and directly to that individual, just as you would in person. At least for the first round!

- Respect others' privacy. Don't forward private messages. When you're having a two-way conversation, don't cc others. Use "Reply All" in email *very* sparingly!
- Set your email preferences NOT to send your messages immediately. Always give yourself a chance to read it over one more time before you press send.
- Check your inbox one more time before you "send" to be sure you haven't received a clarification, apology, or revocation email.
- Use * symbols *, **boldface**, underlining, *italics*, CAPS, and smileys ☺ or other emoticons to indicate emphasis or emotional tone, but use them sparingly. For instance, use ALL CAPS only to emphasize a word or two. A friend told us, "A committee member I correspond with via email writes in all caps and I always feel as if she is YELLING AT ME!"
- Use abbvtns vy cautiously if U R xprssng emotions. They may ezly B msundrstd.
- When you're reading a message you've received, keep in mind that some people don't express themselves well in writing. A typed message can sound stilted or even harsh. Don't take it personally until you check it out.
- Take a look at David Shipley and Will Schwalbe's book, *Send*, for more ideas on making your email communications more effective.

Tools for self-expression online I: Emoticons. An emoticon is an icon typed in text to express an emotion, hence the term **emot**(ion)**icon**. The resulting characters, read sideways, look a bit like the expression on a human face. Professor Scott Fahlman of Carnegie-Mellon University takes credit for this innovative form of digital communication, which he says he first sent in 1982.

The following are a few of the common ones you may have seen or may want to consider inserting in your own messages:

:-) or :)	=	Smile or happy
:-(or :(	=	Frown or sad
:-D or :D	=	Wide or open-mouthed smile — a grin, often denoting laughter
:-p or :p	=	Smile with tongue out — used to denote "tongue in cheek" in English
:-S or :S	=	Confused smile
;-)	=	Wink
>:-(or :-@	=	Angry
8-0	=	Shocked
:-o	=	Surprised
:-$	=	Embarrassed or confused
:-|	=	Disappointed or indifferent

There are dozens more in common usage. And you may find creative symbols to express your own feelings. What about fear, excitement, exhaustion, affection, or assertiveness?

"Emoticons," says professor Clifford Nass of Stanford, "reflect the likely original purpose of language — to enable people to express emotion." They are a handy — though imperfect — substitute for tone of voice and other nonverbal components in the digital environment. And some folks sketch them in handwritten communications also.

Tools for self-expression online (or offline) II: Write clearly. Yeah, OK, we know. Writing style and grammar are boring. You just wanna *say* it, right? Sure, but don't you also want the other person to *get* it?

We heard recently from a high school senior who nearly lost a friend thanks to an email exchange that went astray: "I had someone get very upset at me because they thought I was being sarcastic on a topic I was totally serious about. So, when in doubt, or if you think there could be a doubt, be sure to clarify." Sound advice, in our view.

Eats, Shoots and Leaves was a bestseller in the United States and the United Kingdom in 2005-2006, despite the fact that it was a book about punctuation! Author Lynne Truss used the catchy title to emphasize the importance of the lowly comma (in this case to describe the feeding habits of the giant panda; these bears don't really shoot after they eat, do they?) Truss points up the problem of clarifying one's intent this way:

> "... how often do you hear people complain that emails subtract the tone of voice; that it's hard to tell if someone is joking or not?... Which is why, of course, people use so many dashes and italics and capitals ("I AM joking!") to compensate. That's why they came up with the emoticon, too — the emoticon being the greatest (or most desperate) advance in punctuation since the question mark in the reign of Charlemagne."

To further spell out the point, Truss offers the following example:

"A woman, without her man, is nothing."

"A woman: without her, man is nothing."

As you see, we ignore punctuation at our peril!

Tools for self-expression online III: Shorthand. Text messaging and instant messaging, as well as email, have spawned a whole new shorthand language to speed up communication. Once again, we caution that the further you go from plain language, the more likely it is you'll be misunderstood. With that caveat, the box on the next page lists some of the shorthand items in common usage in online communications.

COMMON SHORTHAND USAGE IN ONLINE COMMUNICATIONS

AFAIK As far as I know	**DETI** Don't even think it	**JOOTT** Just one of those things	**PAL** Parents are listening
ATM At the moment	**F2F** Face to face	**LMAO** Laughing my ass off	**PMJI** Pardon my jumping in
AYT Are you there?	**FWIW** For what it's worth	**LOL** Lots of luck *or* Laughing out loud	**RL** Real life
BBL Be back later	**FYI** For your information		**ROFL** Rolling on the floor laughing
BFN Bye for now	**GAL** Get a life	**MYOB** Mind your own business	
BRB Be right back	**IANAL** I am not a lawyer, but…	**N2M** Not too much	**TTYL** Talk to you later
BTDT Been there, done that	**IMHO** In my humble opinion	**OIC** Oh, I see	**TU** or **TY** Thank you
BTW By the way	**IOW** In other words	**OMG** Oh, my God!	**WFM** Works for me
CUL See you later	**JK** Just kidding	**OTOH** On the other hand	**YT** You there?

CHILDREN ONLINE

If you have children living at home, you know how wedded the upcoming generation is to its cybercommunications. All of the media systems mentioned above — cell phones, iPods, text messaging, MySpace, blogs, etc. — are heavily populated with youngsters. Indeed, most of us over forty probably have been taught how to use the newfangled devices by someone under eighteen (or maybe under twelve!).

One issue that deserves attention in our conversation about assertiveness in "long-distance" communications is that of *safety*. Particularly for young people, the hazards of contact with strangers in cyberspace are very real. Indeed, cautious child safety monitors have even come up with a name for those hazards: "the 4Ps." They are *privacy, predators, pornography,* and *pop-ups*. Simply stated, it is critical that you prepare your children to deal with these online and telephone issues, just as you would instruct them to handle the situations in person.

Don't settle for a simplistic "Don't talk to strangers." You'll need to get specific about some of the things they're likely to encounter and how you want them to respond. For instance, what about a "friend" who responds to a MySpace or Twitter site, begins a friendly correspondence, and then asks for personal information or a face-to-face meeting? What about someone who wants a home address so they can send a "gift" or birthday card? (Hint: the answer is a two-letter word beginning with "N.")

And it's not only strangers who are problems in cyberspace. All the bullies aren't hanging out on the way home from school. Some are waiting at their computers to intimidate and humiliate your kids. One recent estimate is that about 40 percent of teens experience some form of "cyberbullying" in any year. Offensive text messages, nasty comments posted on MySpace or YouTube or another online site, rumors spread on a community or school site, or other forms of harassment are common, and at least as painful for the teen as personal attacks at school.

How to handle the bullies? Just as you would in person: ignore them as much as possible; stand up to them assertively when you must; report them to authorities (for online bullies, that may mean contacting the site or internet service provider); take the initiative and let those who matter to you know the real story.

The best advice we've heard to help your kids handle online intrusions boils down to this:

❖ Online contacts stay only online.

❖ Never give out your last name, home address or telephone number, name of your school or parents' workplaces, or any other personal information online.

❖ Remember that adults can pose as children online. You may be talking to a forty-year-old, not a fourteen-year-old — never mind what he or she says.

❖ It's always OK to say no or no thanks.

❖ Never respond to online "pop-up" ads or invitations.

❖ Use your assertiveness skills with online contacts just as you would in person: say no, play your own game, and protect yourself and your family's privacy.

❖ Keep in mind the guidelines for assertive communication outlined above and elsewhere in this book.

For more suggestions about protecting your children online, visit the web sites of the American Academy of Pediatrics: http://safetynet.aap.org; the National Education Association: www.nea.org/schoolsafety/bullyingparentsrole.html; or the U.S. Federal Trade Commission: www.onguardonline.gov.

In this chapter, we've followed a path off the main road to explore the newer tools for communication because we think it's important not to lose the message in the medium. Regardless of the venue you use to assert yourself — the latest high-tech gadget and/or online system or an "old-fashioned" conversation or letter — we don't want you to forget that the bottom line is to *express yourself while respecting the other person*.

Go ahead and make (or receive) that cell phone call or send (or read) that IM or email or snail mail letter, but be sure your message is clear and heard the way you mean it and that it shows respect for the other person while you attempt to achieve your goals. And accept no less from those who would make contact with you.

10

Thinking Assertively

If a person continues to see only giants,
it means he is still looking at the world
through the eyes of a child.
— Anaïs Nin

O K, YOU SAY, "MAYBE I'M NOT AS ASSERTIVE as I'd like to be.
You can't teach an old dog new tricks. That's just the
way I am. I can't change it."

We don't agree. Millions of people have found that it is possible
to change. Becoming more assertive is a learning process, and it
takes longer for some of us, but you can master the process and
the rewards are great.

Right *thinking* about assertiveness is crucial. Thoughts, beliefs,
attitudes, and feelings set the stage for behavior. Your mind needs
to be ready to respond to each new situation calling for assertive
action. Negative attitudes, faulty beliefs, and self-critical thoughts
hold you back and stop your natural flow. "You are what you
think" (even more than "what you eat"). Getting your thinking
straight will be a great resource to help you generate greater
assertiveness. Start today to rid yourself of self-defeating
thinking!

In this chapter, you will find some "pep talks" and some
specific procedures that will help you to look at your thinking
process in relation to assertiveness. Consider carefully what we

say here. We are probably going to challenge some of your beliefs about how life works.

Speaking of thinking, let's take a look at some exciting new discoveries about how our brains influence our social behavior.

SELF-EXPRESSION AND YOUR BRAIN

We've been teaching and writing about this process for four decades. You'd think just about everything that *could* be said *has* been said. But there always seems to be some new finding, and some of these are quite surprising. In the last two decades, for example, brain researchers — neuroscientists — have done some truly amazing work mapping the patterns of human brain activity associated with a wide variety of life situations and how we feel and respond to them. These brain-behavior relationships are founded on both the brain's "hardwiring" — what we're born with — and a mind-boggling (literally!) series of connections that develop over a lifetime of learning about what it means to get along with other people. The state of the art today makes it clear that although our social behavior patterns are quite firmly established in our brains — because we've repeated them over and over again for years — we can learn new patterns with active effort.

At the risk of *way* oversimplifying what goes on in the brain when we encounter a social situation, imagine two key components of the brain itself talking with each other. The *amygdala* is the tiny, almond-shaped center of emotions located at the base of the brain toward the rear. The brain's *orbitofrontal cortex* — OFC — is the primary (though not the only) regulator of those emotions, which thinks and evaluates as it receives signals from the amygdala. The OFC puts the rational brakes on by regulating the length, intensity, and frequency of such emotions as anger, terror, or shame.

The emotional brain (i.e., amygdala) deals in raw feelings. The rational, cognitive brain (i.e., OFC) specializes in considered understanding. Psychologist Daniel Goleman refers to the two functions as the "low road" (emotions) and "high road" (cognitions) of the brain. The high road works methodically, step by step, with deliberate effort, giving us some control over our "inner life." The two roads are intertwined, working in parallel and virtually simultaneously, although the low road's amygdala fires the more immediate shots.

Picture yourself walking through a primeval forest 100,000 years ago. In the distant shadows you notice a movement. Your brain's first response is likely to be fear. The amygdala is sending survival messages: "Could be a threat. Lots of dangerous predators in these parts. Better run, or take cover or find a weapon." The OFC, decoding these distress signals, takes the long view: "Yes, it could be a threat, but not likely. I've been all over this area today, and I'm confident there are no predators around now. Still, it would be prudent to be somewhat cautious. I'll wait here a while and watch and listen. Besides, if it is a dangerous predator, I probably couldn't outrun it anyway."

That scenario could happen today on the streets of any city, or even in a forest. The point is that our brains are constantly responding emotionally to and evaluating rationally the situations we encounter. Everyday social situations usually do not have the same survival value as our hypothetical encounter in the forest, but our brains do respond both emotionally and rationally to everything that comes along.

What's important about all this is to recognize first that your emotional reaction to a social situation may well be anxiety (fear), but you can handle that emotion if you take time to listen to the rational evaluation of the OFC. If you do, you can learn skills for dealing with those situations effectively. And this book is designed to help you do just that.

Detailed examination of the research findings regarding those very complex brain processes are beyond the scope of this book. Readers who are interested in looking further into the state of knowledge on brain and behavior are encouraged to explore Daniel Goleman's fine book *Social Intelligence* (2006) and such other recommended resources as *Looking for Spinoza* (Damasio, 2003), *The Developing Mind* (Siegel, 1999), *Understanding Emotions* (Oatley, Keltner, & Jenkins, 2006), and another *Social Intelligence* (Albrecht, 2005), all listed in the References.

For now, the important thing to keep in mind is that you have some work to do to overcome a lifetime of brain network patterns that lead you to make less-than-adequate responses to social situations. Time to get started!

YOUR ATTITUDE TOWARD BECOMING ASSERTIVE

Perhaps you, like many folks, have experienced parents, teachers, and peers saying, "You have no right . . ." Now we are telling you "You have a *perfect right* . . . ," and it is *good*, it is *right*, it is *OK* to assert yourself. How to deal with these conflicting messages? Trust yourself. Experiment a little. You owe it to yourself to try!

Your attitude will help or hinder your capacity to grow in assertiveness. If you cooperate with the natural process of self-expression, you can learn to enjoy each new challenge. Don't let negative attitudes stunt your growth.

Maybe you're imagining all the "dire consequences" that may result from taking risks in your relationships. ("Oh, dear. What might happen? Maybe he'll hit me! Maybe she'll leave me!") Recognize that at times it's appropriate to ignore those excessive cautions and take just one small step toward your goal.

You can take charge of your own growth process and guide your development in a positive, assertive direction. You'll find your attitudes can change *because* of your actions. And you may be surprised at the results. Positive responses from others, better feelings about yourself, and accomplishment of your goals will be your reward for expressing yourself and standing up for your rights. Pay attention to these positive outcomes; they offer important support and encouragement as you practice new skills.

Your Attitude toward Yourself

Can you congratulate yourself when you succeed? When you fail, can you accept your foibles with honesty and laugh at yourself? Can you express the feeling of elation you get when you achieve a personal goal, such as completing a college course or a remodeling job on your home? Do you allow yourself the pleasure of feeling satisfied with a job well done? How about when you do something that makes someone else happy?

Maybe your goal in life is to be of service to others. If you don't take care of yourself, you'll have little to give to anyone else! If you continually inhibit your self-expression, you'll gradually lose your effectiveness in helping others as well. Recall that the charge is to "Love others *as you love yourself*." How well do you love yourself? Remember the "Behavioral Model for Personal Growth" in chapter 7? Read it over again now, and consider how you can love yourself better.

Your attitude toward yourself and your behavior are in a continuous cycle. When you are down on yourself, you'll tend to act in self-denying ways. Others will see those actions and respond accordingly — as if you don't deserve much respect. When you see the way they treat you, it confirms your attitude: "I *knew* I wasn't worth a damn! Look how people treat me!" And the self-fulfilling cycle continues.

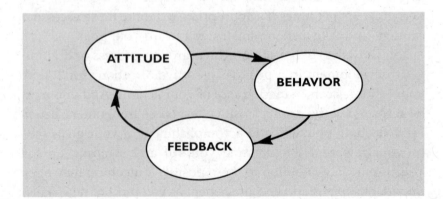

We want to help you break up the cycle by teaching you — and "authorizing" you — to behave assertively. Since you won't do it for yourself, maybe you'll do it when someone else tells you to! The trainer says, "Never mind how strange it feels, go ahead and try this new approach." When you do try it, the result is more positive feedback from other people, which in turn improves your attitude about yourself. You're on your way!

This enhanced sense of self-worth is the beginning of a positive turn in the attitude-behavior-feedback-attitude cycle. You can achieve the same results on your own — or perhaps with some help over the rough spots — by following the procedures described in this book. We'll give you a step-by-step program for behavior change a couple of chapters down the road; for now, let's take a deeper look at this business of thoughts and attitudes.

THOUGHTS THAT GET IN THE WAY OF SELF-ASSERTION

There are some patterns of thinking — both nonassertive and aggressive — that are common obstacles to assertiveness. If you're like most folks, you've heard yourself saying things like these — at least once in a while:

> *I'm a failure.*
> *The world is treating me badly.*
> *I'm a helpless victim of circumstances.*
> *Nobody loves me.*
> *Everybody is judging me.*
> *Other people are in control of my destiny.*

Or, on the other side:

> *When I speak, people listen (or else!).*
> *The world owes me obedience.*
> *I don't need help from anybody.*
> *I'm not going to let them get away with that!*
> *People suck!*

All of these ideas are false. (A few of them may be partly true in your life: you — and everybody else — will fail sometimes. And the world does sometimes treat us badly. And some of us are self-sufficient some of the time.)

The big problem with this kind of thinking is that you may begin to believe it. Distorted views of what's happening in your life may result from a number of circumstances. Sometimes bad events occur coincidentally and create an impression that life has it in for you. That idea can stick in your head and become a "self-fulfilling prophecy."

Most of us don't experience life as a devastating series of downers, but we all have days (and weeks!) that can bring us down on ourselves — at least for a while. Psychiatrist and author Aaron Beck, M.D., has outlined some of the tendencies that commonly occur:

❖ *a predisposition to think poorly of yourself.* Maybe you have been out of a job for a while, or you did poorly in school, or you broke up a romance. Or perhaps you have a rather low opinion of yourself (self-concept). In any case, you are prepared to assume that whatever goes wrong, you're to blame.

❖ *a tendency to exaggerate problems.* Minor emergencies often seem catastrophic at the time. In the total scheme of things, however, most life situations are less critical than we assume.

❖ *an egocentric view of life events.* "Everything happens to me!" is the theme of this tendency. An objective view would tell a different story, but the victim sees everything that goes awry as aimed at him or her.

❖ *a belief that life is either one way or the other.* This notion of good-bad, black-white, yes-no limits your choices markedly. The fact is that there are a number of alternatives in most life situations.

❖ *a view of yourself as helpless or vulnerable.* "How can I possibly do anything about all the problems in my life?" You can begin to deal with them effectively if you break them down into small enough increments.

HELPFUL AIDS FOR HANDLING THOUGHTS

A number of excellent methods have been developed for dealing with your thinking patterns. Three of the most effective are *stress inoculation, thought stopping,* and *positive self-statements.*

Stress Inoculation. This type of "inoculation" not only minimizes expected stress, it can also be used on the spot to deal with stress. (Noted Canadian psychologist Dr. Donald Meichenbaum gets credit for this one.)

Assume you have a situation coming up that you know will be stressful, such as a job performance interview. Your supervisor tends to be a fast talker and not a good listener. In the past, you have become very uptight and upset.

To inoculate yourself this time, start by writing yourself a message about the situation beforehand. Speak to yourself as a wise counselor would. Here is a sample message:

> *When you have your performance evaluation, relax. Don't let yourself be thrown off. It does no good to get upset. Remember your supervisor's style, and be ready for it. When your supervisor says something you question, be firm but polite in asking about it. Ask for time to consider further. Speak up about information the supervisor is forgetting. Be ready to list your accomplishments. You can handle this. Take a deep breath once in a while. You'll be fine. If surprises come, just roll with them. This is only one small event in your total life.*

Once you have a tailor-made message, read it aloud several times before the actual situation arises. Read it especially when you start worrying excessively or when you feel undue anxiety.

Remember the essence of the message so you can repeat key portions silently during the actual event (e.g., an interview). If you find yourself slipping back in confidence, listen within yourself for the key parts.

One of our clients used this method successfully with her estranged husband. They were to meet in court and Cyra knew she would fall apart and perhaps ruin her chances for a fair settlement. She developed a stress inoculation message and practiced it often. When she entered the courtroom, her husband came up and said "Hi," and Cyra immediately broke into tears and ran to the bathroom! While there, she reread her message aloud several times, regained her confidence, and "sailed through" both talking to him again and the subsequent proceedings. Afterward, she was amazed that it worked! In the past, she would have continued to be upset and cry. Stress inoculation helped Cyra through a very emotional event.

Thought Stopping. Have you ever had an annoying tune or thought continually "run through your head?" Nothing you do seems to work to stop it. That's the time to try "thought stopping," another method developed by psychiatrist Joseph Wolpe. Close your eyes right now and conjure up some recurring thought that bothers you. When it comes in clearly, yell "STOP!" out loud. (Make sure no one is nearby or they may think you a bit bizarre!) Your thoughts will actually stop. When they do, shift immediately to a pleasant thought to replace the unwanted one. The unwanted thought will typically return in short order, but if you persistently repeat the procedure, it will be longer and longer before the offender sneaks back in. Soon, the unwanted thought will give up.

No, you don't have to run around yelling "STOP!" continually! The technique works just as effectively when done silently in your head. Of course, you may still want to yell it out loud once in a while because it's so much fun!

One warning: Be careful that the unwanted thoughts are not actually carrying *constructive* messages that you're not catching on to. You need to pay attention to *some* unpleasant thoughts and act on them! They may be offering important guidance. With practice and trial and error, however, the difference between good and not-so-good thoughts will become apparent.

Positive Self-Statements. "The hardest step for most people I know," commented high school counselor Gail Wainwright at an assertiveness group meeting, "is to *be assertive with yourself*: to convince yourself to go ahead and take the action you know is needed!"

If your thoughts are filled with self-denying "rules" and "attitudes," your behavior will in all likelihood be similar. You may think in negative statements: "I'm not important." "My opinions don't count." "No one will be interested in what I have to say." "I'll probably make a fool of myself if I say anything." "I'm really not sure." "I have no right to say that." If so, chances are very good you will act accordingly — that is, you'll keep quiet and let others control the situation!

Try, for a short period of time, to allow yourself to say the *positive* form of those statements: "I am important." "My opinions count." "Someone will be interested in what I have to say." "I have a right to say that." You don't have to *act* on any of these at this point, just get the feel of saying positive things to yourself.

The positive self-statements procedure simply consists of developing complimentary statements about yourself that you memorize and repeat regularly. The purpose is to build self-confidence. Examples:

> *I am respected and admired by my friends.*
> *I am a kind and loving person.*
> *I have a job.*
> *I handle anger well.*
> *I got through school successfully.*
> *I am firm when the situation calls for it.*

Some of the statements you choose may not be totally true of you, but we want you to "fudge" a little at first. (Don't go to extremes, however. We don't agree with those who would have you go around saying "I am rich and beautiful." Unless, of course, it's true.) Then proceed as if they were true. Place these statements on the refrigerator, on the bathroom wall, or in your purse or wallet. Regularly remind yourself that you are a positive and valuable person.

You can use positive self-statements as replacement thoughts in conjunction with thought stopping. Or, they can be part of your stress inoculation message.

After you have practiced the positive thoughts for a while, you may wish to begin — still in your own thoughts — to consider the ways you would act in those situations if you followed through on the thoughts. Perhaps, for example, you were thinking, "Someone will be interested in what I have to say," in regard to joining in on a group discussion. If you were to imagine *acting* on that thought, you might see yourself asking a question of one of the more outspoken participants. Or, maybe you could just start out by saying, "I agree."

Think about ways you could *act* like a person who *thinks* positively!

STOP IMAGINING THE WORST!

Too often people do not respond assertively because they have conjured up dire consequences. "If I do this, she'll be mad." "I could never say that because he'd fire me." "I'll feel guilty." "She'll divorce me." "My mother always cries." "I'd hurt him too much." On and on go the imagined disasters. A part of the brain seems to work overtime to stifle self-expression.

The late renowned psychologist Albert Ellis called this "catastrophisizing," and he did a remarkable job of pointing out how such irrational beliefs hurt our chances of handling life situations well. In his book *Feeling Better, Getting Better, Staying Better*, Ellis suggests that our thoughts always come before our emotional reactions to situations. Ellis describes some of the irrational ideas and beliefs about how life "ought to be" that lead to upsetting emotions, thus blocking adequate responses. These beliefs relate to such life events as rejection, fear, and being treated unfairly. Read Ellis's book, and stop inhibiting your assertiveness by believing (irrationally) that the world should somehow be perfect!

"WHAT ELSE CAN I DO ABOUT MY THOUGHTS?"

UCLA psychologist Gary Emery is another highly regarded specialist in cognitive therapy procedures. He has described a number of effective strategies and techniques for those who wish to make changes in their thinking patterns and "internal conversations."

You may find one or several of the procedures of help:

❖ *Get to know and be aware of yourself.* A continuing quest for greater self-awareness — your goals, dreams, feelings, attitudes, beliefs, limitations, problems — will give you a solid foundation for your self-improvement efforts.

❖ *Recognize and keep track of your "automatic thoughts."* This term is used to describe the involuntary inner dialogue you experience when you face a stressful situation (e.g., "Oh dear, this is going to be . . .").

❖ *Ask yourself questions to clarify your reactions to an event.* Is there good evidence for your assumptions? How logical is your reaction? Could you be oversimplifying things? Exaggerating? Taking the situation out of context?

❖ *Consider possible alternative explanations.* Look at the situation from another viewpoint. Modify one fact at a time and see what happens.

❖ *Ask yourself, "So what?"* Does it really matter? Even if the situation is actually as bad as you suspect, will the consequences be lasting? Will anybody really be hurt?

❖ *Try to substitute positive images.* See if you can come up with a "silver lining." Might the bad news contain (or hide) some *good* news?

❖ *Identify the payoffs for you.* Are you getting some reward for feeling bad? More attention, perhaps? Special help? Excused from work or school? Might there be an even better payoff for changing your outlook?

❖ *Ask yourself, "What if it really does happen?"* What's the worst outcome likely to bring? Can you act for a while as if the feared event had already happened? Is it really as bad as you thought?

❖ *Do some very specific "homework" to change your thoughts.* Go back to the previous section and develop a plan for positive self-statements, stress inoculation, or thought stopping. Write your plan in your log, then do your homework!

ARE SOME MORE EQUAL THAN OTHERS?

One of our most important goals for this book is to help you recognize that you are *equal* to others on a human-to-human level. True, there will always be someone more talented, more assertive, more beautiful, more powerful, more wealthy, more educated . . . But you are just as good, just as valuable, just as important as anyone else *as a human being.* That's a terribly important idea. If you want to read more about it, try the Constitution of the United States of America, or the United Nations *Universal Declaration of Human Rights,* or . . .

11

There's Nothing to Be Afraid Of

*Courage is resistance to fear,
mastery of fear, not absence of fear.*
— MARK TWAIN

*In any social situation, I felt fear. I would be anxious
before I even left the house, and it would escalate
as I got closer to a college class, a party, or whatever.
I would feel sick to my stomach; it almost felt like I had the flu.
My heart would pound, my palms would get sweaty,
and I would get this feeling of being removed
from myself and from everybody else.*
— NATIONAL INSTITUTE OF MENTAL HEALTH

MANY READERS of *Your Perfect Right* — perhaps you, too — find anxiety to be the most significant obstacle to greater assertiveness. "Sure," you say, "I know how to express myself! I just get really uptight about doing it. The risks seem too great. I want people to like me..."

Microsoft co-owner Melinda Gates told *TIME Magazine* that her friend investor Warren Buffett — also a billionaire, of course, and famous for being a natural public speaker on financial matters — had to take extra pains to overcome his own fear of public appearances. Buffett, named by *TIME* as one of "the most influential people in the world," took the Dale Carnegie course in public speaking, says Gates, to get past his anxiety and to develop what has become one of his greatest skills.

Perhaps you find yourself perspiring, your heart racing, your hands icy, as you anticipate a public appearance. Or you get those same feelings as you're about to walk into a job interview. Or maybe you have avoided asking your boss for a raise because you fear the words will catch in your throat. Do you take the long way home so you don't have to confront the neighbor who is always asking favors that you're afraid to refuse?

You may not even be aware of the source of such fears. They may have resulted from childhood experiences — for example, well-meaning parents may have taught you to "speak only when spoken to." Or classmates may have teased you when you stood up to make an oral report.

Or you may be one of the many who have the genetic predisposition to shyness and/or social anxiety that relatively recent research studies have shown to exist. Some people are born with the likelihood that they will be reticent or fearful in social situations. Yet, even for those whose social anxiety is a birthright, it is possible to reduce the level of anxiety to a point where social situations are not so intimidating.

Learning to be assertive is one way to help reduce such fears. Still, when the level of anxiety is very high, it may be necessary to deal more directly with the anxiety itself. And that's the topic of this chapter.

To overcome fear, nervousness, anxiety, and stress about assertiveness, it's necessary to determine what *causes* the reaction. Once you know what you are dealing with, you can learn methods to eliminate the fear. So, we suggest you begin by *tracing* your fear. Narrow down exactly what causes you to feel afraid to express yourself assertively. Use your journal to record your reactions systematically, and keep track of what is causing your anxiety (fear) level to rise.

FINDING YOUR FEARS: THE SUD SCALE

A useful aid in assessing your own anxiety level is the "SUD scale." SUD is an acronym for *subjective units of discomfort* — simply, a way of rating your own physical feelings of anxiety on a scale of 0-100. SUD is an important contribution of the work of the late psychiatrist Dr. Joseph Wolpe (1969).

Because anxiety has physical elements, you can become aware of your degree of discomfort in a situation by "tuning in" to your body's indicators: heart rate (pulse), breathing rate, coldness in hands and feet, perspiration (particularly in hands), and muscle tension. There are others, but most of us usually are not aware of them.

Biofeedback training — the electromechanical measurement and reporting of specific bodily functions, such as heart rate, skin conductivity, muscle tension, and breathing — is sometimes used to allow people to learn when they are relaxed or anxious, since it offers an automated monitor of physical indicators.

Try this: get yourself as relaxed as you can right now — lie flat on the couch or floor or relax in your chair, breathe deeply, relax all the muscles in your body, and imagine a very relaxing scene (such as lying on the beach or floating on a cloud). Allow yourself to relax in this way for at least five minutes, paying attention to your heartbeat, breathing, hand temperature and dryness, and muscle relaxation. Those relaxed feelings can be given a SUD scale value of 0, representing near total relaxation. If you did not do the relaxation exercise but are reading this alone relatively quietly and comfortably, you may consider yourself somewhere around 20 on the SUD scale.

At the opposite end of the scale, visualize the most frightening scene you can imagine. With your eyes closed, picture yourself narrowly escaping an accident or being near the center of an earthquake or flood. Pay attention to the same body signals: heart rate/pulse, breathing, hand temperature and moisture, and muscle relaxation. These fearful feelings can be given a SUD scale value of 100 — almost totally anxious.

Now you have a roughly calibrated comfort/discomfort scale that you can use to help yourself evaluate just how anxious you are in any given situation. Each ten points on the scale represents a "just noticeable difference" up or down from the units above and below. Thus, 70 is slightly more anxious than 60 and by the same amount more comfortable than 80. (The SUD scale is too subjective to be able to define comfort level more closely than ten units.)

Most of us function normally in the range of 20-50 SUDs. A few life situations will raise anxiety above 50 for short periods, and on rare occasions (rare for most of us, anyway!) one can relax below 20.

The SUD scale can help you to identify those life situations that are most troublesome. Once again, being systematic in your observations of yourself can pay big dividends! The procedure described below shows a way to use the SUD scale to develop a "plan of attack" against your fears.

LIST AND LABEL YOUR FEARS

A method developed in the field of creative writing — list/group/label — is another helpful tool you might want to use as you address questions of anxiety.

Start by recording or *listing* life situations when you feel fear or anxiety. Use some space in your journal to list all your reactions that hinder your assertiveness, including the situation or event involved, people, circumstances, and other factors that contributed to your reaction. Assign a SUDS value, as described in the previous section, to each of the items on your list.

Next, find the reactions on your list that are similar, those that seem to have a common theme, and *group* them together. Now see if you can *label* your groups, applying appropriate names to each grouping of anxiety-producing factors. Among your groups may be such common phobias as fear of snakes, spiders, heights, or enclosed places. Interpersonal fears are more

> *Once you know what you are dealing with, you can learn methods to eliminate the fear.*

likely to be the problem in assertiveness. Fears of criticism, rejection, anger or aggression, or hurting the feelings of others greatly hinder your assertive response.

You may find a grouping that centers around one or more of the situations given in the Assertiveness Inventory. Instead of a classic fear like rejection, you may simply experience a good deal of anxiety when standing in line or when facing salespersons. Perhaps people in authority scare you. Obviously, your assertiveness will not be optimum if your anxiety is already working overtime!

Now, one more step in this analysis of your fears. In each labeled group, relist the items in order, according to the SUDS scores you have assigned. Now you have a rough agenda, in priority order (from least to most disturbing), for dealing with your anxieties! Usually it is best to start working to reduce or overcome those that are most disturbing before you attempt to develop your assertive skills further.

The sample journal entry on the next page will help make this process clearer.

We're indebted to Patsy Tanabe-Endsley, who in her book *Project Write* describes this system to list, group, and label ideas. We've adapted her system by simply substituting "fears or anxieties" for "ideas."

METHODS FOR OVERCOMING ANXIETY

Now that you have carefully identified the anxieties that are inhibiting your assertiveness, you will want to begin a program

September 13, 2009

Today I'm going to write down situations when I feel anxious, including a "SUDS" estimate. I want to try the "list, group, label" method to see if I can figure out any patterns of fears.

1. Magazine article about open heart surgery made me nauseous.   SUDS 50

2. I was upset when Jose ignored me at lunch.   SUDS 30

3. The boss looked disgusted when I made several mistakes at work. SUDS 65

4. Elise told me she talked with Connie (ex-wife) about the kids.
    I was so angry that Connie criticized my discipline.   SUDS 80!

5. Roommate didn't help with the dishes.   SUDS 55

6. Cut my finger; seeing the blood made me queasy.   SUDS 35

7. I was embarrassed about being late to the meeting.   SUDS 25

8. Friends teased me about my new haircut.   SUDS 25

Groups:	Labels:
A. 2, 3, 7, 8	Being too sensitive
B. 4, 5	Anger
C. 1, 6	Medical fears

Well, if this is a typical day, looks like I'm more sensitive about criticism than I thought. Maybe I should look into that "desensitization" exercise Dr. G. told me about.

to overcome them. There are many effective approaches. Since this topic is a book in itself, let us briefly describe some popular methods; then we'll refer you to other resources for detailed information.

Systematic Desensitization. This approach, controversial and experimental when introduced forty-plus years ago, is another developed by assertiveness training pioneers psychiatrist Joseph Wolpe and psychologist Arnold Lazarus. Like assertiveness training (AT), systematic desensitization is based on learning principles, declaring that you learned to be anxious about expressing yourself, and you can unlearn it.

It is not possible to be relaxed and anxious at the same time.

Practically speaking, it isn't possible to be relaxed and anxious at the same time. The process of desensitization involves repeated association of an anxiety-producing situation with a feeling of deep relaxation throughout your body. Gradually, your brain learns to "automatically" associate relaxation — instead of anxiety — with the situation. In a therapeutic desensitization, you first learn to relax your entire body completely through practicing a series of deep muscle relaxation exercises or through hypnosis. The anxious situation will be presented in a series of imagined scenes arranged in a hierarchy from least to greatest anxiety.

You are told to imagine yourself in the least anxious scene of your hierarchy and to be aware of the anxiety that results. After five to fifteen seconds you'll switch your visualization back to your relaxing scene, relaxing once again. This procedure is repeated several times for each step of the hierarchy of anxious scenes. The repeated exposure to your anxious scenes while you are relaxed gradually reduces your fear of the anxious situation.

The intricacies of the procedure are somewhat more complex, but that is the essence of systematic desensitization. It has been proven effective for a wide range of fears, including phobic reactions to heights, public speaking, animals, flying, test taking, social contact, and many more.

Exposure Desensitization. Similar to the procedure for systematic desensitization described above, desensitization by gradual exposure to sources of anxiety in the real world is another proven strategy for overcoming anxiety.

A particularly vivid example of this treatment is demonstrated in the case of individuals who are working to overcome agoraphobia — a debilitating fear of "open spaces," the marketplace, or social events. Agoraphobic clients are asked to create a hierarchy similar to that for systematic desensitization (above) then to take very gradual steps of exposure to the feared situations — one step at a time, then back to a "safe" environment. With this repeated gradual exposure — never beyond the point of very mild anxiety — the client becomes able to confront and eventually to overcome the fear of being outside, in the marketplace, and among other people.

As with systematic desensitization, it is important to take only small steps and to build on success by repeating the low-anxiety steps already desensitized as one progresses up the hierarchy to more anxious environments.

As with systematic desensitization, such gradual real-world exposure procedures have been shown to be highly effective with a variety of anxiety-producing situations, including riding in or driving a car, being in high places, riding in elevators, entering school classrooms, riding in public transportation, attending social events, and more. While it is possible for exposure to be self-administered, it is probably best conducted under the guidance of a trained therapist.

Diet, Exercise, and Sleep. In today's world, there is never enough time. Try to cross the street at a busy but unlighted intersection. Cars, trucks, and buses fly by, everyone in a hurry, no one stopping for a pedestrian. We rush to work in the morning, often skipping breakfast ("the most important meal of the day," just as Mom always told you!). We rush out at lunchtime to meet a friend for a quick sandwich, to pick up the laundry, or shop for a new cell phone. "Exercise" consists of scurrying across that intersection, running for the commuter train, or mowing 150 square feet of grass. For a lucky few, it may also include a round of golf or a couple of hours a week at a fitness club.

We know better, don't we? We know that it's vital to our well-being to eat well, exercise vigorously on a regular basis, and sleep soundly. Without those self-care systems and living life at today's speed we're *certain* to be anxious!

Of course, diet, exercise, and sleep are not *treatments* for anxiety as much as they are *preventions*. If you eat a well-balanced diet, full of whole grains, fresh fruits, and vegetables with minimal fat and sugar, you're going to be healthier than if you're grabbing a fast-food snack or a super grande latte on the way to work. (And keep in mind that that the caffeine and sugar in that latte will keep you pumped up even if you don't have any other reason to be anxious!) If you sleep soundly for something close to the recommended six to eight hours, you're more likely to be refreshed — and less anxious — the next day. If you get plenty of heart- and muscle-healthy exercise, you're going to feel better in every way, including in situations that might otherwise cause anxiety. (Hint: as with your growing assertiveness skills, start slowly and build on success.)

Here are some notable comments about exercise and mental well-being:

> *Exercise stimulates various brain chemicals, which may leave you feeling happier and more relaxed than you were before you worked out. You'll also look better and feel better when you exercise regularly, which can boost your confidence and improve your self-esteem. Exercise even reduces feelings of depression and anxiety.*
> — THE MAYO CLINIC

> *Exercise reduces feelings of depression and anxiety* [and] *promotes psychological well-being and reduces feelings of stress.*
> — U.S. CENTERS FOR DISEASE CONTROL

OK, enough of the parental lecture. But don't take our word for it anyway. Read the volumes of literature on the subjects offered by the American Heart Association, the Anxiety Disorders Association of America, the American Dietetic Association, and virtually every other recognized authority on health.

For a very readable and authoritative guidebook on diet and nutrition, take a look at Dr. Andrew Weil's *Eating Well for Optimum Health*.

Meditation, Breathing, and Relaxation Training. Many books have been written on each of these topics, and we won't be able to do them justice here. What's important about meditation, breathing, and relaxation is that they have very positive and lasting effects far beyond their specific benefit as part of an anxiety treatment program.

The systematic practice of meditation is a powerful means of turning off the world around you for short periods in order to focus your attention on your body, your breathing, your thoughts, or your mental image of a most restful and contemplative place. Some folks balk at "meditation" because it sounds a bit mystical. It's not, although the most widely used procedures have roots in Eastern philosophies. If it sounds strange or unusual, it's because we so seldom allow ourselves to retreat from the pressures and distractions of the day into a quiet time. Most forms of meditation in Western societies are not based on mystical content and have been developed as a way of promoting physical and mental well-being.

There are dozens of forms of meditation, breathing, and relaxation practice, including progressive muscle relaxation (Edmund Jacobson), autogenic training (Johannes Schultz), relaxation (Ainslie Meares), relaxation response (Herbert Benson), and biofeedback. One of the most interesting recent findings comes from University of Colorado neurophysiologist Dr. James Austin, whose fMRI studies indicate that Zen meditation actually rewires the circuitry of the brain!

It is widely recognized that anxiety and stress significantly contribute to a lack of physical health, and there is an increasing volume of mainstream medical research in this area. Hospitals, for example, often use meditation as a method of stress reduction for patients with a chronic or terminal illness or a depressed immune system.

Jacobson argued that since anxiety includes muscle tension, one can reduce anxiety by learning how to relax the tension. Benson, whose Mind-Body Medical Institute is affiliated with Harvard and several Boston hospitals, describes the "relaxation response" — a complex of physiological changes that come with deep relaxation, including changes in metabolism, heart rate, respiration, blood pressure, and brain chemistry. Jon Kabat-Zinn at the University of Massachusetts is another active researcher and author in the field who has studied the effects of mindfulness meditation on stress.

Treatment for Panic Attacks. If you are experiencing major anxiety attacks — panic at just the thought of a confrontation, for example, or for no apparent reason at all — you may need to undertake a systematic treatment program with a therapist.

Wisconsin psychologist and author Denise Beckfield has developed a program that helps clients to figure out what leads to their panicky feelings, thought patterns, and the resulting physical reactions: shaking, palpitations, dizziness, chills, nausea, chest pain, and the horrible sensation of losing control or "going crazy." Beckfield also encourages examination of background aspects — like genetics, personality traits, and early experiences — that may have lowered one's anxiety threshold as well as issues like loss and anger that feed into panic attacks.

The good news is that the scary sensations not only do pass; in time, they can be made to disappear completely. Among the simple techniques suggested for panic patients are (1) to keep a journal to note panic episodes, record feelings at the time, and chart positive actions and successes; and (2) to learn and practice a controlled breathing exercise ("Stop, Refocus, Breathe") — a remarkably effective technique in helping to "chill out" quickly during anxious times.

Again, if you suffer from full-blown panic attacks, you're encouraged to see a psychologist or other qualified psychotherapist. If, however, your social anxiety leads to near-panic episodes, anxiety in specific situations, or chronic low-level anxiety, you can use self-help procedures to begin to take charge and stay calm as you face social encounters. Dr. Beckfield's book *Master Your Panic and Take Back Your Life* is a good beginning.

Irrational Beliefs and Self-Talk. We grow up with lots of funny ideas and, as adults, we repeat those ideas until we talk ourselves sick. What kinds of "funny ideas" you may well ask? Well, how about the idea that the world must treat us perfectly. Or that life should be fair. Or that if you don't succeed at everything you do, you're no good. We talked about some of these irrational thoughts back in chapter 10. (You might want to review that material.) One unfortunate result of such ideas is that we upset ourselves unnecessarily, provoking anxiety, panic, depression, frustration, anger... We pay a high emotional price for believing impossible things about how the world should treat us, because the real world will never measure up to those ideals.

To counter these toxic notions and get back on a path to healthier thinking, we recommend the works of our friend the late psychologist Albert Ellis, whose books and other works on Rational Emotive Behavior Therapy will help you learn to dispute irrational thoughts in your life and replace them with realistic ideas that more closely resemble what life will likely present to you. We've listed a couple of Dr. Ellis's books in the Reference section at the end of the book.

Assertiveness. We haven't talked much about it in this book, but the fact is that renowned psychologist Arnold Lazarus and psychiatrist Joseph Wolpe originally devised assertiveness training *as a treatment for anxiety*. In laboratory research in South Africa in the 1960s, working on new treatments for anxiety in animals, they devised careful physiological measures and found that fearful animals became relaxed when the feared situation was paired with food, relaxation, or assertiveness.

Since you've been learning about assertiveness throughout this book, we needn't pursue the topic further here, except to say that, particularly for those who are anxious because they are uncertain about their social skills, AT is well established as an effective treatment for social anxiety.

Eye Movement Desensitization and Reprocessing (EMDR). Developed in the 1990s by psychologist Francine Shapiro, EMDR created a good deal of commotion early on because it seemed a bit "magical." The name was derived from the original procedure, which involved moving the eyes from side to side repeatedly while remembering upsetting memories concerning past traumas or anxiety-provoking situations.

The introduction of EMDR provoked some controversy among mental health professionals, due primarily to the unusual "eye movement" requirement. Concern was also expressed about the apparent very rapid client response to the method and about Shapiro's early demand that the method be employed only by practitioners she had personally trained.

Over time, research with EMDR found that the important element in reducing the disturbance is not the *eye movement* but the *alternating movement*. A more recent technological innovation has most EMDR therapists now using a hand-held electronic vibration device to stimulate the alternating movement.

The EMDR method has been effective in dealing with the anxieties and fears associated with behaving assertively, emotional confrontations, hurting others' feelings, or being the center of attention. EMDR also has been shown to be helpful in overcoming the aftereffects of traumatic stress situations (such as, physical or sexual abuse, war experiences, accidents, natural disasters, and dysfunctional family experiences) and in overcoming the guilt, fear, upset, faulty thinking, and anxiety that often result from traumatic experiences.

(Note: Michael Emmons has been trained in EMDR therapy and has used it in his practice. He has been enthusiastic about the results and correctly predicted years ago that EMDR would gain widespread acceptance as a method for helping people overcome anxieties, fears, and traumas. It has done so, though it is still not universally endorsed.)

Medication. If you go to see your primary care physician or internist about anxiety, you're very likely to get a prescription for an anti-anxiety medication. There are a host of such drugs on the market today. You've surely seen them advertised on television: "Ask your doctor if NoAnx is right for you!"

And well you may ask. If you've had a good relationship with a primary care doc for some time, and anxiety is something new in your life, the doctor may be able to determine that it's due to a chemical change and should be fought with appropriate chemical counteragents.

We don't happen to believe that medication should be your first line of attack, however, unless the anxiety has come out of nowhere suddenly, and there appears to be no likely suspect in your immediate life situation. We encourage you to consider first the other approaches we've described in this chapter.

If you do elect to go the route of meds, prepare yourself well to discuss medications with your physician. Inform yourself. Do some homework on the variety of drugs available for anxiety. Don't simply accept the first one your doc suggests, and by all means don't believe the ads you see, hear, and read. Check carefully — before you fill a prescription — to determine that a recommended drug is *really* "right for you."

Chances are your primary care physician will not have the time or expertise to do a thorough psychological workup. Primary care doctors are usually so busy — and the health care finance system allows them so little time with patients — that they simply write scripts for their favorites — the ones that seem to work for most folks. Don't settle for that. Ask why a particular drug is the *best* one for you.

If your doctor is unwilling to discuss these issues with you, use your assertiveness skills to deal with your need for information and a respectful, cooperative relationship. If your needs go unmet, consult another physician.

For detailed information about medication for anxiety, we suggest you visit one or both of the following authoritative web sites and seek information on anxiety medications:

❖ National Institute of Mental Health, at
   www.nimh.nih.gov/health/publications

❖ Mental Health America, at
   www.mentalhealthamerica.net

Other Therapies for Anxiety. We've briefly discussed several proven approaches to dealing with anxiety, ones we know to be effective and are able to recommend. As you might guess, there are many more. Some therapists would have you spend years examining early childhood experiences and relationships with your parents and siblings. Others would put you in a highly stressful situation immediately (you might call it "sink or swim."). Among the many ideas other therapists often suggest for treating anxiety are psychoanalysis, acceptance and commitment therapy, gestalt therapy, implosion therapy, hypnosis, systemic family therapy, and more.

If you need special help overcoming anxiety about expressing yourself assertively, we suggest you examine the procedures we've discussed above and identify one that best fits your own circumstances and style. Start that process by doing some further reading. Two good books on the topic are *The Stress Owner's Manual* by Michele Haney and Ed Boenisch and *The Anxiety and Phobia Workbook* by Edmund Bourne. Both books explore self-help procedures for anxiety and describe further resources available. Another excellent self-help book that may help you to deal with anxiety that results in panic attacks is *Master Your Panic and Take Back Your Life* by Denise Beckfield. (See the References at the end of this book for more information.)

Once you commit to an intervention for your anxiety, expect to invest some time — probably several weeks — practicing your choice of the methods of anxiety relief, with or without a therapist. It took time for you to become anxious; it will take time to overcome it.

We don't mean this discussion of anxiety about assertiveness to discourage you. On the contrary, most readers will find themselves able to handle their mild discomfort about self-expression without major difficulty. There are some of us, however, who do need some extra help in overcoming obstacles. Don't be embarrassed or hesitant about asking for help just as you would seek competent medical aid for a physical problem. Then, when you've cleared up the anxiety obstacle, turn back to the procedures outlined in this book for developing your assertiveness.

Summing Up about Anxiety
Feelings of nervousness, anxiety reactions, and fear are common when thinking about and acting assertively. Often, practicing assertive responses will reduce these uneasy reactions to manageable levels. Practice will make assertion feel more natural to you. If you feel that you are still too afraid, there are

systematic ways to identify the situations that trigger fearful reactions and to reduce the level of anxiety.

Simply understanding a fear is seldom powerful enough to reduce it significantly. Self-help methods that help eliminate or lower the fear to manageable levels are often successful. Professional therapy is recommended when your own efforts are not enough.

We've called this chapter "There's Nothing to Be Afraid Of." Actually, life hands all of us situations we find fearful at times. What we want you to remember is that *there are effective ways to deal with anxiety*. If it's a problem for you, we urge you to read this chapter again, learn as much as you can about your anxiety, and seek out methods — including professional therapy if necessary — that will help you overcome it.

12

It's a Skill You Can Learn

Energy and persistence
conquer all things.
— BENJAMIN FRANKLIN

IT'S AN OLD JOKE IN PSYCHOLOGY. When two engineers (lawyers, housekeepers, plumbers, nurses) are talking together and a psychologist walks up and joins the conversation, there are now two engineers and a psychologist. But when two psychologists are talking and an engineer (substitute your own favorite) walks up and joins them, there are now three *psychologists!*

Everyone believes she or he is a psychologist in some sense. Indeed, we all have some practical first-hand knowledge of human behavior, beginning with ourselves. Unfortunately, a lot of what *seems* true is not.

CHANGING BEHAVIOR AND ATTITUDES

Popular wisdom often suggests that to improve yourself you need to "change your attitude." In contrast, until late in the twentieth century, behavioral psychologists argued that it was more important to change *behavior*, that attitude change would follow.

In early editions of this book, back in the 1970s, we supported the position of traditional behavior therapy, that it is easier and more effective to change behavior first, then attitude change would slowly follow. While there is still little doubt that attitude change is the "tougher nut to crack," psychologists have learned that thoughts and beliefs can be modified by procedures such as those described in chapter 10 and that such changes will powerfully affect behavior.

Positive self-statements provide a good example. By consciously telling yourself "I have the ability to succeed in this situation," you greatly enhance your chances of success, even without any other changes. Everyone views and interprets life events through her or his own unique attitudes and beliefs about "how life is" and acts according to those interpretations. If I go around believing that "I'm no damn good," I'll approach life situations with an outlook of failure — and thus increase my chance of failure. If I tell myself I am capable of succeeding, my actions will be more likely to follow a pattern of success — and I'll be more successful.

For a time, the "cognitive folks" seemed to have everyone convinced that such changed thinking was all-important. That usually happens when a new idea emerges from psychological research. In recent years, the "pendulum" has swung back toward a more moderate position, and that is the view we hold: *Both thinking and behavior are vital elements in the process of bringing about personal growth.* (Funny how psychological research catches up with common sense if we allow enough time to pass!)

Some people respond more readily to cognitive (thinking) interventions, others to behavioral (action) interventions. In any comprehensive program for growth, therefore, *both* areas must be dealt with. Put most of your energy into whichever is most helpful for *you!*

And let's not forget that the most recent work — from the field of neuroscience — has demonstrated that the brain itself is the most powerful factor of all in determining our attitudes and behaviors. While that's not surprising, as we've discussed earlier, it has led to some remarkable findings about how our patterns of thinking and behavior have developed — and how they can be changed.

GETTING THERE FROM HERE

As you begin the process of becoming more assertive, don't expect to wake up some morning and say, "Today, I'm a new, assertive person!" You will find, spelled out in detail in the following chapter, a systematic, step-by-step guide to change. The key to developing assertiveness is *practice*. It has taken you a lifetime to develop the neural pathways in your brain and the resulting thinking and behavior patterns. You'll need to give it a little while — and quite a bit of *practice* — to make the changes you want.

Cycles of behavior tend to repeat and to perpetuate themselves until a decisive intervention occurs. People who have acted nonassertively or aggressively in relationships for a long time typically don't think much of themselves. Their behavior toward others may be inhibited or abusive — either one is usually met with scorn, disdain, or avoidance. When those inevitable responses come, such a person says, "See, I knew I was no damn good!" The person is confirmed in a low self-evaluation, and the cycle is repeated: self-defeating behavior, negative feedback from others, self-critical attitude, self-defeating behavior, and so on . . . (Remember the illustration of cycles in chapter 10?)

The cycle can be reversed, becoming a positive sequence: more appropriately assertive *behavior* gains more positive responses from others; positive feedback leads to an improved evaluation of *self-worth* ("Wow, people are treating me like a worthwhile person!"); and improved attitudes about oneself result in further assertiveness.

Or, the cycle may be entered at the point of *thoughts:* by saying positive things to yourself and beginning to think of yourself as a valuable person, you'll begin to act more appropriately. Your more effective action will usually produce more positive responses from others and the resulting confirmation of the original thought: "Maybe I *am* a good person, after all!"

JB had been convinced for years that he was truly worthless. He was totally dependent upon his wife for emotional support and, despite his handsome appearance and ability to express himself, he had literally no friends. Imagine his utter despair when his wife left him! Fortunately, JB was seeing a psychologist at the time and, after several months of therapy working on recovery from his loss, he was willing to begin to make contact with other people. When his first attempts at assertiveness with eligible women were successful, you can imagine how rewarding it was for him! JB's entire outlook toward himself changed, and he became much more assertive in a variety of situations.

Not everyone will experience such an immediate "payoff" for assertion; and not all assertions are fully successful. Success usually requires a great deal of patience and a gradual process of handling more and more difficult situations.

Generally speaking, however, *assertiveness is self-rewarding*. It feels good to have others begin to respond more attentively, to achieve your goals in relationships, to find situations going your way more often. And you can make these changes happen.

Remember, *begin with assertions where you are more or less sure of success* before proceeding to more difficult ones requiring greater confidence and skill. You'll find it helpful and reassuring to obtain support and guidance from a friend, practice partner, teacher, or professional therapist.

Keep in mind that changed behavior will lead to changed attitudes about yourself and your impact on people and situations. And changed thinking leads to changed behavior.

The next chapter presents the steps involved in bringing about these changes. Read all the material carefully first. Then begin to follow the steps in your own life. You'll like the difference in you!

WHEN YOU ARE READY TO BEGIN

First, make certain that you understand thoroughly the basic principles of assertion. Recognizing the differences between assertive and aggressive behavior is important to your understanding and success. Reread chapters 4, 5, and 6 if you need to.

Second, decide whether you are ready to begin trying self-assertive behavior on your own. If you have chronic patterns of nonassertiveness or aggression or if you are highly anxious, be more cautious. We recommend slow and careful practice and work with another person, preferably a trained therapist, as a facilitator. This recommendation is particularly strong for those who feel *very* anxious about beginning, as we discussed in chapter 11.

Third, your initial attempts at being assertive should be chosen for their high potential of success, so as to provide reinforcement. The more successfully you assert yourself at first, the more likely you are to be successful from then on!

Begin with small assertions that are likely to be rewarding, and from there move on to more difficult situations and relationships. Be very careful about attempting a difficult assertion without special preparation. And don't instigate an assertion where you are likely to fail and discourage your further attempts at assertiveness.

If you do suffer a setback, which very well may happen, take time to analyze the situation carefully and regain your confidence. Get help from a friend or facilitator if necessary. Especially in the early stages of assertion, it is not unusual to experience difficulty. You're still perfecting your technique, after all! Or you may overdo it, to the point of aggression. Either error is likely to cause a negative response, particularly if the target of your assertion becomes hostile and highly aggressive. Don't let such an occurrence stop you. Consider your goal again, and remember that although success requires lots of practice, the rewards are great.

Expect some failures. These procedures will not turn you into a 100 percent success in all your relationships! There are no instant or magic answers to life's problems. The fact is assertiveness does not *always* work — for *us* either! Sometimes, your goals will be incompatible with the other person's. Two people can't be at the head of the same line. (Letting the other person go first can be an assertive act, too!) At times, others may be unreasonable or unyielding, and the best of assertions will be to no avail.

Also, because you're human, you'll blow it sometimes — as we all do. Allow yourself to make mistakes! And allow others their right to be themselves as well. You'll be uncomfortable, disappointed, discouraged. Reassess, practice, then try again. (More about "failure" in chapter 22.)

The key to all of this, of course, is *choice*. If you choose to express yourself but don't succeed in gaining your goals, is that failure? We don't think so. The choice itself was an assertive act, as was the attempt. Outcomes are never guaranteed in life!

If you feel your assertions are failing a bit too often, take a close look at what's going on. Are you setting your goals too high? Take small steps to ensure success! Are you overdoing it and becoming aggressive? Monitor your behavior carefully — refer to your journal and check yourself. (Some aggression may be expected at first. The pendulum will balance in a short time.)

We all want our assertions to work, and we all want to achieve our goals. Nevertheless, the greatest value of self-assertion is the good feeling that comes from having expressed yourself. To know that *you have a perfect right to self-expression* and to feel free to say what you're feeling are the best benefits of all.

Usually, you'll find assertiveness will make things happen. But whether it works or not, remember how good it felt to speak up for yourself! You did what you could, even if the outcome wasn't what you hoped for. If you have genuinely tried and done all you can, that's all you can ask of yourself!

One final caution: Nothing turns people off faster than a self-righteous attitude. Avoid the trap some new assertiveness trainees fall into — feeling you *must* assert yourself in all situations, at all costs. Let moderation, consideration for others, and common sense prevail! (More on this in chapter 24.)

Ready to move ahead? Chapter 13 shows how — step by step.

13

Take It One Step at a Time

Believe in life!
Always human beings will live and progress
to greater, broader, and fuller life.
— W. E. B. DuBois

O K, YOU'RE READY TO MOVE ON. You've done your homework, found out what it means to be assertive, looked hard at how greater assertiveness might change your life, thought about your goals, and begun to deal with your anxiety. Now it's time to start the process of actually changing your behavior. In this chapter, you'll follow the step-by-step process that has been so effective for four decades in helping others to become more assertive in expressing themselves. Take it slowly, and let each success strengthen the foundation for your next steps.

THE STEP-BY-STEP PROCESS FOR INCREASING YOUR ASSERTIVENESS

Step 1. Observe your own behavior. Are you satisfied with your effectiveness in interpersonal relationships? Are you asserting yourself adequately? Look over your personal journal and the discussion in chapters 1–6, and assess how you feel about yourself and your behavior.

Step 2. Keep track of your assertiveness. Keep your journal very carefully for a week without trying to change the way you act. Each day, record those situations in which you found yourself responding assertively, those in which you blew it, and those you avoided altogether so you would not have to face the need to act assertively. Be honest with yourself, and systematic, following the guidelines for self-assessment described in chapters 2 and 3.

Step 3. Set realistic goals for yourself. Your self-assessment will help you select specific targets for your growth in assertiveness. Pick out situations in which or people toward whom you want to become more effective. Be sure to start with a small, low-risk step to maximize your chances of success. (See "When You Are Ready to Begin" in chapter 12.)

Step 4. Concentrate on a particular situation. Spend a few moments with your eyes closed, imagining how you handled a specific incident (being shortchanged at the supermarket, having a friend "talk your ear off" on the telephone when you had too much to do, letting the boss make you feel like "two cents" over a small mistake). Imagine vividly the actual details, including your specific feelings at the time and afterward. Appendix A offers many sample situations for your practice.

Step 5. Review your responses. Get out your journal and write down your behavior in step 4. Make use of the components of assertiveness noted in chapter 8 (eye contact, body posture, gestures, facial expression, voice, message content, etc.). Look carefully at the components of your behavior in the recalled incident, including your thoughts. Note your strengths. Be aware of those components that represent nonassertive or aggressive behavior. If a major element of your response involves anxiety, refer to the discussion in chapter 11. Do not attempt to force yourself into very painful situations. On the other hand, do not avoid new growth if it is only moderately uncomfortable!

Step 6. Observe an effective model. At this point it would be very helpful to watch someone who handles the same situation very well. Again, watch for the components discussed in chapter 8, particularly the *style* — the words are less important. If the model is a friend, discuss her or his approach and its consequences.

Interestingly, while such "modeling" has been an important step in assertiveness training for years, only recently have brain researchers weighed in. They've learned that we all have "mirror neurons" in the brain that encourage us to virtually mimic the behavior of others we're engaged with. For instance, we almost always smile back at someone who smiles at us. You can put your brain's natural ability to work to help you mimic the effective assertiveness of your model person.

Step 7. Consider alternative responses. What are other possible ways you could handle the incident? Could you deal with it more directly? More firmly? Less offensively? Refer to the chart in chapter 5, and differentiate among nonassertive, aggressive, and assertive responses.

Step 8. Imagine yourself handling the situation. Close your eyes and visualize yourself dealing effectively with your practice situation. You may act similarly to the model you observed in step 6 or in a very different way. (You may find it helps to "act as if" first, mimicking your model's style. Then adjust your voice, face, gestures, etc. to find a style that's more your own.) Imagine being assertive but as much your natural self as you can.

Develop strategies or ways of coping with any blocks in your visualization. If you notice yourself feeling anxious, calm yourself. If negative thoughts interrupt your assertion, replace them with positive statements. "Self-correct" as you proceed.

Cope with disruptions of your assertive response in your visualization. Repeat this step as often as you need to until you can imagine yourself handling the situation well.

Step 9. Practice positive thoughts. Spend some time going over the material in chapter 10 again. Develop a list of several brief positive statements about yourself that are related to this situation (e.g., "I've had job interviews before and have done all right"). Practice saying those statements to yourself several times. Remember, this is not a "script" for what to say to someone else, it is a "prompter" for what to say to yourself. As with most things in life, it's best to begin by being assertive with yourself! ("I can do this!")

Step 10. Get help if you need it. As we have noted before, the process of becoming more assertive may require you to stretch yourself considerably. If you feel unable on your own to deal with the situations you have visualized, seek help from a qualified professional. (We suggest a licensed mental health professional — psychologist, clinical social worker, or marriage and family therapist — not someone who simply offers "assertiveness training" or "communication skills" or "executive coaching.")

Step 11. Try it out. You have examined your own behavior, considered alternatives, observed a model of more effective action, practiced some positive thoughts about yourself, and obtained any help needed to overcome obstacles. You're now ready to begin trying out for yourself new ways of dealing with the problem situation. (Don't skip over a repeat of steps 6, 7, 8, and 9 if needed to be sure you're prepared, but don't get bogged down "getting ready.")

It's important to select an alternative, more effective way of behaving in the problem situation. You may wish to follow your model and enact that person's approach. That's an OK choice, but don't forget that you're a unique person. You may or may not find your model's style one that you want to adopt for yourself.

After selecting a more effective alternative behavior, role-play the situation with a friend, practice partner, teacher, or therapist. Try to follow the new response pattern you have selected. As in steps 2, 4, and 5, make careful observation of your behavior, using an audio or video recording to review your actual behavior whenever possible. Don't worry about not having your goals absolutely clear. As you try out new behavioral skills, you'll become more aware of what you want in the situation.

Step 12. Get feedback. This step essentially repeats step 5 with emphasis on the positive aspects of your behavior. Note particularly the strengths of your performance, and go to work on your weaker components (review chapter 8 as needed).

Step 13. Shape your behavior. Repeat steps 8, 9, 11, and 12 as often as you find it helpful to "shape" your behavior — by this process of successive approximations of your goal — until you feel satisfied that you're able to deal with the situation effectively. These repetitions may seem unnecessarily drawn out, but it's this practice of new responses that will make it possible for you to create new neural pathways in your brain, change your old style, and act more effectively "when push comes to shove."

Step 14. Give yourself a "real world" test. You are now ready to give your new response pattern a real test. Up to this point your preparation has taken place in a relatively safe environment. Nevertheless, careful training and repeated practice have prepared you to react almost automatically. You should be ready to proceed with an actual trial. If you are unwilling to give it the test, you may need further rehearsals or help. (Repeat steps 8-12.) Moving from intention to action — being assertive with yourself — may be the most important step of all!

And remember to select a situation that is not too "loaded." That is, *pick a test at which you're very likely to succeed*, not an important encounter with your life partner or your boss!

Step 15. Evaluate the test. Make notes in your journal to record how your "real world" trial(s) go. Note the overall result, your general impressions of your effectiveness, your SUDS level (chapter 11), and details on the specific components of your behavior (chapter 8). If a friend observed you, get feedback from him or her. If you used a pocket digital or microcassette recorder to capture your verbal effectiveness, listen to the recording. This step is an important part of the learning process. Don't ignore it!

Step 16. Continue your training. Repeat the procedures described above to help develop your desired behaviors in other specific situations that have given you trouble. Gradually increase the difficulty and importance of your practice situations, continuing to build on your successes and learn from your mistakes. Look over the *Assertiveness Inventory* in chapter 2 and the vignettes in chapter 6 and in Appendix A for examples that may be helpful in planning your own program for change.

Step 17. Set up "social reinforcement." As a final step in establishing an independent behavior pattern, it is very important that you understand the need to provide ongoing support and rewards for yourself. In order to maintain your new assertive skills, set up a system of rewards in your own environment. For example, you now know the good feeling that comes from a successful assertion and you can rest assured that this good response will continue. Admiration from others will be another continuing positive response to your growth. Write down in your journal a personal checklist of specific reinforcements — rewarding results — that are unique to your own environment and relationships. And reread earlier entries in your journal to track your progress over time.

We have spelled out this step-by-step process in detail because we know it works. No one system is right for everyone, of course. We've emphasized the importance of systematic procedures, but we know it will only work for you if you take into account your own personal needs, objectives, and learning style. We want you to create a learning environment that will help *you* grow in assertiveness.

There is no substitute for *active* practice of assertive thoughts and behavior in your own life, when you choose to, as a means of developing greater assertiveness and enjoying its rewards.

In the chapters that follow, you'll find many ideas for developing and applying your growing assertiveness. We urge you to keep at it and to apply the principles and procedures you've learned — at least a little every day.

The Step-by-Step Process for Increasing Your Assertiveness

17. Set up "social reinforcement"

16. Continue your training

15. Evaluate the test

14. Give yourself a "real world" test

13. Shape your behavior

12. Get feedback

11. Try it out

10. Get help if you need it

9. Practice positive thoughts

8. Imagine yourself handling the situation

7. Consider alternative responses

6. Observe an effective model

5. Review your responses

4. Concentrate on a particular situation

3. Set realistic goals for yourself

2. Keep track of your assertiveness

1. Observe your own behavior

14

Assertiveness Builds Equal Relationships

Unity is plural and, at minimum, is two.
— R. BUCKMINSTER FULLER

"STAND UP FOR YOURSELF" is the slogan often equated with being assertive. But there's much more to assertive living than defending your rights. We've observed that positive, caring feelings are even more difficult for many people to express than "standing up for yourself" behavior. Expressions of warmth are often held back, particularly by adults. Embarrassment, fear of rejection or ridicule, and the idea that reason is superior to emotion — all are excuses for not expressing warmth, caring, and love spontaneously. Effective assertiveness can contribute much to greater freedom in your communication of positive feelings toward others.

The first edition of *Your Perfect Right* was devoted almost exclusively to fostering "stand-up-for-yourself" behavior. In a critical review of that first edition, published in the professional journal *Behavior Therapy*, the late psychiatrist Michael Serber noted our oversight. Serber, a colleague who had substantial influence on our work, wrote in that early review (1971):

Certainly, behavioral skills necessary to stand up to the multiple personal, social, and business situations confronting the majority of people are imperative to master. But what of other just as necessary skills, such as being able to give and take tenderness and affection? Is not the expression of affection toward other people also assertion? . . . The ability to express warmth and affection, to be able to give and take feelings, including anger, badly needs . . . special attention. . . . Humanistic goals and behavioral techniques can yield both meaningful and concrete new behaviors.

In this chapter, we'll give special attention to the expression of affection and other positive feelings.

YOUR SOCIAL BRAIN

Research on the human brain, as we've discussed in earlier chapters, has brought us exciting insights into why we humans think and act as we do. One of the most exciting aspects of those findings has been the discovery of the brain connections and pathways that help to define us as social beings. Neuroscientists have been able, via such newer high-tech systems as functional magnetic resonance imaging (fMRI), to actually view the brain activity patterns, which "light up" during social contacts.

Nature plus nurture. Some of those patterns are "hardwired" — born in us in the form of *temperament* — and some we learn from *life experiences*, particularly in our early years. Temperament is the term used to label inborn personality predispositions, such as one's tendency to shyness, social facility, or aggression. Those qualities are not irreversible but will persist into adulthood if reinforced by the person's upbringing and other life experiences along the way.

The development of our social brain centers on a complex interaction of the neural connections and patterns that come from both "nature" and "nurture." Thus our social attitudes and behavior are governed by an integration, in the developing brain, of pathways that are there from day one with those that develop through learning over the lifespan. Our ability to sense, understand, and respond to each other's feelings comes from the way our brains put together these extremely complex networks.

Social learning. Since we can't do much about our temperaments, let's focus on the learning process. Children who learn early in life that manipulating, overpowering, and intimidating others (aggression) pays off will use those techniques to get what they want, rather than developing socially appropriate (assertive) skills. In fact, the brain must learn those appropriate social patterns in childhood, say some researchers, or they may not develop at all.

Similarly, children who grow up very insecure or fearful — perhaps from early loss of a parent — also seem to have difficulty developing appropriate assertiveness. They don't recognize, or don't trust, their own emotions. They tend to be very anxious in social situations, and they don't learn effective social skills.

Thus it seems clear from research in neuroscience that individuals who are temperamentally inclined to be aggressive or fearful, or who fail to learn socially appropriate attitudes and behaviors in childhood, will find it difficult as adults to develop social sensitivity and effective social skills — "social intelligence."

Does that mean you can't learn to be assertive if you fit into one of those groups? Not at all. It does mean that you may have to work a bit harder to achieve the changes you seek.

It's well beyond the scope of this book to offer a detailed explanation of the impact of brain on attitudes and behavior — and we certainly don't claim expertise in neuroscience! What's important in the context of our discussion of relationships is to recognize that:

❖ We humans are hardwired to be social beings.

❖ There are very important differences in our individual "social intelligence."

❖ We can develop greater social sensitivity and skill through learning.

So let's press on and learn more about how you can develop more effective social skills, with or without a temperament that predisposes you to social facility. If your interest leads to learning more about this topic, we again invite you to examine the books recommended in chapter 10.

"What the World Needs Now..."

More than four decades ago, psychoanalyst Eric Fromm defined five types of love in his excellent book *The Art of Loving*. The book is old, but Fromm's perspective on love is timeless. He discusses at length the concepts of fraternal love, maternal love, erotic love, love of God, and self-love.

Fraternal love, for example — caring for other members of the human family — is a very different quality than the popular romantic idea of "love." It is a vital and critically important aspect of our lives on this small planet. However independent we may become, we humans are fundamentally interdependent and social creatures!

Effective assertive communication can build positive, equal relationships between people — the most valuable assets any human being can have.

Reaching Out

Expressing your warm feelings for another person is a highly assertive act. And, as with other assertions we have noted, the action itself is more important by far than the words you use. This is even more true for expressions of caring. Nothing represents a more personal, individual expression than that which says, "You mean a great deal to me at this moment."

Here are some ways of communicating that message:

> *Expressing your warm feelings for another person is a highly assertive act.*

❖ A warm, firm, and extended handshake

❖ A hug, the squeeze of an arm, an arm around the shoulders, an affectionate pat on the back, the squeeze of a hand held affectionately

❖ A warm smile

❖ Extended eye contact

❖ A gift of love (made by the giver, or uniquely special to the recipient)

❖ And, yes, sincerely warm words, such as
   "Thank you."
   "You're great!"
   "I really understand what you mean."
   "I like what you did."
   "I'm here."
   "I believe you."
   "I trust you"
   "I love you."
   "I believe in you."
   "I'm glad to see you."
   "You've been on my mind."

None of these messages is new to you. Yet you may find it difficult to allow yourself to do or say them. It is too easy to be hung up on embarrassment or to assume: "She knows how I feel" or "He doesn't care to hear that." But *who* doesn't care to hear that? All of us need to know we are cared about and admired and needed. If those around us are too subtle in their expressions of positive regard, we may begin to doubt, and perhaps to look elsewhere for human warmth.

We asked a group of university students to tell what makes each of them feel especially good. Some of their favorite experiences are in the following list (notice how many involve someone else caring!):

Acceptance of my invitation	Greeting someone else	Personal satisfaction with myself
Achievement	Having a friend	Positive comment
Affection	Having someone say "hello"	Praise
Approval	Helping others	Receiving a compliment
Assurance	Implementation of ideas	Recognition
Compliments from the opposite sex	Independence	Recognition when speaking
Encouragement	Jobs completed	Request to repeat a job previously done
Expressed interest of another	Keeping my plants alive	Satisfaction
Friendliness	Laughter	Security
Getting an A on an exam	Making new friends	Singing
Giving a compliment	My boyfriend's/girlfriend's actions of love	Spoken affirmation
Good grades	toward me	Touch

We all need positive contacts with others. Therapists encounter many, many clients who are unhappy precisely because they are not getting such "strokes" in their lives.

Imagine the following scenes:

❖ While you are wandering alone at a large gathering, a stranger walks up to you and starts a conversation, and you no longer feel anxious and lost.

❖ Three days after you arrive in a new neighborhood, the couple next door comes to welcome you with a pot of coffee and a freshly baked cake.

❖ During your visit in another country, you are looking in vain for a street sign. A native appears and asks, "May I help you find something?"

Take a few moments to jot down in your journal how you would feel in each of those situations.

Such initiative involves concern for the other person and some courage of your own. Yet, people often hesitate to make contact for fear of rejection — a common excuse for avoiding assertions! Realistically, when you think about it, who could reject such a kindness?

Often actions like these are easier than you might suppose. As you enter a classroom, a meeting, or a bus, think how easy it would be simply to approach a vacant seat and ask the person sitting nearest, "Is anyone sitting here?" Not only have you found a place to sit — assuming the seat is available — *you have begun a conversation!* Having thus opened contact, you may easily proceed to find out more about the other person: "Where are you headed?" "Have you heard this lecturer before?" "My name is . . ."

Thoughtful acts like these are not only strokes for the receiver, they also produce warm feelings for the person who reached out assertively. And not just warm feelings. Check this out: Psychologist-author Daniel Goleman (*Social Intelligence*) reports recent brain research showing that certain parts of the brain "light up" (under fMRI scanning) in special moments of human contact, such as hearing the voice of an old friend. What's more, not only do good feelings result, such connections actually stimulate the immune system. Result: those with good social support systems — such as warm friendships — live healthier lives.

Don't wait for others to take the initiative. Take the risk of reaching out! It's a key means of caring about yourself and about others and an important step toward greater assertiveness and more fun!

"Thanks, I Needed That!"

Compliments are a frequent source of discomfort — both giving and receiving — sadly enough. To praise someone as a person or to recognize something someone has done may be a difficult thing for you. Again, we encourage practice. Go out of your way to praise others — not dishonestly or insincerely, but whenever a genuine opportunity presents itself. Don't concern yourself with waiting for the right words either. Your thoughtfulness — the honest expression of what you are feeling — will convey itself, *if you act!* Try simply, "I like what you did" or "Great!" or a big smile.

Saying thank you is difficult for some people. As the CEO of an organization with thousands of employees, Geoffrey was quick to criticize, but rarely expressed appreciation directly to the people on his staff. He seldom openly rewarded, recognized, or even acknowledged a job well done. Because the chief executive was afraid to act in warm and positive ways (perhaps he might appear "soft," or others might come to *expect* rewards?), staff turnover in the firm was high, and morale was low.

Accepting compliments — receiving very supportive statements directed toward you, or about you to a third person — is perhaps an even more challenging task, particularly difficult if you are not feeling good about yourself. Nevertheless, it is an assertive act — and mutually enhancing — to accept praise from another person.

Think about it: you really have no right to deny another person's *perception* of you. If you say, "Oh, you just caught me on a good day!" or "It wasn't anything special" or "It was an accident that it turned out well," you have in effect said the compliment giver has poor judgment. It is as if you told that person, "You're wrong!" Try to allow everyone the right to feelings; if they are positive toward you, do others — and yourself — the courtesy of accepting.

You don't have to go around praising yourself or taking credit for achievements that are not your own. However, when another person sincerely wishes to convey a positive comment about you, *allow* the expression without rejection or qualification. Try saying at the least, "It's hard for me to accept that, but thank you," or better yet simply, "That feels good" or "I like to hear that."

Supermodel Kathy Ireland has this to say about how to take a compliment:

> *A compliment is a gift. It's not relevant that you may not agree with the giver's opinion of you. In some ways, the compliment is not even about you; it's about the fact that someone else cared enough to think of you and to share his or her thoughts in a positive way. So the best way to handle one? With a heartfelt, "Thank you."*

We agree. And, incidentally, it doesn't hurt to offer a polite, "You're welcome," in response. What is it with "No problem"? Sounds pretty dismissive of the other person, don't you think?

APOLOGIES

One of the early issues that assertiveness trainers used to focus on back in the 1970s and 1980s was the tendency many nonassertive people had to *apologize* too much. In fact, it used to be pretty common for women especially to open a conversation with "I'm sorry, but . . ." A correction was clearly needed for those who seemed to be sorry about their very existence.

These days, however, we may have gone overboard in the other direction, leading many people to avoid an apology when one is clearly in order. It's not self-demeaning to admit you've made a mistake or screwed up. In fact, it's downright courageous and ethical to accept responsibility for your actions. You needn't wallow in it, however.

NBC TV's Al Roker has some straightforward advice on how to say you're sorry:

> *Look the person straight in the eye and say, "I'm sorry." Don't embellish it by making excuses or trying to explain why you screwed up. Just ask for forgiveness.*

The important thing here is not to apologize for *being yourself*. You're human; you make mistakes and come up short at times. So does everybody else. When you do mess up, apologize briefly — following Al Roker's model — and get on with your life.

FRIENDSHIP

"Nancy has seen me at my worst, watched me make stupid mistakes, felt the sting of my unjustified anger, and been there when I was coming apart at the seams. It's amazing; she's still my friend!"

There is no relationship quite like that of friendship. Not so irrational as love; yet far more intense than acquaintance, friendship is perhaps the least understood of human interactions.

Actual *knowledge* about friendship continues to be sketchy at best; most relationship research involves strangers or lovers. Yet some popular wisdom is useful in examining the bond between friends:

. . . Friends have some interests in common.

. . . Friends share an ongoing relationship, with periodic (although not necessarily regular) contact.

. . . Friends trust one another, at least to some extent, with information, money, safety, and other relationships.

. . . Friends can say no to each other and still remain friends.

. . . Friends can see — and accept — the worst in each other.

. . . Friends rarely feel they "owe" each other anything; give and take is without obligation between them (perhaps with some limits!).

. . . Friendship is also characterized by understanding, communication, acceptance, lack of embarrassment, and trust.

Friendship is held within us, an attitude toward another person much like love, anger, or prejudice. It requires no regular outward expression. It requires merely a *feeling of commitment* to the relationship. Often the belief that the other person cares about you, that the other values the relationship as well supports such a feeling. If we believe that we are important to each other — important enough that we think of each other warmly now and again — we will likely remain friends, even if we don't see each other for years.

> *Effective assertive communication can build positive, equal relationships between people*

It's common to see tearful reunions at airports, parties, and homecomings between friends who have not seen each other for years. Friendships often survive no more contact than an annual ritual holiday card! What keeps them going? Can such a relationship really be called a "friendship?" Why not?

"True friendship," says Letty Cottin Pogrebin in her book *Among Friends*, "describes a feeling... best captured by the word 'soulmate' in Aristotle's sense of 'a single soul dwelling in two bodies'... a feeling that can happen to any two people who are caught up in the act of being themselves, together, and who like what they see."

But what has this to do with assertiveness? How does assertive action contribute to friendship or vice versa?

Consider this hypothesis: *If you act assertively most of the time, you are more likely to have satisfying relationships than if you act in nonassertive or aggressive ways*. We can't prove that idea. In fact, we have not even dreamed up a research study that would allow us to test it. But our observation of assertive people over many years leads us to conclude that it's a pretty good bet!

Acting on that idea, then, and assuming that you would like to have satisfying relationships, we invite you to apply the assertive skills you are learning to the development of friendship:

❖ Take the risks necessary to build an acquaintance into a friend.

❖ Allow your friend to see you as you are.

❖ Share something of yourself you would not ordinarily tell someone else.

❖ Be spontaneous with your new friend, suggest an activity on the spur of the moment, really listen to what is important in your friend's life, give a gift for no special occasion.

❖ Ask your friend's advice with a problem or help with a project (remembering that an assertive friend can say no and still like you!)

❖ Simply tell the person you like her or him.

❖ Clear the air between you; if you are annoyed or suspect that your friend may be, bring it up.

❖ Get *honest*. Don't allow assumptions to define your relationship. If the relationship can't handle it, it probably would not have lasted anyway; if it can, you'll be miles ahead!

As adults, friendship helps to define who we are, much as family does when we are children. (The absence of friends also says a great deal about us.) Assertive action on your part can make all the difference in nurturing friendships. Maybe you've put it off long enough?

GENDER MENDERS
One of the most obvious realms of concern about equality in relationships has been that of the "battle of the sexes." The last quarter of the twentieth century saw major changes in how we view male-female relationships — at home, at work, in society.

In times of upheaval in such ingrained social traditions as sex roles, of course, misunderstandings are abundant and stress levels are high. After all, both genders had been conditioned for generations to behave toward each other in certain ways. What's more, there are certain hereditary, biological, and biochemical factors that have influenced each differently. The abandonment of traditions and movement toward equality has come with a price, and each of us may choose to pay that price with impatience and conflict or with patience and cooperation.

Some popular writers — Deborah Tannen (*You Just Don't Understand* and *Talking Nine to Five*) and John Gray (*Men Are from Mars, Women Are from Venus*) among them — have taken the position that men and women are raised in different cultures. We have no doubt of that, yet we don't agree that there are *consistent differences* that characterize males and females. In fact, most research in the field shows that the similarities among us are greater than the differences.

There are inequalities, biases, prejudices, myths, and false beliefs within both male and female cultures, and it doesn't help anything to assume that any of us consciously sets out to cause difficulties for each other.

We suggest an assertive effort — based on patience and cooperation — to mend, not bend, whatever "gender gap" you may experience in your relationships:

❖ Make equality your goal.

❖ Let each person become more aware of the characteristic attitudes, needs, and behaviors of the other, but don't assume, "because he's a man" for instance, that he'll be like all the other men you've known.

❖ Work on your assertive communication skills, especially listening, in order to understand and explore the uniqueness of each person, regardless of gender.

❖ Remember that, while there are a few accurate generalizations about each gender, there are even more unique things about each person.

❖ Discuss with each other what you can do differently in your relationships with the opposite gender to bridge any gap. Work on accepting and respecting each other.

❖ Learn about the masculine and feminine parts of yourself so you can improve your relationship with both genders.

❖ Treat every other person with respect, regardless of gender.

ASSERTIVENESS IN A SHRINKING WORLD

A final note before we leave this chapter on relationships. All of us live in networks that begin with ourselves as individuals, touch family and friends closest to us, and include neighbors, membership groups, community, region, nation, hemisphere, world (even the universe?). Events that happen in the next block, the next town, a nearby state, even across the world can have lasting effects upon our lives.

And we know about those events within moments thanks to the internet, CNN, cell phones with built-in cameras, blogs, YouTube, shortwave radio, the local evening news, even the print media. The changes, and the speed with which they come at us, are mind-boggling.

People all over the globe are asserting their independence — declaring their rights of freedom and self-determination. As local autonomy, nationalism, and independence are increasingly asserted worldwide, let's remember our own *world citizenship* in the process. The earth is small; we can't afford to be arrogant about political boundaries, despite the ideas and actions of political officials in some countries. Relationships with others begin at home, on the block, and in town; but they must extend to our fellow human beings all over this tiny globe. At risk is our continued existence as a species.

15

All in the Family: Assertiveness for Parents, Children, and Seniors

When you have a problem because my behavior
is interfering with your meeting your needs,
I encourage you to tell me openly and honestly
how you are feeling. . . . I will listen. . . .
— THOMAS GORDON

H OW LONG HAS IT BEEN SINCE YOU WERE ON A SEESAW? Remember how you could affect the ride of the person on the other end by shifting your weight forward or back? If you moved forward quickly, your friend would likely drop with a solid bump! By leaning way back, you could keep the other person suspended in mid-air.

Families and other interpersonal systems have a balance system not unlike that of the seesaw. A change in one member of the family will generally upset the balance of the total system, affecting everyone. Often families are strong "resistors" of change because of the delicate balance in family relationships, even though the system may be painful — or even destructive.

Becoming more assertive is clearly a change that may upset the family balance.

A passive wife and mother for years who begins to express a new assertiveness introduces severe strains into the family system. The children, previously able to manipulate her easily, must find new and more direct avenues to achieve their goals. A reluctantly supportive husband will soon be ironing his own shirts and sharing in household chores, since his formerly passive wife may have gone back to work or school full time.

Renowned psychologist Raymond Corsini tells a story of just such a client. She told Corsini she was "wiped out" each morning by 9:00 after preparing separate breakfasts and lunches for her husband and each of their three children, cleaning the house, helping with homework, and driving the youngsters to school. "Tell your family," Corsini prescribed for her, "that your doctor has ordered you not to get out of bed until 9:00 a.m. every weekday." She followed the "doctor's orders," and when she returned for her appointment the following week, "she was a new woman. . . . The children had fought to get her out of bed, but she refused. In a month the husband and children were doing fine taking care of themselves."

Such changes present a difficult adjustment for everyone. The prospect of such disruption of the family balance can be a considerable obstacle to the person who wishes to become more assertive. A traditional partner may actively resist changes that demand a greater share of responsibility for the family's well-being. For the children, a whole new set of challenges is introduced, as they learn to deal with the requirements of increased self-reliance.

OUT OF THE MOUTHS OF BABES . . .

It has been said that "the last frontier of human rights is that of the rights of children." Despite the history of apparent dedication to individual rights in the United States, and even despite the hard-won gains in rights for minorities, women, and others who have been denied and oppressed, our society has made very few changes in our basic notions that children are second-class citizens. The glorification of "youth" in popular media, dress styles, music, and literature has not carried over into a comparable respect for the *rights* of those who are very young.

Without debating the relative concerns of innocence and inexperience vs. age and wisdom, let us simply suggest that assertive children, like assertive adults, are likely to be healthier and happier, more honest, and less manipulative. Feeling better about themselves, these youngsters are headed toward more self-actualized adulthood.

We favor a conscious effort in families, schools, churches, and public agencies to foster assertiveness in young people. Let's create conditions that will tolerate — even support — their natural spontaneity, honesty and openness, rather than sacrificing it to parent anxiety and school authority.

Let us be clear — we do not suggest that parents ignore discipline and adopt totally permissive child rearing. The real world places limits upon us all, and children need to learn that fact early if they are to develop adequate life s-u-r-v-i-v-a-l skills. However, we consider it vital that families, schools, and other child rearing social systems view children as human beings worthy of respect, honor their basic human rights, value their honest self-expression, and teach them the skills to act accordingly.

Assertive skills are valuable for children in dealing with their peers, teachers, siblings, and parents. When Mike Emmons led assertiveness groups at a local elementary school (grades 1-6), the youngsters got enthusiastically involved and volunteered a few situations from their daily experience:

- *What do you do if someone pushes in front of you in the lunch line?*
- *My sister borrows my things without asking. What should I say?*
- *When it's Joe's turn to be "out" in handball, he won't leave.*
- *What do you do if someone teases you or calls you names?*
- *The woman I babysit for forgot to pay me. I told my Mom, and she said I should call her, but I'm too embarrassed.*

The children easily understood the meaning of assertiveness. They practiced the skills and especially enjoyed being videotaped in the process. Even the children's feedback to each other was specific and helpful. Children can learn the basics of assertiveness and apply them to situations in their own lives.

Parents often have difficulty discriminating between assertion and aggression when disciplining or dealing firmly with their youngsters. The definition of assertiveness applies to parent-child relationships! Although each situation is unique, the key to defining assertiveness in family interactions is *mutual respect.* Children, like parents, are individual human beings. They deserve fair treatment and nonaggressive discipline.

Most of the principles and procedures advised elsewhere in this book apply to the development of assertiveness in children, so we won't present any specialized material here.

How about your kids? Have you taught them appropriate assertive skills? Can they handle themselves with their peers, with neighborhood bullies, with pushy salespeople, with privacy questions online, with adults who might take advantage of them? Can they openly express affection and appreciation to friends and relatives? Let them tell you about the difficult interpersonal situations they face every day. Use those situations to teach and practice assertive skills, using the procedures you've learned in this book. You'll learn a lot about them — and yourself — in the process!

THEY DO GROW UP, DON'T THEY?
Independence may be the single most important life issue we all face, certainly it is the core around which growing up revolves. Some rebelliousness is normal and healthy for teenagers and facilitates their developing independence. Families with dominant parents and inhibited teenagers may find the teens' necessary steps toward independent adulthood are delayed.

Unresolved ties with parents — unfinished work from the teen years — sometimes restricts independence in the lives of adults of all ages. In our experience, an appropriately assertive approach by the adult child can clear the air, make the situation clear to the parent, and allow needed expression of feelings on both sides.

Such a confrontation is almost inevitably painful, and it is a considerable risk for both parent and child to open up old wounds. Despite this obstacle, we believe continued silence exacts much too high a price. Adults who avoid dealing with their parents or adult children as they would any other adult with whom they feel a special closeness can suffer unmeasured guilt, self-denial, inhibition, repressed anger, and often depression.

New York psychologists Janet Wolfe and Iris Fodor have done excellent work with the relationship of adult mothers and daughters, and their five steps toward a new assertive mother-daughter relationship are useful for anyone who is dealing with this issue:

❖ Recognize the life cycle issues each party is dealing with (e.g., economic independence, menopause, retirement, etc.)

❖ Identify attitudes or beliefs that inhibit assertive communication (e.g., "Don't talk back to your father.")

❖ Figure out the rights and goals of each party.

❖ Identify emotions (e.g., anxiety, guilt) that interfere with pursuing goals.

❖ Try out new forms of relationship (e.g., adult-to-adult, rather than parent-to-child).

Can Seniors Be Assertive Too?

"Whatever happened to respect for your elders?" a seventy-two-year-old retired engineer asked recently. "In my generation, kids held the door for older people. Now they crash through first and knock down anybody in their way. Same thing when you're standing in a line, driving down the freeway, or trying to find a seat on the bus. 'Me first, and the devil take the hindmost.'"

Yep. Those of us who are "of a certain age" pretty much have to look out for ourselves, like everyone else. It's not likely these days that anyone — at least in the United States — will step aside or hold the door or say "you first," unless you're obviously disabled. So what's a senior to do? Well, you know the answer you're likely to get from us: "When it's really important to you, be assertive!"

And the approach to assertiveness we would advise for seniors doesn't really differ from what we've been saying throughout this book. The real difference comes in terms of the situations older people are likely to experience. In addition to the usual encounters with store clerks, social groups, pushy salespeople, noisy neighbors, and so on, seniors find themselves patronized by medical office personnel, ignored by politicians, neglected by their adult children, mistreated by caregivers, and dismissed by the courts when they seek contact with grandchildren after an ugly divorce. (For an entertaining look at some of the issues and joys of aging, we recommend Eugenie Wheeler's book, *The Time of Your Life*.)

Some of these circumstances — the political and medical establishments come to mind — are not likely to change much, despite your best assertive efforts. You may, however, be able to teach your adult children and caregivers a thing or two about responding to your needs. We suggest you start by reviewing your goals. What are you after? Do you really want to change the world or just to live better in your corner of it? Do you particularly want your children to spend more time with you, or are you just lonely for any company?

In an interesting recent study, researchers at the University of Waterloo (Ontario, Canada) examined seniors' responses in a conversation with health care workers (Ryan, Anas, & Friedman,

2006). Seniors who responded assertively were evaluated as more competent than those who were passive or aggressive.

The many challenges seniors confront that have implications for assertive action include such situations as:

❖ Confronting ageist remarks.

❖ Discussing family issues with your adult children and grandchildren.

❖ Campaigning for senior rights, including those of grandparents.

❖ Receiving better treatment in the health care and insurance systems.

❖ Getting more time with grandchildren.

❖ Teaching youngsters (including children and grandchildren!) to respect elders.

If you are old enough to belong to AARP, or maybe even to collect Social Security, we urge you to add such situations to your list of goals for assertiveness. Review the fundamentals of assertive behavior in chapter 5 and the step-by-step process in chapter 13, and apply those principles and procedures to situations that are the special needs of seniors.

Finally, consider this: *it's not all about you!* We urge our own gray-haired generation to keep in mind a couple of caveats:

❖ *You're the one who taught your children (and others) how to treat you.* You showed them both by the way you've treated them and by the way you behaved toward your own parents and other elders.

❖ *We seniors have no more right to be treated with respect than anyone else,* just because our hair is gray. Deal with clerks, caregivers, and your children as equals. They are not your personal servants. Give them the same respect that you expect to receive.

ASSERTIVENESS AND BALANCE IN THE FAMILY SYSTEM

Let us sum up this discussion of assertiveness in the family this way:

❖ Assertive behavior enhances both individuals and relationships for people of all ages.

❖ Honest, open, and nonhurtful assertive communication is desirable and highly valuable in families.

❖ Children and adults of all ages should learn to be assertive within the family — and beyond it.

❖ The key to successful relationships in the family — and beyond — is mutual respect.

❖ The principles and procedures for defining and learning assertiveness described in this book are applicable to adults, children, and seniors (i.e., modeling, rehearsal, feedback, practice, reinforcement, mutual respect, and individual rights).

Change in family systems is more difficult, more time and energy consuming, and potentially more risky (families can and do break up) than is change in individual behavior. We encourage you to evaluate carefully, to proceed slowly, to involve everyone openly, to avoid coercion, to tolerate failure, and to remember that nobody and no approach is perfect! Do what you can to develop respectful assertive relationships within your family and beyond.

16

Assertiveness, Intimacy, and Sexuality

I'm feeling great, and I have sex almost every day.
Almost on Monday, almost on Tuesday,
almost on Wednesday . . .
— JACK LaLANNE, FITNESS GURU, AT NINETY-THREE

I LOVE YOU," according to author Judith Viorst, "can be translated into his willingness to lace my ski boots, and to listen to my discussion of infant diarrhea, . . . and to not say anything at all when I've just done something spectacularly stupid."

Jack's pun on sex, and Judy's thoughts on love, are bookends for this chapter's discussion of sex and intimacy. You'll find that greater assertiveness can improve both intimate and sexual relationships in your life. ("Wait! Aren't those the same thing?")

ARE INTIMACY AND SEX THE SAME THING?

Many people use the words *intimacy* and *sex* interchangeably. They define sexual expression and intimate expression in the same breath, as if they were equivalent.

They're not.

Intimacy includes much, much more than sex. Think of it this way: if you put a tiny pinch of cinnamon into a bowl filled with a host of other ingredients, it adds a zing of flavor to the final outcome. Sex is like that touch of cinnamon. It adds zing, but it is far from the whole recipe.

As a result of our interest in assertive, equal relationships, we've devoted intensive study to the factors that contribute to healthy intimate partnerships. In our book, *Accepting Each Other*, we described six vital dimensions of intimacy. Sex didn't make the first team. It's important, of course, but it's a second-string player.

Don't misunderstand. We don't underestimate the significance of the sexual relationship. It's just not the all-important factor lots of folks make it out to be.

When anybody bothers to ask couples how important sex is to their overall happiness most rank it below such intimacy variables as communication, understanding, and commitment. You can guess why. True intimate sexual expression is a *result* more than it is a *cause* of overall healthy intimacy. While the prevailing myth would have us believe that sex is the best indicator of a happy couple, the reality is that happiness is dependent upon the total relationship. Sex is a part, but a small part.

If not sex, then what is intimacy?

Here's our definition:

> *Intimacy is a quality of a relationship between two people who care deeply about each other that is characterized by mutual* **attraction**, *open and honest* **communication, commitment** *to continuation of the partnership,* **enjoyment** *of their life together, a sense of* **purpose** *for the relationship, and mutual* **trust** *that honors and respects both partners.*

Genuine intimacy is a complex blend of those six major dimensions, which also (not by accident) fit the acronym *ACCEPT*. This model of intimacy embodies the idea of *acceptance* of yourself, of each other, and of your relationship. Acceptance is truly the heart of intimacy.

It's worth noting, too, that all intimate partnerships are *interdependent systems* in which the two individuals, the six dimensions of their relationship, and their environment are constantly interacting.

Intimacy is a vital thread that weaves through virtually every aspect of a love relationship. When it's healthy, it helps increase a couple's happiness, satisfaction, and fulfillment, improving their communication, attitudes, love for each other — and sex life. As you think about assertiveness in intimate relationships, keep sexuality in perspective.

Is That All There Is?

The importance of sexuality varies with the couple involved, of course, and without a sexual relationship, a key way to express love is lost. If sex is primary, however, the relationship may be shallow — and fragile.

In very intimate relationships, as between lovers, it is often *assumed* that each partner knows the feelings of the other. Such assumptions may lead to the marriage therapist's office with complaints such as, "I never know how he feels," "She never tells me she loves me," "We just don't communicate anymore." Therapists often help couples to build communication patterns that allow each partner to express caring feelings openly. The expression of caring won't solve all the ills of an ailing marriage, but it can "shore up the foundation" by helping each partner remember what was good about the relationship in the first place!

Author Robert Solomon, in his book *About Love*, looks at love as "shared identity." In his view, healthy couples build the self-esteem of each partner by providing each other a sense of wholeness or completion that neither can have alone. Such couples are engaged in a joint effort to bring out the best in each other, and love represents a process of mutual self-improvement. Thus love is reciprocal, equal, active, dynamic, and a process that nurtures itself: *love creates love*. Solomon is obviously an idealist, but his notions represent a worthy — and surprisingly attainable — goal for loving relationships.

Psychologist Arnold Lazarus of Rutgers University has identified two dozen "myths" that create major problems in many relationships. In his book, *Marital Myths Revisited*, Lazarus suggests that the myth, "True lovers automatically know each other's thoughts and feelings," is particularly destructive of intimate relationships. Lazarus's advice? Don't take it for granted! Don't assume! Communicate!

But it doesn't help to beat your partner over the head with "self-disclosure." The most basic fact about intimacy is that, by its very nature, it is shared with another person; but taking the idea of "sharing" to extremes can get you in trouble. Telling your partner "everything" under the guise of "total honesty" is an exercise in emotional self-indulgence that may result in greater distance between you, rather than increasing closeness. Don't sacrifice your relationship on the altar of *unreserved* self-expression. And if you do, don't bother to call it "assertive"!

YOU'RE NOT ALONE!

In 1975, the World Health Organization recognized the complexity of sexual well-being in a formal definition:

> *Sexual health is the integration of the somatic, emotional, intellectual, and social aspects of sexual being in ways that are positively enriching and that enhance personality, communication and love.*

As if your own personal sexuality were not intricate enough, society — government and the prevailing mores —gets into the act too. (Duh! Doesn't it always?) Intimate relationships weave together the two individuals, their partnership, and the society in a highly complex fabric of attitudes, emotions, physiology, mores, customs, values — even politics and economics.

Nobody ever said it would be easy.

Amazing, isn't it? You'd think that the complexity of sexual expression combined with the complexity of intimate communication would be enough to deter any sane person from engaging in either, let alone both!

But it doesn't, of course.

ARE "MARS AND VENUS" REAL?

In the late twentieth and early twenty-first centuries, we have moved from a time of heavy emphasis on the physical aspects of sex to a focus on the relationship aspects. Instead of exploring for new erogenous zones, we are talking about true intimacy, about devotion and commitment. Some see all this as a swing back to the "good old days." It seems more accurate to consider the entire process an evolution, of which the so-called "sexual revolution" — at least greater freedom to discuss sexual topics — was a key part. The new emphasis on commitment incorporates the gains. There is no return to the old times or forgetting about recent discoveries.

Whatever we call them, the changes of the late twentieth century dug deeply at the closely held attitudes, beliefs, stereotypes, and behaviors that inhibited complete sexual expression. Although traditional values were questioned, they were not abandoned. Now we are moving ahead with newfound abilities, openness, awareness, and equality.

The "Intimacy Attitudes and Behaviors" chart on the following page is a shorthand view of society's former and current sexual expectations for men and women.

And the process of change continues.

Both women and men are still overcoming blocks to healthy sexuality. Couples today are able to build their sexual relationships on the foundation of knowledge and techniques, freedom of sexual expression, and equality between the sexes.

INTIMACY ATTITUDES AND BEHAVIORS

FEMALES

Former Expectation	Current Expectation
Passivity	Equality
Misguided Compassion	No-nonsense Compassion
Silence and Suffering	Outspoken Enjoyment
Giving In	Initiation
Doing Your Duty	Active Participation
Hinting	Straightforwardness
Manipulation	Honesty
Shyness, Embarrassment	Confidence, Playfulness
Fragility, Weakness	Strength, Helpfulness

MALES

Former Expectation	Current Expectation
Silence	Expression
Lack of Emotion	Openness, Flow
Insulation	Involvement
Strength	Vulnerability
Control	Mutuality
Machismo	Gentleness
Inflexibility	Patience
Exploitation	Equality
Score Keeping	Responsiveness

Where are we headed? The cornerstones of the new intimacy are *communication* and *commitment*. The new vocabulary includes words like *assertiveness, adult-to-adult, negotiation, devotion, faithfulness,* and *fidelity.* We have entered a new era of togetherness.

ASSERTIVE SEXUALITY

In earlier chapters, we discussed self-expression as a need of all humans. Sexual expression is a special application of the principles of assertiveness we have presented throughout this book. Anxiety, skills, attitudes, obstacles . . . all are elements of sexual communication, along with the components of verbal and nonverbal behavior described in chapter 6. What you have already learned about assertiveness is a good foundation for your assertive sexual communication.

One element that does seem to come up more frequently in sexual relationships than elsewhere is indirect aggression — so-called "passive-aggressive behavior." This is the style that is designed to make the other person feel guilty or bad, to put responsibility on the other, or to manipulate the other into doing something. A variety of inventive methods are employed: false flattery, coyness, pouting, seeking sympathy, whining, crying, finding fault, playing "hard to get," even lying.

The "Sexual Communication Types" chart (pages 174–175) depicts four styles for expressing feelings about sexual interaction. For each style, five subcategories help narrow down our meaning: trait descriptions, inner thoughts, outer expressions, affect, and body language.

There are several important considerations to keep in mind about the four styles of sexual communication:

First, *none of us is purely one type or another.* Each person may lean heavily one way, but we all exhibit all four behaviors at times. Come on now, admit it, even you! You have been known to pout a little or come on too strong or ineptly fumble around, haven't you? And, of course, there are times when you are quite confident, direct, and assured. We would all like to be purely assertive, but no one is perfect!

Second, *the goal in sexual communication is to have the capability and choice to respond as you like.* Many of us respond by default,

SEXUAL COMMUNICATION TYPES

BEHAVIOR	TRAIT DESCRIPTIONS	INNER THOUGHTS
Nonassertive	Hesitant, shy	"She's being way too rough with me during sex."
		"He hurt my feelings when he said I wasn't much into sex tonight."
Indirectly Aggressive	Devious, manipulative, sneaky	(Upset that he's been told no) "I'll get her goat... insinuate she's been having an affair."
		"Ugh, sex tonight! I'll pretend to be terribly ill."
Aggressive	Demanding, pushy, insistent	"That's a stupid way to caress me!"
		"Why doesn't he ever want to have intercourse a different way? He is so straight!"
Assertive	Honest, open, straightforward	"Our foreplay has been really short recently."
		"She hasn't seemed to be as responsive to me lately."

lacking the skills, attitudes, or behaviors necessary to be fully aware and in control of our sexual expressions. Those who keep working at it, however, do begin to find their relationships more satisfying and fulfilling.

Third, *the motivation for some behavior is beyond our awareness.* We fool ourselves. Of course, we think that we always understand why we react in certain ways, but depth psychology

OUTER EXPRESSIONS	AFFECT	BODY LANGUAGE
"Did you think you were a little bit rough tonight?"	Irritated	Obscure
"I'm sorry, I wasn't very good tonight."		Hidden
"Did you read in the paper that people who aren't interested in much sex with their spouses are usually having affairs?"	Angry	Incongruent
Yawns, looks distressed, sighs, frequently rubs stomach and makes a face.		Subversive
"You're so clumsy tonight!"	Hostile	Abrasive
"Are you crazy? Everyone is into this!"		Oppositional
"It seems to me that our foreplay has been really short lately. I enjoy it; I'd like it to last longer."	Bright	Forthright
"I've been feeling that you aren't as responsive during intercourse lately."		Direct

(which explores the relationship between the conscious and the unconscious) says, "Don't be so sure!" Feelings that are unresolved seem to appear in unexpected forms of behavior.

Fourth, *all sexual communication is two-way, of mutual concern.* This brings us back to devotion and commitment. Keep in mind your purpose. It isn't manipulation, deceit, always pleasing the other person, or always being right. It is working things out together, realizing that you both play an equal part in your sexual communication.

Fifth, *body language and spoken language are both vital in sexual expression*. The chart hints at the key components. Keep in mind that sexual assertiveness is much more than the words you use. Perhaps here, more than in other situations, body language is vital!

SEX IS A SOCIAL ACTIVITY

New knowledge and greater sexual expressiveness brings increased responsibility. Safe sex, teen pregnancy, HIV-AIDS, abortion, promiscuity, prostitution, assault — the social issues around sexual behavior are almost overwhelming. Sex is not just something that happens between two people in the privacy of their relationship.

A book on assertiveness is not the place for an extended discussion of these issues, but in encouraging an assertive lifestyle, including assertiveness in sexual matters, we must address a few of our major concerns, especially when they are topics in the news virtually every day. We don't presume to offer solutions to these major social problems, but a few comments are in order:

❖ *Sex education for children belongs in the home, AND in the schools, AND in the media.* There is *no legitimate evidence* that educating our young people about their bodies and about the sexual and reproductive processes increases the likelihood that they will engage in sexual activity prematurely. There is abundant evidence that lack of adequate sex education leads to unwanted teen pregnancies and sexually transmitted diseases.

❖ *Young people must learn to speak to others openly about sex.* Acquaintances, friends, and — unspeakably — family members commit the vast majority of sexual assaults. Each of us must learn to respect and protect our bodies and to say no directly and assertively to unwanted sexual advances. That learning should begin at an early age, preferably at home.

❖ *Each person has a fundamental human right to self-determination.* It is a basic tenet of assertiveness, as discussed throughout this book, that each of us has the right to be and to express ourselves, and to feel good (not powerless or guilty) about doing so, as long as we do not hurt others in the process.

❖ *Knowledge of safe sex practice is critically important to every adult and young adult.* The statement on "safer sex" at the end of this chapter provides guidelines on this topic.

SAMPLE SEXUAL SITUATIONS CALLING FOR ASSERTIVENESS

Here are a few examples to help you understand each type of sexual communication better, including a "typical" response for each type.

BEACH BLANKET ROULETTE

Richard was really excited. He had been pursuing Susan for weeks now, and they finally had agreed to a picnic at his favorite — virtually private — spot on the beach. It was a beautifully warm afternoon, and Susan had worn a particularly sexy bikini. As the day waned into evening and their ardor warmed, Richard asked, "How about making love here on the beach?"

Susan wasn't sure. She liked Richard, but . . . She said:

(a) "Are you sure you're man enough, Mr. Hotpants?"

(b) "That sounds like fun, but I really need to be home in twenty minutes."

(c) "Uhh, sure, if you want to . . ."

(d) "I'd like that. I have a condom and spermicide in my purse if you didn't bring them."

BEDROOM BOREDOM

During the past six months Marisol's husband, Lucho, has become less sexually attentive. They have been having intercourse less often, and Lucho has not seemed as enthusiastic or caring when they do. Marisol tries hard to provide motivation, but to no avail. Her frustration leads her to try this:

(a) She decides to be more patient. It crosses her mind that she is not sexy enough. She tries being more attentive to Lucho's every need.

(b) She tells Lucho that her doctor told her that her hormone levels were low. She hints that more intercourse would be helpful.

(c) She lashes out irrationally. Her feelings of upset have built to a boiling point. This evening's dull sexual encounter was the "last straw." Lucho retaliates. The verbal explosion lasts for hours. Marisol seethes and spends the night on the couch and the next week sulking.

(d) She tells Lucho that her patience is exhausted and that there must be a change in their sexual relationship. Her style is firm, but not confrontational. She suggests alternatives: a new self-help book she read about; a weekend workshop conducted by a sex therapist; an appointment for relationship counseling. Lucho is reluctant, replying, "You go; it's your problem." Marisol persists, acknowledging that some of the difficulty lies with her, but pointing out that it affects them both. She repeats her desire that they both work on the problem.

ALCOHOL AMOUR

Lan routinely drinks too much before she and Dinh have intercourse. Dinh feels that her drinking interferes with the quality of sex and that it's time to take action:

(a) He hesitantly asks if there is "any chance that you might be drinking a little too much before intercourse?" Lan is offended and responds defensively, "It's just normal social drinking."

(b) He begins talking about the "evils of alcohol" to others in front of Lan at social gatherings. At home he "misplaces" the alcohol; when he does serve drinks, he "accidentally" drops Lan's drink.

(c) In the middle of intercourse he yells out, "You're a drunken slob!", dramatically pulls away, and storms off to sleep on the couch.

(d) Talking directly to Lan at a relatively calm and private moment, he expresses his concern that the drinking before intercourse is interfering with the quality of sex for him. He gives more details in a straightforward way, emphasizing that their relationship together is very important to him.

SOME BASIC SKILL AREAS OF ASSERTIVE SEXUALITY

There is a basic landscape of sexual communication, involving key situations that repeatedly arise in relationships. Here are several, along with a few suggested "words of wisdom" that you may find useful.

❖ *Saying No.* Because of the sensitive nature of sexual communication, it doesn't hurt to use a little empathy and understanding in the process of saying no.

> *"I am not trying to hurt your feelings, but no, I don't want to do that."*

> *"I love you, but I am really too tired tonight. How about tomorrow night?"*

(We discuss situations that call for more than a simple no in the next section.)

❖ *Saying Yes.* We all like a little enthusiasm, especially when we propose something amorous!

> *"Sure. I'll go for that!"*

> *"That sounds neat. Yes."*

> *"Yes, let's have intercourse tonight."*

❖ *Being Playful/Breaking New Ground.* Why should sex be dull and boring or the same all the time? Why not take risks, explore with each other, and try something new? We need a freer, more imaginative and playful approach to sexuality.

> *"Honey, I've been reading this new book and I'd sure like to try position number 85 tonight."*
>
> *"How about a massage with almond oil? We'll even light some incense!"*
>
> *"Let's only kiss and fondle tonight. No intercourse."*

❖ *Listening.* The above situations involve speaking out. The other side, listening, is a lost art — especially when it comes to close, personal, intimate relationships. Take time to *hear* what your partner is saying.

Marital therapists often assign homework to help couples improve their listening skills. For example, try repeating back what your partner says and getting confirmation that you have heard the message correctly before you reply. Then have your partner do the same thing: fully, accurately listen to you before replying. It certainly can help you to feel heard and valued!

❖ *Negotiating/Compromising.* These are skills that are helpful in all aspects of a marriage or relationship. Learning to give and take, to let it be known what you desire, and to take turns are all necessary in assertive sexuality.

WHEN NO IS NOT ENOUGH

Sexual coercion of and assault on women is a major social problem in our society. Estimates and research findings vary widely, but it appears that at least a quarter of all women over age eighteen have experienced some form of unwanted sexual activity. Most such unfortunate events involve friends, relatives, or dates. Only a small percentage is actually committed by strangers. Too many women cannot say no and make it stick — and too many men are behaving like spoiled children who won't take no for an answer.

Since women are most often the victims of unwanted sexual advances, the vast majority of programs for dealing with the problem have been directed to them. Until men learn to accept responsibility for treating women with respect, such efforts will continue to center on arming women with self-protection techniques. Assertiveness training has been used with great effectiveness in this area.

Here are a few suggestions for developing your own assertive approach to preventing unwanted sexual advances:

- Prepare yourself by building your assertiveness skills.

- Talk about it openly with dates and co-workers.

- Be clear from the onset — set limits.

- Don't create expectations.

- Don't send double messages.

- Say no firmly when limits are exceeded.

- Demand that your partner (date, co-worker) take responsibility.

- Leave yourself an out (don't get trapped).

- Raise your voice if you are ignored.

- Report violations to appropriate authorities.

If you are a woman reading this, we urge you to take steps to improve your assertiveness in responding to such situations. Practice your "saying no" skills in a variety of circumstances, particularly those that would involve you in situations you prefer to avoid. For our male readers, we offer a strong invitation to reconsider your own attitudes about women, about sexuality, about the rights of each person to self-determination, and about respect for each other. If you tolerate or encourage other men to "prove themselves" sexually, you are contributing to the problem even if you yourself do not engage in coercive behaviors. If you assume that dinner and a show, or a few dates, or even a promise of a future relationship "earns" you the right to a sexual relationship against the will of your partner, you are still caught up in the "macho mode," and we urge you to think about how you might act if you *really* accepted a woman as your equal in the relationship and if you were to treat her with the respect that equality demands.

ASSERTIVENESS AND EQUALITY IN INTIMATE RELATIONSHIPS

We have often pointed out in this book that genuine assertiveness is a means for establishing equality in a relationship, not simply for expressing your own needs. Nowhere does that fact have more direct application than in the realm of intimate partnerships. In a relationship characterized by equality, love, and honest assertive expression, the intimate dimension can grow to immense mutual satisfaction. Without those qualities, a fulfilling intimate relationship is unlikely.

IMPACT PUBLISHERS STATEMENT
ON SAFER SEX

The management, many authors, and the editorial advisors of Impact Publishers, Inc. — predominantly professionals in health care and human services — recognize safe and healthy approaches to sexual expression as one of the principal health and social issues of our time. We offer the following statement for your serious consideration.

❖ Sexual expression is a basic, normal, positive, intensely personal, and highly satisfying human activity. Although social mores, religious values, and the law often publicly regulate sexual practices, individuals and couples decide privately how they will live their sex lives.

❖ In addition to important choices about personal moral values, responsible sexual practice requires good information, including knowledge of the fundamentals of human sexuality, responsible family planning, contraceptive choices, and protection against sexually transmitted diseases.

❖ Sexually transmitted diseases, such as Acquired Immune Deficiency Syndrome (AIDS), Chlamydia, various forms of Herpes, Hepatitis B, and the several other sexually transmitted diseases (STDs), are serious and widespread public health problems, both in the United States and throughout the populated world.

❖ "Safer sex" — minimizing the risks of sexually transmitted diseases — includes at minimum an absolutely certain, long-term, exclusively monogamous relationship between two partners who have tested negative for HIV infection, or *ALL of the following:*

- regular periodic physical examinations;
- conscientious, unfailing use of condoms (preferably with spermicides) during intercourse;
- awareness and avoidance of common risk factors in STDs (e.g., sex with members of high-risk populations including but not limited to intravenous drug users);
- honest and open discussion of sexual habits and preferences with potential partners; infrequent changing of partners.

❖ Each individual — married or single — has the right to freedom of choice in sexual expression, as long as the practice involves consenting adults and consciously avoids physical or psychological harm to any person.

❖ No one is obligated to have a sexual relationship with another person — including a marriage partner — unless he or she wishes to do so.

❖ The following AIDS facts are reproduced from the brochure, *Understanding AIDS: A Message from the Surgeon General* [a U.S. government publication]:

- *Who you are has nothing to do with whether you are in danger of being infected with the AIDS virus. What matters is what you do.*

- *There are two main ways you can get AIDS. First, you can become infected by having sex — oral, anal, or vaginal — with someone who is infected with the AIDS virus. Second, you can be infected by sharing drug needles and syringes with an infected person.*

- *Your chances of coming into contact with the virus increase with the number of sex partners you have.*

- *You won't get AIDS through everyday contact...a mosquito bite...saliva, sweat, tears, urine, or a bowel movement...a kiss...clothes, a telephone, or from a toilet seat.*

- *A person can be infected with the AIDS virus without showing any symptoms at all.*

- *The AIDS virus may live in the human body for years before actual symptoms appear.*

- *Condoms are the best preventative measure against AIDS besides not having sex and practicing safe behavior.*

RISKY BEHAVIOR

- Sharing drug needles and syringes.
- Anal sex, with or without a condom.
- Vaginal or oral sex with someone who shoots drugs or engages in anal sex.
- Sex with someone you don't know well (a pickup or prostitute) or with someone you know has several sex partners.
- Unprotected sex (without a condom) with an infected person.

SAFE BEHAVIOR

- Not having sex.
- Sex with one mutually faithful, uninfected partner.
- Not shooting drugs.

- *If you know someone well enough to have sex, then you should be able to talk about AIDS. If someone is unwilling to talk, you shouldn't have sex.*

17

Anger Is Not a Four-Letter Word

When angry, count five;
when very angry, swear.
— MARK TWAIN

TWAIN WAS HALF RIGHT, AT LEAST. Counting to five — or fifty — may be a pretty healthy way to deal with angry feelings after all. (Just don't allow your hostility to escalate as you count!) Turns out that swearing, on the other hand, may not be such a good idea.

For nearly forty years at this writing, we've taught and written about ways to spontaneously and assertively express anger. In the last decade, however, some research indicates that *expressing* anger — assertively or otherwise — may not always be the way to go. In this chapter, we'll take a look at what's known about anger, what you can do about your own anger, and how you can handle anger directed at you.

ALAS, THERE ARE NO EASY ANSWERS ABOUT ANGER
We'd like to offer you a simple, three-step method for dealing with anger in your life. We'd like to, but we can't. Anger is complicated, and handling it is complex as well.

We all love simple answers. We elect public officials who offer glib solutions to the incredibly complex issues of the day. If only the good guys and the bad guys — like in the old Western movies — could still be identified by the color of their hats. We try to oversimplify relationships between apparent "causes" and their "effects." We want the answer to "Why do I behave that way?" to be simple: "because you were toilet trained too early," "because your family was dysfunctional," "because you're a middle child." We search for effortless equations to "explain" the mysteries of the complex human organism.

Anger is one of those things that's an easy target for such simplistic psychology. It is variously seen as "sinful" (and therefore to be avoided at all costs), "freeing" (and therefore to be expressed at all costs), and all of the options in between. The correct answer is, "none of the above."

What Do We Know about Anger?

Although there is considerable controversy among professionals who work in the anger field, there are some important points of agreement:

❖ Anger is a natural, normal, human emotion.

❖ Anger is not a style of behavior (although it is common to confuse emotions and behavior).

❖ A modest level of anger arousal is healthy — a signal that there is a problem to solve.

❖ Chronic anger can be a major health hazard.

❖ We can — and should — learn to defuse most anger even before it begins.

❖ When we must express anger, we should learn to do so effectively — toward resolution, not revenge.

What Do We "Know" That's Not So?

The six points above give us a solid foundation from which to examine a half-dozen popular *myths* about anger. Let's take a close look at some popular ideas about anger that turn out to be false.

Anger Myth #1: Anger is a behavior. Let's begin our exploration of anger myths by clearing up one widespread misconception. Anger is not a *behavior*, it's an *emotion*. The confusion of angry feelings with aggressive behavior has made it difficult for many people to effectively handle this natural, universal, and useful human emotion.

Some folks say, "I never get angry." We don't believe it! Everyone gets angry — that is, everyone experiences the *feeling* of anger. However, some people have learned to control themselves so that they do not openly *show* anger; they choose not to *express* their anger. By minimizing anger in your life and developing nondestructive ways to deal with the anger you do experience, you can make aggressive actions unnecessary.

Anger Myth #2: You should be afraid of your buried anger! Anger remains one of the most difficult emotions for many people to express. Assertive behavior training groups often lose members when expression of anger becomes the topic. Many people have "buried" their anger for years and are terrified of the potential consequences should they ever "let it out." They assume that any anger brought into the open will be hurtful to others. "I'd sooner suffer in silence than hurt anyone" is the common, unfortunate plea.

Yet much pain in human relationships results from anger that is unresolved. Both persons suffer. The angry one silently fumes. The other person continues to behave in ways that are upsetting and wonders why the relationship is deteriorating.

But the answer to dealing with long-buried anger may not be what you think. It does not lie in pillow pounding or shouting at an empty chair but rather in finding ways to resolve — within yourself or outside — the problem that caused the anger in the first place.

Anger Myth #3: An angry person is a human steam kettle. For many years, psychologists and the general public believed the old Freudian myth that strong emotions build up inside us somewhere, and if we don't vent them somehow, they'll eventually explode. The popular expression of this was "You need to get the feelings out!" The idea was that by *expressing* the anger, the feelings would be released and prevent health problems associated with "building up inside."

Contemporary research has shown the steam kettle idea to be false. We now know it doesn't work that way. What does happen is that we *remember* annoying events, and our feelings of anger can be experienced again when those memories are tapped. There are important differences between a "steam kettle" of simmering emotion and a "memory bank" of stored experiences. A steam kettle, for example, needs only release its pressure build-up; memories can be satisfied only by resolving the problem somehow.

Anger Myth #4: Venting is good for your health. One of the most persistent points of disagreement among anger researchers has to do with the value of "venting" angry feelings. Many theorists favor the use of pillows, foam bats, and other "harmless" devices, or shouting at an empty chair, as tools for physical "release" of angry feelings. Others point to research that demonstrates that teaching people such means of expression *strengthens* the angry feelings and teaches them to vent their feelings aggressively even at "unsafe" times (such as when the other person is present and a violent fight may ensue).

What's more, contrary to the popular myth, angry feelings are not "released" through aggressive acts. The result of pillow pounding, shouting obscenities — and, yes, football or boxing — is that one simply learns ways to handle anger aggressively.

The best and most current evidence clearly supports the view that *venting angry feelings is not psychologically healthy.*

Physical expressions of hostility *do nothing to solve the problem.* Banging the table, stomping the floor, crying, striking at the air, hitting a pillow — all are devices for temporary expression of strong feelings without aggression toward another person. However, they are not effective methods for *dealing with* your anger.

A subset of the venting myth is described in the important work of Dr. Carol Tavris, a social psychologist whose studies of anger as a social phenomenon are widely recognized as accurate and authoritative. Among the myths Dr. Tavris has identified are:

Myth: Aggression is instinctive catharsis for anger. *Reality:* Aggression is an acquired cathartic habit.

Myth: Talking out anger gets rid of it. *Reality:* Overt expression can focus or even increase anger.

Myth: Tantrums are healthy expressions of anger. *Reality:* Tantrums, if rewarded, teach the child a method of controlling others. "Emotions are subject to the laws of behavior."

Dr. Tavris's highly acclaimed *Anger: The Misunderstood Emotion* is one of the few books on the subject that we can recommend for your further reading. (We'll talk more about a couple of others in a page or two.)

Anger Myth #5: Anger needs to be expressed. In early editions of this book, more than a quarter century ago, we encouraged readers and our clients to try *physical* approaches when learning how to express strong emotions, including pounding a pillow, shouting "NO!" or "I'm really ANGRY!", and tug-o-war with a towel.

Later research — to our dismay — showed that when people *learned* those techniques, they *used* them — in therapy or out — often destructively. If no pillow was at hand, they might pound the nearest person!

So we shifted our emphasis to "nondestructive" *verbal* expression of anger, teaching folks to speak up without inhibition at injustices — real or perceived.

But research on human emotions doesn't stand still. Now, we must once again respond to new evidence about anger. This time it's medical science that has thrown us a curve and questioned some aspects of the "spontaneous expression" approach. The latest research comes from long-term studies of the effects of hostility on the heart. We'll take up that topic later in this chapter. Bottom line: it *may* be better *not* to express your angry feelings.

Anger Myth #6: Tell other people but not the person you're angry with. All too often, people express anger, frustration, or disappointment with another person by indirect, hurtful methods. If you want to change the behavior of the other person, these approaches are rarely successful.

> *Newlyweds Martha and John are a "classic" case. In the first few months of their marriage, Martha discovered at least a dozen of John's habits that she disliked. Unfortunately for both, she was unable — or unwilling — to find the courage to confront John openly with her concerns. Martha instead chose the "safe" way to express her dissatisfaction with John's behavior; she confided in her mother. Worse yet, not content with almost daily telephone conversations with mother about John's shortcomings, she also used family get-togethers as occasions to berate John before the rest of the family.*

This "see-how-bad-he-is" style — telling a third person (or persons) about your dislikes of another — has disastrous effects on a relationship. John felt hurt, embarrassed, and hostile about Martha's attacks. He was angry that she didn't choose the privacy of their own relationship to tell him directly. He was not motivated to change his habits. Instead, he responded to her aggressive approach with bitterness and a resolve to strike back — by intensifying the very behaviors she would have him change.

Had Martha asserted herself directly by telling John her feelings, she would have created a good foundation for a cooperative effort to change both John's behavior and her ineffective response to it.

Relief from anger comes only by some resolution to the problem.

If John had responded assertively early in the process, he might have prevented the escalation of Martha's attacks and avoided the bitterness and growing resentment. Instead, his determination to get revenge is sure to drive a further wedge into the relationship. John and Martha seem sure bets for marital therapy and/or the divorce court.

"OK, OK. ENOUGH WITH THE MYTHS. WHAT ARE THE FACTS ABOUT ANGER?"

Now that we've explored a few of the most popular myths about anger, let's consider how those and other false ideas fit into the larger scheme of things.

On the following page is a chart that summarizes some current notions about anger, classified under three headings: facts — findings that are clearly demonstrated by careful research or are self-evident; theories — ideas for which there is some solid evidence but that lack clear validation and sometimes lead us astray; and myths — ideas like the six we've just discussed and that, despite their acceptance, have been proved wrong or that appear on the surface to be accurate but contain false assumptions. The chart represents a summary of what is known about anger, according to our analysis of the most recent careful studies.

ANGER MAY BE HAZARDOUS TO YOUR HEALTH

Have you ever heard about "Type A" behavior?

Back in the 1970s, California cardiologists Meyer Friedman and Ray Rosenman came up with the term "Type A" to describe the

ANGER: FACTS, THEORIES, AND MYTHS

FACTS	THEORIES	MYTHS
Anger is a feeling, with physical components, not a mode of behavior.	Anger should always be contained until it can be expressed in a calm, rational manner.	Venting (by yelling, pounding pillows, hitting with foam bats) "releases" anger and therefore "deals" with it.
Anger is universal among human beings.	Men in our culture are able to express anger more easily than women.	
What really matters is resolving the issue. Thus, the method of anger expression is important.	Women in our culture are generally inhibited in anger expression by their social conditioning.	Anger should always be expressed spontaneously/ immediately.
Venting of anger — "catharsis" — is rarely a good idea, unless it sets the stage for resolution.		Women are less angry than men.
		Some people never get angry.
Aggressive expression leads to further aggressive expression, not resolution.		Anger is always a "secondary" emotion, with another "real" feeling behind it.
Anger is not a "steam kettle" phenomenon: it does not "build up" finally "exploding."		TV violence, active sports, and/or competitive work "releases" anger.
Most anger is directed toward those close to us, not strangers.		Aggressive behavior is instinctive in humans.
Chronic hostility increases the risk of heart attack.		Anger is always a destructive, sinful, undesirable emotion.
Defusing anger is the healthiest way to deal with it.		Verbal expression of anger is always desirable.

behavior of hard-driving, ambitious, angry men. These so-called "Type A" personalities were significantly more heart-attack prone than their "Type B" brethren — those whose style is more laid back, relaxed, and easygoing. The concept was widely accepted, and tens of thousands of men tried to convert themselves from Type A to Type B. Later research, however, failed to confirm the Type A hypothesis, and it lost respectability for a time.

Type A made a comeback around the turn of the century, qualified by an important new finding from the heart patient studies. Seems it's not Type A behavior *as such* that causes heart problems, but *hostility* that is the key factor in heart disease. Psychiatrist Redford Williams and his colleagues at Duke University identified a "hostility syndrome" — a collection of attitudes and behaviors — that predicts heart disease with astonishing accuracy.

The Duke hostility research with a large number of patients, based on such well-established psychological tests as the *Minnesota Multiphasic Personality Inventory*, showed three major factors in toxic anger: *cynical thoughts, angry feelings,* and *aggressive behavior.*

Incidentally, most heart research over the decades has studied men, but more recent studies have turned up limited data on women, showing similar patterns.

Williams's work was presented to popular audiences in 1994 in a national bestselling book, *Anger Kills,* co-authored with his wife, Virginia Williams. (This is another book we recommend on anger.) Although the facts are not quite as dramatic as the title would suggest, the picture is not pretty. Chronic anger can be deadly.

Colorado State University psychology professor Charles Cole is another researcher who has found a definite health risk for people who are chronically angry. Cole studied fifty heart patients and learned that the large blood vessels constricted — causing reduced blood flow, thus increasing blood pressure and

risk of a heart attack — for some
patients when they merely *discussed*
subjects they were angry about. For
the chronically angry — those who
are angry most of the time — says
Cole, the constriction of blood flow
is also chronic, and heart attacks
may be much more likely.

> *Everyone gets*
> *angry. Some*
> *people do not openly*
> *show anger.*

Psychologists Howard Kassinove (Hofstra University) and
Chip Tafrate (Central Connecticut State University), in their fine
book *Anger Management*, offer a useful "anger thermometer,"
which presents a rough scale for measuring the intensity of one's
anger. You'll find it helpful to refer back to the thermometer
(on the next page) from time to time as you reflect on your own
anger and what to do about it.

"WHY DO I GET SO ANGRY?"

You'd probably like to know more about your own angry
reactions to people and events. Here are some elements to look
for as you answer that question for yourself. Some factors you
can't do much about, of course, but don't get discouraged.
Several are largely subject to your control:

Your genes. The data is not all in yet — indeed, it may never
all be in — but the best evidence in psychological science now
suggests that about half of our personalities is genetically
hardwired. That is, we're born with certain behavioral
predispositions. To some extent not yet fully understood, our
"anger threshold" is among those in-born traits.

Your brain. Anger is another realm in which the brain plays a
key role. (Duh!) But it may not be as obvious as that sounds.
Among the many extremely complex dimensions of our brains
is a complementary relationship between the brain's emotional
center (the *amygdala*), the memory coordinator (the *hippocampus*),

KASSINOVE AND TAFRATE'S ANGER THERMOMETER

This is a tool to help you learn about the appropriate communication of annoyance, anger, and rage. The goal is to express your feeling state directly to another person, with a word that expresses the true intensity of your feeling. After all, there is no value in exaggerating or minimizing what you feel.

Consider the problem you are dealing with, and examine the words listed below. Then, complete the following sentence:

"When I consider what we are talking about, I feel _____"

100° Rabid – Crazed – Maniacal – Wild – Violent – Demented

90° Frenzied – Vicious – Unhinged – Untuned – Up in arms

80° Incensed – Infuriated/Furious – Enraged – Hysterical

70° Irate – Inflamed – Exasperated – Fuming – Burned Up

60° Fired-up – Riled up – All worked up – Peeved – Indignant – Nuts

50° Mad – Angry – Agitated – Pissed off – Irked – Aggravated

40° Provoked – Impelled – Cranky – Crotchety – Distressed – Disturbed

30° Annoyed – Bothered – Irritated – Perturbed – Flustered – Uneasy

20° Jogged – Moved – Stirred – Ruffled – Challenged

10° Aroused – Actuated – Alert – Awakened – Kindled

0° Sleepy – Dead – Drunk – Comatose

(Howard Kassinove, Ph.D. and Raymond Chip Tafrate, Ph.D. *Anger Management: The Complete Treatment Guidebook for Practitioners* © 2002)

and the reasoning center (the *orbitofrontal cortex* — OFC). An angry, emotional reaction to a perceived offense may be moderated by more rational evaluation *if* the person has learned to "check with the OFC" before responding aloud. In short, *you can train your brain to refrain from the flame and avoid the pain!* (OK, so poetry is not our strong suit. You get the point, anyway, right?)

Your upbringing. Early life experiences, primarily within your family of origin, are likely one of the most powerful influences on how you currently experience and express your anger. How did Mom and Dad handle anger? Were they quick to express it? Did they act out anger by yelling or throwing things? Or did they suppress their anger and/or avoid situations that might lead to conflict? Or perhaps they modeled appropriate anger expression, maintaining respect for everyone's rights. What about your siblings? Did they treat you with respect, or were they bullies? Reflect on your early life experiences and how they may have influenced your thinking and behavior about anger.

Your environment. Let's set the scene for anger. Where and when do you get angry? Consider the temperature, pollution, weather. Were you caught in a traffic jam? Pushed around in a crowd? Waiting in a slow line? Do you live under political oppression? Economic hardship? Are you a member of a minority that is often treated unfairly? Lots of folks have good reasons to *start the day* angry.

Your health. Do you have any significant disabilities? Are you fatigued much of the time? Under tension? Do you eat a balanced nutritious diet? Have you had a physical exam recently enough to be sure that your internal chemistry is right? Any of those factors can make it more likely that you will get angry if the right situation comes along.

Your attitudes and expectations. Do you believe the world should treat you fairly? Is it important to you to have people recognize your accomplishments? Do you have a strong sense of justice? Are there certain "right" ways things should be done? Rules everybody should live by? Such attitudes, beliefs, and expectations — while very human — can set you up to get angry at the way the real world treats you and others. And what do you think about anger expression itself? What's OK and what's not? Is it all right to yell at your spouse but not your boss? Do you think it's OK to throw insults but not lamps?

Your relationships. Are you happy in your personal and intimate relationships? Is there lots of stress at home? Are you lonely? Satisfying friendships, love, and family relationships are among the most important factors in good emotional health.

Your job. Do you work with unreasonable people? Is your work satisfying and rewarding? If you are *out* of a job, you may be close to anger all the time.

Your substance use — and abuse. Does alcohol or drug use play a role in your anger expression? Various chemical substances lower your normal inhibitions and may lead to problem behaviors. Has a loved one complained about your drinking and/or anger? You'd better take any such complaint seriously — even if you don't think you have a "problem." It's difficult to deal effectively with your anger if you're under the influence. Clear thinking is a prerequisite to effective social behavior.

Spend some time thinking — and writing in your journal — about the anger in your life. Look for patterns, triggers, and targets of your anger; they're the keys to understanding — and dealing with — your emotional response. You may discover that you have more control over your anger than you thought!

"So What Can I Do about My Anger?"

"I'm confused. On the one hand you're saying, 'It's not healthy to express anger.' On the other, you say, 'You need to resolve your anger; don't let it become chronic.' Which is it? Do we show anger or not? Are we simply to 'take a deep breath' and forget the feelings? Is it really healthiest not to even *talk* about our anger?"

We warned you that there are no simple answers. Human emotions are incredibly complex, and there aren't any "one-size-fits-all" solutions. There are some guidelines, however, and the rest of this chapter is devoted to helping you sort out the complexities.

To begin our examination, let's go back to the Williamses and their book *Anger Kills* and note their guidelines for deciding how to respond to angry feelings:

❖ "Is the matter worth my continued attention?"

❖ "Am I justified?"

❖ "Do I have an effective response?"

They're suggesting that when you begin to feel angry, you take a moment (as Twain said, "count five") to consider just how big a deal this *really* is and how right you *really* are. (In chapter 19 we provide a detailed guide to choosing when to take assertive action.) Then, if you decide that your angry feelings *must* be expressed, do so *assertively*, without hurting someone else (physically or emotionally) in the process.

WORK IT OUT!

Honest and spontaneous expression *aimed at resolving the disagreement* can help to prevent inappropriate and destructive anger later and may even achieve your goals at the outset. When you do choose to express your anger, one of the most constructive steps you can take is to *accept responsibility for your own feelings*. Keep in mind that you feel the anger, and that doesn't make the other person "stupid," "an S.O.B.," or the cause of your feeling. (The sidebar on page 204 has some ideas for language that may help you say what you're feeling in an assertive way.)

The central objective of effective anger expression should be to achieve some *resolution of the problem* that caused the anger. "Getting the feelings out" — even in appropriately assertive ways — only sets the stage. Working out the conflict with the other person, or within yourself, is the all-important step that makes the difference. That doesn't mean pounding a pillow until you are exhausted; it means working out some *resolution* of the issue yourself — through relaxation, forgiveness, attitude change, negotiation, constructive confrontation, or psychotherapy.

If you take action that doesn't help you to cope or to resolve the problem, your anger may actually increase, *whether you've expressed it or not*. So, focus your energy on problem-solving actions. Work to resolve the issue through assertive negotiation of solutions with the person with whom you have been angry. If direct resolution is not possible, find satisfaction within yourself (perhaps with the aid of a therapist or trusted friend). In either event, don't stop by saying, "I'm mad as hell!" Follow through with "and here's what I think *we* can do about it..."

Keep your anger in perspective. Don't take it too lightly, or too seriously. Learn what triggers it, teach yourself to "lighten up" in the face of situations that usually set you off, and develop effective ways to deal with it when it comes. Focus on working out your issues.

Fortunately, there are some really helpful procedures that are of proven value. As it happens, they fall naturally within three general guidelines: (1) minimize anger in your life, (2) cope before you get angry, and (3) respond assertively when you get angry.

MINIMIZE ANGER IN YOUR LIFE

Our first ten steps are borrowed from the Williamses' recommendations in *Anger Kills* (we told you we like their work!):

1. *Improve your relationships* with others through community service, tolerance, forgiveness, even caring for a pet. Brain research has shown that good social support systems reduce the brain's production of cortisol (bad for the heart), boost the immune system (good for everything), help good moods, and limit bad moods.

2. *Adopt positive attitudes* toward life through humor, belief in something beyond yourself, and acting as if today is your last day.

3. *Avoid overstimulation* from chemicals, work stress, noise, and traffic.

4. *Listen to others.* Practice trusting others.

5. *Have a confidant.* Make a friend and talk regularly, even before you feel stress building up.

6. *Laugh at yourself.* You really are pretty funny, you know. (It goes with being human.)

7. *Meditate.* Calm yourself. Get in touch with your inner being.

8. *Increase your empathy.* Consider the possibility that the other person may be having a *really* bad day.

9. *Be tolerant.* Can you accept the infinite variety of human beings?

10. *Forgive.* Let go of your need to blame somebody for everything that goes wrong in life.

To the Williamses' ten, we add three of our own to this "minimize-anger-in-your-life" section:

11. *Work toward resolution* of problems with others in your life, not "victory."

12. *Keep your life clear!* Deal with issues when they arise, when you feel the feelings — not after hours/days/weeks of "stewing" about it. When you can't deal with it immediately, arrange a specific time when you can and will!

13. *Use alcohol in moderation; controlled substances not at all.* Alcohol and drugs may offer a temporary escape from anxiety, depression, and the stresses of life, but they lead away from problem solving. Moreover, they reduce inhibitions and may contribute to inappropriate and unnecessary anger expression.

COPE BEFORE YOU GET ANGRY

Anger is a natural, healthy, nonevil human emotion and, despite our best efforts to minimize its influence in our lives, all of us will experience it from time to time, whether we express it or not. So, in addition to the steps above, you'll want to be prepared before anger comes:

14. *Remember that you are responsible for your own feelings.* You can choose your emotional responses by the way you look at situations. As psychologists Gary McKay and Don Dinkmeyer put it, *How You Feel Is Up to You.*

15. *Remember that anger and aggression are not the same thing!* Anger is a feeling. Aggression is a style of behavior. Anger can be expressed assertively — aggression is not the only alternative.

16. *Get to know yourself.* Recognize the attitudes, environments, events, and behaviors that trigger your anger. As one wise person suggested, "Find your own buttons, so you'll know when they're pushed!"

17. *Take some time to examine the role anger is playing in your life.* Make notes in your journal about what sets you up to get angry and what you'd like to do about it.

18. *Reason with yourself* (another good idea from the "Williams collection"). Recognize that your response will not change the other person. You can change only yourself.

19. *Deflect your cynical thoughts.* Learn effective methods for thought stopping, distraction, meditation (ideas in chapter 11).

20. *Don't "set yourself up"* to get angry! If your temperature rises when you must wait in a slow line (at the bank, in traffic), find alternate ways to accomplish those tasks (bank online, find another route to work, use the time for problem solving).

21. *Learn to relax.* Develop the skill of relaxing yourself, and learn to apply it when your anger is triggered. You may wish to take this a step further by "desensitizing" yourself to certain anger-invoking situations (review chapter 11 for more on desensitization).

22. *Develop several coping strategies* for handling your anger when it comes, including relaxation, physical exertion, "stress inoculation" statements, and working out resolution within yourself.

23. *Save your anger expression for when it's important.* Focus instead on maintaining good relationships with others. Remember what brain research tells us about the importance of good social connections (noted in item 1 on the previous page).

24. *Develop and practice assertive ways to express your anger*, so these methods will be available to you when you need them. Follow the principles you've learned in this book: be spontaneous when you can; don't allow resentment to build; state your anger directly, without accusing or blaming the other person; avoid sarcasm and innuendo; use honest, expressive language; let your posture, facial expression, gestures, voice tone convey your feelings; avoid name-calling, put-downs, physical attacks, one-upmanship, hostility; and work toward resolution.

Now you've developed a healthy foundation for dealing with angry feelings. Go on to the following section, and get ready to handle your anger when it comes.

RESPOND ASSERTIVELY WHEN YOU GET ANGRY

25. Take a few moments to *consider if this situation is really worth your time and energy* and the possible consequences of expressing yourself.

26. *Take a few more moments* to decide if this situation is one you wish to work out with the other person, or one you will resolve within yourself.

27. *Apply the coping strategies* you developed in step 21 above and those listed at the end of the chapter.

If you decide to take action:

28. *Make some verbal expression of concern* (assertively). The sidebar below may give you some helpful ideas. Focus on "I" statements (see chapter 8).

29. *"Schedule" time for working things out.* Do it spontaneously if you can; if not, arrange a time (with the other person or with yourself) to deal with the issue later.

30. *State your feelings directly.* Use the assertive style you have learned in this book (see #24 above), with appropriate nonverbal cues. (If you are genuinely angry, a smile is inappropriate!)

31. *Accept responsibility for your feelings.* You got angry at what happened; the other person didn't "make" you angry.

32. *Stick to specifics and to the present situation.* Avoid generalizing. Don't dig up the entire history of the relationship!

33. *Work toward resolution of the problem.* Ultimately you'll only resolve your anger when you've done everything possible to resolve its cause.

WHEN SOMEONE ELSE IS ANGRY WITH YOU

OK, now you have a roadmap for dealing with your own anger. But one of the most important needs expressed by assertiveness trainees is for ways to deal with the anger of *others*. What can you do when someone is furious and directing her full hostility at you?

As noted in the text, it's often best not to express anger overtly. Nevertheless, there are times when it *is* appropriate — even necessary — to express your anger. Here are a few verbal expressions others have found useful for putting their anger into words when those times come up. Readers who may be put off by some of the "angry language" are urged to note that in each case the speaker is taking responsibility for his or her feelings — not blaming the other person.

"I'm very angry."

"I'm getting really mad."

"I strongly disagree with you."

"I get damn mad when you say that."

"I'm very disturbed by this whole thing."

"Stop bothering me."

"That's not fair."

"Don't do that."

"That really pisses me off."

"You have no right to do that."

"I really don't like that."

"I'm mad as hell, and I'm not going to take this anymore!"

Try these steps:

1. Allow the angry person to express the strong feelings.

2. Respond only with acceptance at first. ("I can see that you're really upset about this.")

3. Take a deep breath, and try to stay as calm as possible.

4. Offer to discuss a solution later — giving the person time to cool off. ("I think we both need some time to think about this. I'd like to talk with you about it . . . in an hour/ . . . tomorrow/ . . . next week.")

5. Take another deep breath.

6. Arrange a specific time to pursue the matter.

7. Keep in mind that no immediate solution is likely.

8. Follow the conflict-resolution strategies described below when you meet to follow up.

THIRTEEN STEPS TO EFFECTIVE CONFLICT RESOLUTION

How can we improve the process of resolving angry conflict between people or groups? Most of the principles are parallel to the methods of assertiveness training presented throughout this book, and many overlap our discussion earlier in this chapter of ways to deal with anger.

Conflict is more easily resolved when both parties want to work things out, of course. Here is a set of proven guidelines for those who are willing to try:

1. Act honestly and directly toward one another.

2. Face the problem openly, rather than avoiding or hiding from it.

3. Avoid personal attacks; stick to the issues.

4. Emphasize points of agreement as a foundation for discussion of points of argument.

5. Employ a "rephrasing" style of communication to be sure you understand each other. ("Let me see if I understand you correctly. Do you mean . . . ?")

6. Accept responsibility for your own feelings ("I am angry!" not "You made me mad!").

7. Avoid a "win-lose" position. The attitude that "I am going to win, and you are going to lose" will more likely result in *both* losing. If you stay flexible, both can win — at least in part.

8. Gain the same information about the situation. Because perceptions so often differ, it helps to make everything explicit.

9. Develop goals that are basically compatible. If we both want to preserve the relationship more than to win, we have a better chance!

10. Clarify the actual needs of both parties in the situation. I probably don't need to *win*. I do need to gain some specific outcome (behavior change by you; more money...) and to retain my self-respect.

11. Seek solutions rather than deciding who is to blame.

12. Agree upon some means of negotiation or exchange. I probably would agree to give on some points if you would give on some!

13. Negotiate toward a mutually acceptable compromise, or simply agree to disagree.

ADD IT UP: 33 + 8 + 13 = 4 — KEYS FOR COPING WITH THE ANGER IN YOUR LIFE

Almost everybody has trouble with anger and, as we've shown, it's not easy to deal with this complex emotion. There are some things that help, however. We've offered lots of lists in this chapter, but we can boil it down for you. If anger is a problem in your life, you'll want to go back and review the "fine print" above.

Meanwhile, here are four key guidelines to remember:

❖ *Minimize the anger in your life.*

❖ *Cope before you get angry.*

❖ *Be assertive when it's important to express your anger.*

❖ *Work to resolve conflict whenever it occurs.*

18

Must We Put Up With Put-Downs?

He that respects himself is safe from others;
he wears a coat of mail that none can pierce.
— HENRY WADSWORTH LONGFELLOW

THINK ABOUT AN INCIDENT IN YOUR LIFE when you felt belittled. The way somebody looked at you, something somebody said, a facial expression or shrug — any of these small acts may have provoked you to question yourself: "What's wrong with me? Why did she say/do that?" Suddenly, instead of feeling up, you start to doubt yourself, to feel down, perplexed, dissed.

Put-downs can provoke a cloud of darkness or confusion and may stick in your mind for years.

Maybe you're already criticizing yourself: "Of course I get a lot of put-downs. That's because there is so much to criticize!" Easy there. While it's true that people scowl at looks, dress, lifestyle, mannerisms, work performance, and speech, you don't need to compound the insult by agreeing! It's easy to come up with ways to let others know they are not OK. Too many of us add to the problem by putting ourselves down as well.

Here's a familiar example: You're traveling to a distant location and suddenly remember that you've forgotten to bring something you'll need when you get there. What do you do? If you're like most of us, you'll likely let go with some expletive or caustic comment about yourself. "Stupid @#$%^! How could I have forgotten?" Only the most sensitive and self-disciplined among us are able to step back, take a deep breath, forgive ourselves for being human, and look for a way to solve the problem and move on — in short, to "deal with it."

In this chapter, we'll explore some of the most common put-down behaviors and what to do about them, specifically the *direct verbal* put-down, the *indirect verbal* put-down, the *nonverbal* put-down, and the *self* put-down. But first, let's take a look at the general idea of criticism.

DEALING WITH CRITICISM — WITHIN AND WITHOUT

"I'm my own worst critic" is a comment that appears often in the writing and speaking of artists, musicians, and writers — most all of us at one time or another. In fact, a Google search turns up 36,000 hits for the phrase — not a huge number in Googleland, but notable.

Most of us carry around an "inner critic," ready to punish ourselves for the least mistake. And maybe it's true that we are our own *worst* critics — as contrasted with our *best* critics. The best critic is one who can offer objective feedback, factual comments that may help us to correct mistakes and improve our behavior. The worst critic is one who criticizes simply for the sake of criticizing, rather than offering useful feedback for improvement.

As you consider how to deal with criticism in your life — both giving it and getting it, we suggest you apply a five-part evaluation to separate the best from the worst. Ask yourself:

❖ Is the criticism based on fact, or opinion?
❖ Is the criticism likely to correct errors and improve performance or to put down?

❖ Is the criticism expressed in positive terms that will help motivate change?

❖ Would an objective observer consider the criticism to be fair?

❖ Is the criticism delivered in private or in front of others?

The best criticism, of course, is based on fact, corrective, expressed in positive terms, fair, and offered in private. The worst criticism is based on opinion, intended to put down, discouraging, unfair, and expressed in front of other people.

You could even use a simple "rating scale" for criticism, rating a critical comment from 1-10 as to whether it is factual, corrective, motivational, fair, and private. When you receive critical comments — from a friend, a loved one, a boss, a co-worker, whoever — do a quick rating. Then respond accordingly. If the criticism scores on the "best" end of the scale, accept it gracefully with an assertive "Thanks. I'll give that some thought." If the comment falls into the "worst" category, you can still be assertive, but you needn't take it to heart: "That's an interesting comment, but it doesn't apply to me." And remember that the criticism you offer to others should be subject to the same evaluation. Offer it assertively, and make it factual, corrective, positive, fair, and private.

Now let's examine some typical types of put-downs and how to handle them.

THE DIRECT VERBAL PUT-DOWN: "YOU FOOL!"

This type of behavior is obvious: another person is verbally "dissing" you. Imagine, for example, that you're leaving an elevator and accidentally bump into someone. That person responds immediately in a hostile manner: "Watch yourself, damn it! You fool! You could have hurt me!" The intent of such an in-your-face overreaction is obvious. Should you respond? How?

Here are the steps we have found effective in dealing with a direct verbal put-down:

❖ Wait a moment, allow the other person to vent feelings and to slow down.
❖ Acknowledge the other person's feelings.
❖ When you're wrong, admit it, even in the face of insult.
❖ Assert yourself about the way the other person is reacting.
❖ Make a short comment to bring the encounter to an end.

These steps will help resolve a put-down encounter where the intent is out in the open.

In the elevator incident you could first let the person vent until the angry feelings calm down. Then, as the outburst subsides, try this: Take a deep breath, then say, "Sorry I bumped into you. It was accidental. I understand that you're upset." Try to stay calm, and avoid a confrontational tone, facial expression, posture, or gestures.

INDIRECT VERBAL PUT-DOWNS: "NICE WORK, FOR A WOMAN."

How about this one from your boss? "You did a nice job on that project you turned in yesterday. All the grammatical errors gave it a folksy quality." Or, what if your spouse says, "I love the way you look when you wear that outfit; old clothes become you." Do you do a double take? Are you confused? What are the real meanings behind statements of this kind?

Such indirect verbal put-downs are *indirect aggression*. In their book, *The Assertive Woman*, Stanlee Phelps and Nancy Austin describe indirect aggressive behavior by observing: "... in order to achieve her goal, she may use trickery, seduction, or manipulation." They note that others react with confusion, frustration, and a feeling of being manipulated. Indirect aggressive behavior comes out as a concealed attack; Phelps and Austin label the person who behaves in this manner a "mad dog in a lamb's suit."

Handle an indirect verbal put-down first by asking for more information. In either of the situations given above, you might reply with, "I'm not sure what you mean." Such a response allows the other person to clarify the true intent (you may have misunderstood).

Your next response will depend upon the other person's answer. Part of your goal in the situation is to teach the person a new way of behaving toward you. If the boss responds, "Oh, I think you did a good job," you might still want to say, "Thank you. I was a little confused. If you're really concerned about my grammar, I hope you'll say so. I couldn't tell if you thought the project was good or bad." You're trying to teach the boss to be straightforward with you.

In marriage relationships, some good-natured teasing can be fun. Too often, however, underlying hostilities come out in the guise of teasing. Your spouse may have been kidding, but there are more direct and less destructive ways.

What if your spouse isn't kidding? Imagine that her next response is even more aggressive. Remain assertive, following the steps above for direct verbal put-downs. Be prepared to go further with your assertion if the response is another put-down.

When you ask for clarification, you may get some valuable information about your own behavior. Remember that a major goal of assertiveness is to level the playing field, to permit *both* people to express themselves openly and honestly. It's difficult for most of us to give direct feedback about another person's upsetting behavior, so we often camouflage our comments in an indirect put-down. Digging further may help your future relationship with that person.

NONVERBAL PUT-DOWNS:
DIRTY LOOKS AND OBSCENE GESTURES

"Sticks and stones may break my bones, but words will never hurt me" is a taunt children long have used to rebuff name-callers. What's the best way to respond to a put-down *without* words — an obscene gesture or a dirty look? How should pouting and silly grins or smirks be dealt with when the person uses no words to help you verify the meaning?

Nonverbal put-downs are much harder to deal with; there are no words, and you can't be sure you accurately read the nonverbal message.

If another person aims an obviously *aggressive* nonverbal put-down toward you, try to get the person to use words instead of gestures. You might say assertively, "I'm not sure what your look/gesture meant. Could you translate that into words for me? I don't want to misunderstand what you're trying to say." Again, remember to avoid confrontational nonverbal behavior yourself. Be prepared for a verbal put-down at this point and respond according to the suggestions above.

The *nonassertive* nonverbal put-down is the least direct of all. If someone begins to stare off into space or grin, the intent is not so obvious as if the person aggressively shakes a fist in your face. Imagine you are about to pay for a purchase when the cashier looks at you, rolls her eyes, and sighs in an exasperated way. You may wish to write it off as nothing personal, or merely assume the cashier is having a bad day. If you're bothered by the incident, however, why not deal with it directly? Ask him to explain: "I didn't understand your expression," or, "I'm not sure what you mean by that," or, "Did I do something to provoke that look?" or perhaps, "Hard day?" This puts the nonverbal action out in the open, giving a chance to clear the air.

If you've done something that bothers somebody else, you deserve to know. Your next response will depend on what happens then, but we think it is a good idea to point out to others that it's difficult to interpret their nonverbal messages.

SELF-PUT-DOWNS: "I'M SUCH A JERK"
Conflict with others, such as those described above, is only half of the picture. Inner conflict can also result in put-downs. The offender in this case is *you*. Put-downs are generated by

conflicts, external or internal. The solution is the same — be assertive.

You can behave nonassertively or aggressively *within yourself* as well as toward others. Be careful how you deal with yourself. Don't ignore (nonassertively) your inner put-down behavior, but don't condemn (aggressively) your inner thoughts and feelings either. Be assertive — honest, open, and straightforward — with yourself. Use the situation as a chance to get to know yourself better. You're not stupid, but you likely do "stupid" things at times. You're not a jerk, though once in a while you may do something to embarrass yourself. Don't exaggerate your faults. It's not awful or terrible if you screw up once in a while. It's human. Get over it.

GET PAST IT AND MOVE ON

No one likes to be criticized, but if the criticism is factual, corrective, positive, fair, and private, we can handle it, and we're likely to be motivated to make changes for the better.

No one likes the conflict generated by put-downs, but by risking an open and straightforward clarification, with the other person or yourself, the upset can be resolved. "Put your assertive foot forward."

Don't ignore or run away from criticism or put-downs — your own or another's. Turn the situation positive. Be persistent, clarify, bring your feelings into the open. It takes some effort to get past feeling hurt and withdrawing, or lashing out, in response to a put-down, but the rewards are worth the effort.

Do you have to put up with put-downs? No! You can learn ways to respond assertively, clear the air, express your feelings, resolve the conflict (real or imagined), and gain new information about yourself and your relationships.

19

Assertiveness Works at Work Too

*Worthy are the labors which
give us a sign other than age
to show that we have lived.*
— LEON BATISTA ALBERTI (1424)

D O THE RIGHT THING," says Dr. Gretchen Bataille, president of the University of North Texas, "even if it causes you grief at the time." Bataille served as chair of the Iowa Civil Rights Commission in the late 1970s and found herself in the center of controversy as an advocate for equal opportunity for girls in school basketball programs. Her efforts cost her the Commission spot — the governor did not reappoint her — but were instrumental in long-term changes that opened doors for girls seeking to play in a full-scale basketball program and thus qualify for college scholarships. "Although unpopular at the time, our actions made [the] future possible," she observes.

Most of us are not in a position of influence comparable to Dr. Bataille's, but we can agree that being assertive on the job can be difficult at best. Fear of reprisals from supervisors or co-workers, even fear of losing the job itself, are formidable obstacles.

In recent years there has been a lot of press about difficult relationships between employees and employers. Stories of whistleblowers, Supreme Court decisions limiting employee rights, employee petitions for flextime and part-time assignments to accommodate family needs, parental leave for both men and women, on-the-job safety and protection for hazardous occupations, shrinking health and retirement benefits, job stress, work-family integration, racial and gender discrimination in hiring and wages ... the list goes on. Does assertive behavior have a role in any of this?

There are, in fact, countless ways to express yourself assertively at work. Realistically, we recognize that the obstacles can be major, but we have seen many successes, and once again we encourage you to assess the potential for making things better in your own work life. In this chapter, we'll explore several dimensions of on-the-job assertiveness and offer some examples to help you see how assertiveness can "work" for you.

ASSERTIVENESS IN THE WORKPLACE

Let's start with a few general ideas about how you can practice assertion on the job:

- ❖ Put off procrastination.

- ❖ Improve your decision-making skills.

- ❖ Negotiate more effectively.

- ❖ Deal with angry customers, bosses, co-workers, and other difficult people assertively.

- ❖ Learn to say no so you'll not lose yourself. (Most organizations will take all you'll give and expect more. If co-workers know you can say no, they won't be reluctant to ask you because they know they'll not be "imposing.")

- ❖ Be persistent: plant a seed and nurture it.

❖ Be patient. Assertiveness is not necessarily being in a hurry.

❖ Speak up about health and safety issues in the workplace. You may risk your job, but that beats risking a limb or a life.

❖ Improve your time management by taking more control of yourself and your schedule.

❖ Stay well informed. Read everything you can about your field; innovations in manufacturing, marketing, IT, or service delivery. If someone in your department is to be caught by surprise with a new idea, make sure it isn't you!

❖ Be assertive about goal-setting on the job. Realistic goals, assertively pursued, are more likely achieved.

There are, of course, those who would make it difficult for you to express yourself openly on the job (no news there!). Such obstacles may come in the form of manipulation (ignore these), unreasonable requests (you can simply point out the unreasonableness), and reasonable requests (that you may not be able to handle, and you will need to say so).

Sometimes performance anxiety becomes a problem in the workplace. Overcoming anxiety was the original reason for assertiveness training and is still an important application of the process. Making public presentations, for example, is reportedly the number one fear of Americans. That fear can be "desensitized" by taking gradual steps toward expressing yourself to others, beginning with one or two friendly folks, and working up to a larger group of co-workers and/or strangers.

Problem solving, negotiation, and conflict resolution on the job can be aided through creating an atmosphere that allows — even encourages — constructive disagreement. As different ideas are expressed, it becomes possible to work out compromises that build in the strengths of everyone's contributions. Solutions that are the result of a number of people brainstorming are often winners; letting all thoughts come out without censorship or critique stimulates creative juices.

We've arranged the balance of this chapter in its natural sequence, from the process of job and career search, through landing a job, working well with others, to being a supervisor. The chapter concludes with some questions about your priorities and a potpourri of work situations for your own assertiveness practice. It may help to read all of the material, or you may prefer to turn directly to that aspect of job-related assertiveness that fits your specific interests and needs.

JOB SEARCH

When we graduated from college (back in "olden times"), jobs were plentiful for anyone with a degree. Things have changed a lot. While government statistics suggest that unemployment is down at this writing, jobs can still be tough to get in many fields, with or without a college education. Widespread layoffs result as large corporations outsource jobs abroad, merge, or downsize. Smaller firms, the source of most jobs, are finding it difficult or impossible to stay afloat among the giants. Competition among job hunters can be fierce, particularly for those who are looking for work after a couple of decades of experience in a shrinking field.

Looking for a job can be a full time "job" in itself. Many people seem to expect to put out a few applications, make a few calls, have an interview or two, and land the job of their dreams. Unfortunately, that *is* a dream. Finding the work you want takes work — and assertiveness can be one of your most useful tools.

Richard Nelson Bolles, in his bestselling book *What Color Is Your Parachute?*, presents a comprehensive plan for "Job Seekers and Career Changers." His counsel is as good as you'll find anywhere and applies the concepts of assertiveness with a broad brush. Bolles's innovative and practical ideas will help you learn about your own career desires and needs, locate opportunities, make contact with employers, handle interviews, and land the job you want.

Among Bolles's recommendations for an assertive approach to careers:

❖ Plan your career and your job search with a clear goal in mind: decide what you want to do, where you want to do it, and for whom.

❖ Seek out activities you enjoy: you'll go after them with more enthusiasm, do them better, and be satisfied longer.

❖ Claim the highest level of skill you legitimately can: you are more likely to find a job, and the job can be more uniquely tailored to you.

❖ Find and meet the employer you want to work for: show the person who has the power to hire you just how you can help fill the needs of that organization.

INTERVIEWING

Even if you have followed Bolles's advice and created your own job, you'll likely go through some traditional interviews along the way.

Now at last an employer has offered you an opportunity to meet and discuss an opening! You've worked hard for this chance to tell what you can do, and you are really looking forward to it. You are pretty anxious too. After all, getting the job depends largely upon how well you present yourself in that short meeting.

Assertiveness can help. We suggest you take it as it comes:

BEFORE THE INTERVIEW . . .

Follow the principles we've described in this book to develop your own ability to present yourself well.

Prepare yourself to deal with anxiety by practicing cognitive restructuring and relaxation (chapters 10 and 11). Everybody has some pre-interview jitters; don't let them be a major obstacle for you.

Write down and memorize three or four key strengths you want to be sure the interviewer remembers about you; be sure to relate them specifically to the job in question.

Practice interviewing with a friend or counselor. If you can, use a video camera and recorder to capture a sample of your own style. Watch the video, and let that feedback help you become even more effective. Pay attention to the nonverbal components of behavior we described in chapter 8.

Do your homework. Find out all you can about the company before the interview from its web site, product catalog, employee friends, public relations, and human resource offices...

AT THE INTERVIEW...

Approach the interviewer with a friendly but not-too-well-rehearsed style.

Remember that most employers would rather hire someone with a strong desire to work and to contribute to the organization than a "star" who may try to outshine the current staff.

Try to relax, enjoy yourself, and get acquainted!

Let the interviewer know you've done your homework, prepared for the interview, and learned something about the company.

Ask good questions about the working environment, staff morale, advancement, employer expectations, and future directions for the firm.

Avoid asking obvious questions you should have answered for yourself in your advance preparation (company product line, details about retirement and health benefits, etc.).

Leave the interviewer with a sample of your work or some other device that will cause him or her to remember you and your talents. (Don't assume a standard "resume" or application will do this job for you.)

AFTER THE INTERVIEW . . .

Drop a note to the interviewer, expressing your appreciation for the meeting, calling attention to any important facts about you, and mentioning details that may have been missed in the interview.

Spend some time assessing and critiquing your own performance, so you'll be ready to do even better next time.

Continue to contact other employers and to arrange other interviews until you land the job *you* want!

After you accept the job, dedicate yourself to doing it well, but don't cut off the contacts you've established with other employers. You never know . . .

CAN THE "NEW KID ON THE BLOCK" BE ASSERTIVE?

When you do get that new job, it is important to start out by *listening* a lot. You'll need to find out as much as possible about the rules of the workplace, the attitudes and opinions of your supervisors and colleagues, the safety factors of the job, the expectations of your role and how it fits into the larger scheme of things, and much more.

But listening alone probably will not be enough to give you all the information you'll need. As you begin to learn your way around a new place of employment, it will be important to ask questions as well. And that's where assertiveness comes in once again.

Remember to maintain *balance.* You want to seem interested in the job, to show the boss and others that you are conscientious. At the same time, you don't want to be a constant nag, demanding more and more information — much of which may not even be relevant to your own work.

We suggest the following guidelines:

Be prepared. Don't expect your boss or co-workers to fill the gaps in your preparation for the job (unless you are clearly in a training program).

Ask your supervisor and co-workers the questions to which you must have answers in order to do the job.

Don't be too quick to ask, since you may be told when the subject comes up in turn.

Make notes of other items that occur to you, and ask them when the subject comes up.

Ask your boss about asking questions. Does she or he prefer that you ask immediately, or in a regular conference, or when...?

When you do ask questions, be assertive. Don't beat around the bush, don't start out defensively ("This may be a dumb question..."), try to focus your question on the specifics, use good eye contact, voice, timing, etc.

Avoid suggesting changes until you are well acquainted with the operation.

Avoid the temptation to describe "how we did it at Acme Widget" (or wherever you worked before) unless you're asked. Better to let it be your own idea — or let it go altogether.

ON-THE-JOB RELATIONSHIPS

Getting along with others at work is essentially a process of making a place for yourself in the work group. At home, the family has little choice but to accept you. In school, although acceptance of your peers can be a tough burden, *you're* the one without choice: you *have* to be there.

The job, for most of us, does offer some choices. Unlike family or school ties, one *can* quit, although the price for doing so may be high. Getting along becomes a matter of deciding to make a place for yourself. And that means developing a relationship of mutual respect with your co-workers.

Here are some ideas that may help:

Stay honest; avoid game playing.

Count to ten before you sound off in anger (refer to chapter 17).

Listen to what the other person has to say — even if you disagree.

Ask yourself, "How would I feel in this person's shoes?"

Express your opinions, but remember they are opinions. Others will have different ideas.

Consider: Is it more important to be a "star," or to get the job done? One of the most famous motivational lines ever — often quoted but first credited to President Harry S. Truman — goes like this: "It's amazing what can be accomplished if no one cares who gets the credit."

Be assertive when it matters.

Accept responsibility for your mistakes — and credit for your successes.

A couple of practice situations for you to think about:

A co-worker has been taking company supplies home for personal use. She knows you are aware of this and expects you to say nothing.

The woman at the next desk loves to chew gum — loudly. You find the noise annoying and distracting.

A senior colleague has made repeated sexual comments and suggestions and frequently finds opportunities to touch you inappropriately.

A couple of your co-workers spend lots of company time gossiping and chit-chatting about their gardens and their children. You see their productivity suffering.

DEALING WITH SUPERVISORS

Some bosses act as though they would have been happier in an earlier era, when all employees were virtual slaves. For the most part, however, the workplace has become quite civilized — even humanized. Supervisors still oversee, but they generally follow modern law and custom — and their own good sense — in treating their workers with respect.

Nevertheless, there are inevitable situations in which it is necessary, as an employee, to express an idea, opinion, or objection firmly in the face of opposition from the boss.

Be prepared for criticism. Don't get caught in the trap of coming down on yourself every time you are criticized on the job. You may be wrong, but the way to deal with the situation is to correct the problem, not to kick yourself. Help your boss to make criticism *specific*, so you can make the adjustments needed to improve.

Assertive efforts to clarify the boss's expectations and criticisms will help clear the air and will enable you to become more effective. If instead you act like a "victim" — mumbling to yourself or backbiting — you'll make no progress and likely will make a powerful enemy along the way.

Try to identify *patterns* in your boss's critiques. If you think you discover one, ask assertively if that *is* what the boss wants ("You'd rather have all the supporting data presented *with* my recommendations, wouldn't you?"). If you clear up any possible misunderstanding in this direct way, you'll save time — and similar criticism — in the future.

Timing may be the most important component of your on-the-job assertiveness — especially with the boss. If you confront a supervisor in front of others or when the boss is very preoccupied with another problem, you aren't likely to gain a favorable audience. Instead, plan — and schedule if necessary — your feedback to the boss so that you can be alone and relatively uninterrupted.

It bears repeating: do your homework! These days, with the almost infinite amount of information on virtually every possible subject that's available online, there's no excuse for "incomplete staff work." When you approach the boss, don't offer only questions or complaints. Be ready to present — and defend with facts — specific recommendations. Instead of, "What do you think I should do?" try "Here are three possibilities. I recommend Plan B because . . ."

Here are a few other examples:

You want to offer an innovative suggestion for simplifying a routine procedure.

Your boss is making unreasonable demands on your time, without offering additional compensation.

You believe you are being unfairly criticized for the quality of your work.

You know more about the job than your boss does, yet she wants you to do it her way.

Your boss is asking you to do jobs that you believe are his responsibility.

Your boss expects you to prepare "phony" expense accounts.

You've been asked — at 4:45 — to stay this evening and prepare a report for tomorrow's board meeting. You have plans for the evening.

SUPERVISING ASSERTIVELY

Now you've done it! You've been so effective with your on-the-job assertion (along with some pretty good work!) that you've been promoted. Now *you're* the boss. New responsibilities, new opportunities, . . . new headaches!

How do the principles of assertiveness apply in the supervisory role? Can you get the job done, treat your staff with respect, and exercise appropriate authority — all at once?

There are many theories of management, and hundreds of good ideas about how to supervise others. While this is not the place for a comprehensive survey, the following guidelines blend our concept of assertiveness with some of the best:

Build your assertive managerial style on the foundation of good on-the-job relationships described earlier in this chapter: honesty, responsibility, cooperation, teamwork, mutual respect.

Listen — and pay attention — to what your people have to say.

Roll up your own sleeves and work *with* your staff.

Walk around — and find out first-hand what is needed.

Remember that we're all equal on the human-to-human level.

Make your instructions clear and direct.

Accept the responsibilities of leadership, including decision making.

Criticize fairly, focusing on the performance — not the person. (Take another look at the discussion of criticism in chapter 18.)

Praise often, focusing on the performance — not the person.

Consider: a manager must both *lead* the staff and provide necessary *support.*

Include the following resources in your supervision "toolkit": team building skills, clear communication of your expectations, skills in employee motivation, encouragement of assertiveness in your staff, and clear performance standards.

Here are a few supervisory situations for practice — and to help you keep things in perspective:

One of your employees has made a thoughtful proposal for a new work procedure. You recognize the idea as one the general manager would probably veto because of its start-up costs.

A supervisor of your rank from another department comes into your area and wants to borrow some equipment. Company policy prohibits such transfers.

You are confronted by a young trainee who refuses to follow your directions.

An employee under your supervision is not working up to your standards. You wish to improve his performance.

Performance reviews are due next week. You must critique a long-time colleague whose work is weak in several areas.

As a new crew chief at an assembly plant, you are responsible for the work of several men old enough to be your father. At least one of the men believes his ways are right and refuses to accept your authority.

A long-time employee in your department has been coming to work late nearly every day this week, with no explanation.

You recognize that one of your workers is an alcoholic, but she won't admit it or seek treatment.

KEEPING YOUR PRIORITIES STRAIGHT

Work can be really seductive. If you enjoy what you do and if you are good at it, you'll probably be advancing in salary and responsibility frequently. As a result, you'll feel motivated to take on even more, and the cycle will go on.

That sort of involvement with your work can play havoc with your personal life — if you let it get out of hand. More and more, you'll take work home, stay late at the job, go in on weekends, and take business trips. You could wind up with little time left for yourself or your family.

Can you be assertive with yourself? Can you elect to pass up career advancement opportunities in favor of more time for home and family? What are your priorities? It's easy to *say*, "My family comes first." It's harder to act accordingly.

Others won't settle for less than "having it all." Career, family, community, self — all are juggled like oranges, at least for a while. The stresses of the real world seldom allow us to maintain that precarious balance for long.

Being assertive with yourself means clarifying your personal priorities, recognizing you cannot do everything — at least not all the time — making appropriate choices, and saying no when you've reached your limits. Keep your own goals in mind (refer to chapter 7 and your journal as you need to).

Test yourself with a few related situations. What's *really* important to you?

You've been offered an important promotion with your present firm. Actually, you'd been thinking of leaving, but the outside job you want is not yet available.

You spend more and more evenings and weekends working on job reports. Your family is beginning to complain that you have no time for them. You think you have an opportunity for a major promotion if you keep up the pace.

You want to continue your successful career, but you know that your only step up in the company will require going back to school for additional course work in business — maybe an MBA. Such a step will require postponing plans to have children — which you and your husband want very much.

MORE ON-THE-JOB SITUATIONS FOR PRACTICE

Use the step-by-step process in chapter 13 as a guide to build your skills and practice handling the following work-related situations:

Your boss suddenly turns cool toward you but offers no explanation. You want to ask what's going on.

Although you have been in your job longer than anyone in your department, you are a part-time worker. Nevertheless, you are often called upon to train others or answer questions as if you were a supervisor. You are paid less and have no real authority.

You've had several job interviews recently but keep finding yourself acting in a very passive way. The interviewers seem disappointed that you do not "sell" yourself.

A manager in another department — very powerful in the company — has been making not-so-subtle sexual advances toward you.

After you've spent many hours on a special report, your boss's supervisor is highly critical of your results.

You've been asked to handle a job that is clearly outside your responsibility and beyond your competence. You think it may be a "test" of how well you know your own limits.

You'd like to start working at home — telecommuting — at least a couple of days a week. Your boss has been resistant to the idea, but you have kids and it's hard to get good child care every day. You do much of your work on computer anyway.

Even if you are not working regularly now, chances are you will be sooner or later. Give some thought to the issues raised in this chapter. Use your journal to keep track of your own on-the-job assertiveness and how you can improve it. You'll be more effective in your work and more highly respected by your peers and supervisors, and you will enjoy yourself more!

20

Dealing with Difficult People

> *Don't interrupt me*
> *when I am interrupting!*
> — WINSTON CHURCHILL

YOU KNOW THE TYPE:

❖ He leans on your desk, glares, and says loudly, "Just how long is it going to take me to get some help around here?"

❖ She comes over from next door whining, "Are you folks ever going to clean up your yard? You know, your place is the only one on the block that..."

❖ He calls your business and demands immediate service, an extra discount, and extended terms. "And if you can't help me, I want to speak to the owner."

❖ She can't wait to corner you at the open house: "Did you hear about Fred and Betty?" she hisses. "Wilma told me that they..."

What is a "difficult person"? *Anyone who doesn't behave as expected.* We do, after all, have some unwritten "rules" about appropriate behavior in our society: be fair; wait your turn; say "please" and "thank you"; talk in conversational tones and volume. Difficult people ignore those mores or act as if they are exempt — often while they expect *you* to live by the standards they're flaunting. They're usually loud, intrusive, impolite, thoughtless, selfish, and, well, *difficult!*

What do difficult people get out of being that way? A workshop participant gave one of our all-time favorite answers to that question: "The biggest cookie." They also usually gain control, get their way, and get attention.

Why do we give these troublesome folks what they want? Well, for one thing, it's usually easier than hassling with them. Most of us don't have the skills, the time, the energy, or the inclination to try to put such people "in their place." Sometimes, they show up in a business context where the policy may be that "the customer is always right."

(Incidentally, we don't happen to think that's an enlightened perspective. Nobody is always right. A more workable view is that "the customer is always the customer," and the business is advised to treat customers well, fairly, and promptly.)

Other times, it seems more trouble than it's worth to try to confront such people. After all, it's highly unlikely that you'll change them, and you may even get into trouble for taking them on. So, what to do?

Actually, there are a few approaches that can pay off. In this chapter, we'll consider some of the possibilities.

WHAT DO YOU THINK?

What are your thoughts when a "difficult" customer, neighbor, or co-worker confronts you? What goes through your mind?

- ❖ "Here comes that S.O.B. again."
- ❖ "Uh, oh, I'm in trouble now."
- ❖ "What does he mean?"
- ❖ "We've got to fix that problem."
- ❖ "Let me out of here!"
- ❖ "No problem — I can handle it."

- ❖ "Take a deep breath."
- ❖ "How embarrassing!"
- ❖ "That's the funniest thing I've heard today."

Your thoughts set the scene for how you'll respond to a difficult situation. Consider your own first reactions — and reread chapter 10 for ideas on developing more constructive thought patterns — as you take a look at the options for action outlined below.

HOW TO DEAL WITH BOZOS

The following discussion offers a "smorgasbord" of action steps you can take when confronted by someone who's trying to push you around. Draw on those that seem to fit your style and life situation, and put together a response plan for your own "difficult people." You may never need to fear them again!

1. CHANGING YOUR COGNITIONS (ATTITUDES, THOUGHTS...).
"IT'S ALL IN HOW YOU LOOK AT IT."

Preconceptions, attitudes, beliefs, prejudices — all kinds of preconditioned thoughts are influential in determining our responses to daily situations. Those ideas may be about the way life is in general, the way your life is, or the way this particular person is.

For example, if you believe that life is fair, and that things work out for the best, and that people are basically good, you'll probably respond very differently than you would if you believed that life is not fair, things usually go wrong, and people are no damn good.

Stress Inoculation is one procedure for dealing with cognitive responses. It involves systematic development of self-statements that will help you change your thoughts related to specific situations and people. The following examples are grouped according to four stages of a difficult event. (Refer also to the discussion of this technique in chapter 10.)

Preparation	Coping Response
There's nothing to worry about.	*Relax, breathe deeply.*
I've handled tough situations.	*Fear and anger are expected.*
I'll play my own game.	*I can control myself.*
Confrontation	**Reprise**
Stay calm and focused.	*I got through it OK.*
This guy is human too.	*The problem will be resolved.*
I know my job.	*It's over; I can relax.*

2. DEALING WITH YOUR ANXIETY. "DENTIST'S CHAIR SYNDROME" OR "IF YOU'RE GOING TO GET DRILLED ANYWAY, YOU MIGHT AS WELL LIE BACK AND ENJOY IT."

A hostile confrontation usually causes the adrenaline to pump — at least at first — and raises the anxiety response. There are several actions on the "anxiety track," including:

- ❖ Run away
- ❖ Tense up and freeze in place
- ❖ Relax and breathe deeply
- ❖ Systematic desensitization (Preparation before an anxiety producing event by deconditioning.)

You'll recall that chapter 11 has helpful ideas for dealing with your anxiety before and during a difficult situation.

3. TAKING DIRECT ACTION. "DON'T TALK TO ME LIKE THAT!"

Assertive and aggressive responses fall into this category of action options: standing up to the attacker, saying you will not put up with such abuse, asking why he is so upset, ordering him out of your office, asking who the hell he thinks he is, telling him to go to hell . . . Handling the situation this way involves facing the person directly, speaking up in a firm voice, using posture, gestures, and facial expression that appropriately convey your determination not to be pushed around, and taking the risk of possible escalation.

"When you come at me that way, I'm not moved to do what you ask."

4. SYNTONICS. "TUNE IN, TURN ON, TALK BACK."

We discussed "verbal self-defense," developed by Suzette Elkin, in chapter 8. Syntonics procedures involve getting in tune with the attacker, acknowledging her point, and indicating your empathy with her emotion — but not giving in. Techniques include:

❖ Matching sensory modes (e.g., sight, smell, hearing)
  "Do you *see* what I mean?" "I *hear* you." "That doesn't suit my *taste*."
❖ Ignoring the bait, while responding to the attack.
  Attack: *"If you really wanted to do a good job..."*
  Response: (Ignoring bait) *"When did you start thinking I don't want to do a good job?"*

Our late friend psychotherapist Andrew Salter said it this way: "Never play another person's game. Play your own." This process is a sort of "applied go with the flow" — letting the other set the pace and style but not going along with her or his intent. Your action is firm but not oppositional. Such behavior makes you definitely not "fun" to pick on. Your objective here is to take control — to play your own game.

5. LIFEMANSHIP. "WHAT'S THAT ON YOUR CHEEK?"

Stephen Potter's "lifemanship" systems, including "one-upmanship," offer ways to get your antagonist off-balance. Among other things, Potter suggests in his books getting the advantage *before* you are attacked:

❖ "Is something wrong?" (looking at spot on the other's forehead)
❖ Staring at some spot on the other person without saying anything, then denying, when asked, that anything is "wrong."
❖ "That ball was out!" (tennis)
❖ "Of course I had a reservation, guaranteed on my VISA."
❖ "When I had lunch with the Lt. Governor last week, he suggested..."

6. SOLUTIONS. "NO-FAULT INSURANCE."

Your response is to ignore any emotional content of an attack, simply dealing with the substantive issues involved, and seeking solutions to the problem:

- ❖ "I can see we need to work out a solution to this situation."
- ❖ "There really is a problem here. What do you suggest we do to avoid similar circumstances in the future?"
- ❖ "Let's take a look at the data and see if we can come up with some answers."

7. WITHDRAWAL. "THE ENGAGEMENT IS OFF!"

This approach involves either saying something simple and direct, such as "I'll be glad to discuss this with you another time — when you're not so upset," or saying nothing at all and simply leaving the scene.

Some situations are not worth the energy it would take to resolve them at the time. This is especially appropriate when the attacker is rational but totally unreasonable (*but not if violent*).

8. HUMOR. ". . . AND THE WORLD LAUGHS WITH YOU."

Humor is appropriate on almost any occasion. This works best, of course, if you have a natural joking style and are pretty good with one-liners, so you can disarm anger or attack with a funny line. It doesn't mean telling jokes that might be funny under other circumstances!

Ask yourself: "How would Jon Stewart handle this?" "How would Rosie O'Donnell handle this?" "How would Bill Cosby handle this?"

9. KNOWING YOUR AUDIENCE. "NOT IN FRONT OF THE CHILDREN!"

"A time and a place for everything" applies here. You may wish to offer an opportunity to discuss the matter at length in private, but point out your unwillingness to pursue it in front of others, since both parties may find it awkward and a rational solution may be less likely.

10. REQUESTING CLARIFICATION. "SAY WHAT . . . ?"
A simple, direct request for clarification — especially if it is repeated a couple of times — can de-escalate a situation and help put you in control.

- ❖ "I'm not sure I understand."
- ❖ "What exactly is it that you want?"
- ❖ "Would you explain that to me again?"

Again, your goal is to gain a measure of control — to prevent manipulation — to play *your* game.

11. CHANGING THE SCENE. "BUILD A LEVEL PLAYING FIELD."
Particular *individuals* — maybe even some in positions of power — may regularly, predictably cause you grief. Or perhaps specific re-occurring *situations* — such as a routine on your job — are likely to produce certain kinds of problems. Then you may need to work with others to establish some institutional or departmental support systems that "cut 'em off at the pass." Such systems might include:

- ❖ Behavioral ground rules for meetings.
- ❖ Standard procedures for how you'll serve people.
- ❖ Policies you apply uniformly.
- ❖ Collective/departmental action to get institutional change.

THE SITUATION IS SERIOUS, BUT NOT HOPELESS
Here is a summary of guidelines and procedures that can help when you're confronted with a particularly difficult person or situation:

❖ Direct your efforts at *solving a substantive problem,* not "taking care of" a difficult person. If you insist on one "winner," there probably won't be one. (And if there is, it may not be you!)

❖ *De-escalation* of loud voice and angry gestures is usually best accomplished by modeling; lower your own level of emotional behavior and you'll probably affect the other person's actions.

❖ *Your approach to these situations should be your own* as much as possible — a good fit with your natural style. All the ideas here are legitimate, but only some will work for *you*.

❖ *Preparation in advance* is a big help. Learn deep breathing and relaxation techniques, cognitive restructuring, and assertive skills. A confrontation is not the time to start practicing!

❖ If you're going into a situation where it's likely you'll confront a difficult person, *set up some ground rules* in advance to cover typical problems (e.g., time limits for talkers in a group meeting).

❖ If there are particular individuals in your life who are predictable problems, you can *practice methods that are custom designed* for responding to them.

❖ *Get to know yourself* and your own triggers for emotional response. As someone said, "Get to know your own buttons, so you'll know when they're pushed!"

❖ So-called *"I-messages" really can help* — take responsibility for your own feelings without blaming the other person. (For more on this, refer to chapter 8.)

❖ *Acknowledging the other person's feelings while seeking a resolution* is usually helpful. ("I can see you're really upset about this.") But be especially careful not to patronize or come off sounding like a too-empathetic counselor.

❖ It's often not possible to solve a situation on the spot. *Look for a temporary way out* so you can seek a solution in a calmer moment.

❖ Remember, *you do have some options* for action. Any of them can cause you *more* trouble with a difficult person if you become a manipulator, so apply them sensitively — but firmly — and with the main goal of getting on with your life.

21

Deciding When to Be Assertive — or Not

Two roads converged in a wood, and I —
I took the one less traveled by,
And that has made all the difference.
— ROBERT FROST

REMEMBER THOMAS FRIEDMAN'S AIRPORT BOOKSHOP STORY in chapter 5? You'll recall that Friedman asserted his place in line a few years ago ("Excuse me. I was here first."), but says he'd handle the situation differently today. Things have changed.

Throughout this book, we've emphasized that assertiveness is, first and last, a matter of personal *choice*.

Don't "assert yourself" just because you can. Don't "assert yourself" every time life rankles you a bit. Don't go out of your way to look for opportunities to "assert yourself." When — as will happen from time to time — the natural course of things produces a situation in your life that you could really *improve* by speaking out, that's the time to put your assertive talents to work.

"So how do I know when action is called for?"

In this chapter we've outlined a "baker's dozen" questions to ask yourself when you're considering, "What do I do now?"

Honestly consider each of these questions, and use the answers to help you decide when to be assertive . . . and when to let it go.

1. What really happened?

Are you sure you understand the situation clearly? Have you heard both sides?

2. How much does it matter to you?

How does this situation relate to your life goals? Will assertive action now achieve something important for you? Have your values been violated? Have you acted on similar situations in the past? Is someone's safety or well-being involved? A job? A promotion? Is an important principle at stake? Have you thought about your motivations for action in the situation? Would you be acting just to "be assertive"? Is this something you feel "should" be done, or will you and others actually benefit?

If your spouse leaves the top off the toothpaste, it may irritate you, but how important is it in the larger scheme of things? How about making a game of it, rather than allowing it to become a big issue between you? Hide the cap occasionally. Put foil or plastic wrap on the tube. Buy your own tube. Write on the mirror with the toothpaste. Approach minor discomforts creatively, not angrily!

On the other hand, if the well-being of others is involved, it's time to act. Maybe your community has created a safety hazard by ignoring a dangerous intersection; don't wait for someone else to take action. You could save a life by being the first to call the situation to attention.

3. What is the probability that you'll get what you want?

Is the change you want even possible? Is the other person likely to pay attention to your assertive action? Are you trying to "teach a lesson" that won't likely be learned anyway? Can you make it clear what you want? What's in it for the other person to do what you want?

If your boss doesn't give clear instructions, you'll want to let her know. When you do, however, *you* are going to have to be clear in your feedback. By telling her exactly what you need to know in order to fulfill her assignments to you, you'll make it more likely that she'll pay attention and give you what you need. And she knows that's in her best interests as well.

4. ARE YOU LOOKING FOR A SPECIFIC OUTCOME OR JUST TO EXPRESS YOURSELF?

Can you express what you want in the form of a tangible change in the other person's behavior? Is there any actual *measurable* change you want to happen? Do you even want something to change, or do you just want recognition of your position?

When your local paper runs a story full of errors — and they all do from time to time — are you moved to let them know about it? If you write a "letter to the editor," is it your goal to let your neighbors know how smart you are, or do you want the paper to run a correction so everyone has the facts? The tone of your letter will tell.

5. WHAT ARE YOUR OPTIONS?

Let's see. You can choose to go along and say nothing. You can speak up "softly." You can voice a firm objection. You can shout your feelings. You can write a letter (to someone involved, to a responsible agency, to the editor, to the president of the company...). You can do some research and present your view of the real facts to everyone involved. If it's a public matter, you can organize a group of people to express a collective opinion in any of several ways.

It's likely that you really do have some choices in the matter. But not always. Sometimes there is simply nothing you can do.

6. ARE YOU LOOKING FOR A POSITIVE OUTCOME?

Is your goal in acting assertively likely to benefit everyone concerned? Are you trying for the greatest good for the greatest number, or just for yourself? Might your assertion make things worse?

Let's assume you live in a relatively small town in which one large company is the biggest employer. You work there yourself, and you know the firm mistreats its employees. Wages are low (you know, because you have friends who work in the same industry elsewhere), benefits are the minimum required by law, sexual harassment by management is widespread, and safety hazards are common. Can you allow this to go on? Can you improve it? Isn't a "whistleblower" likely to be fired? These are tough questions and loaded with consequences whatever you do. (We would encourage you to act, of course, but we don't have to live with the possible results of that action: firing, layoffs, plant closure, legal action . . .) Here's where your careful consideration of the issues raised in this chapter will really pay off.

7. DO YOU HAVE ASSERTIVE ATTITUDES, SKILLS, AND INTENT?

Are you prepared to act in an appropriately assertive way? Have you practiced with less important assertions? Have you taken into account any special circumstances that will influence the situation (e.g., cultural differences, physical or emotional disabilities, age differences)?

8. HAVE YOU COUNTED TO TEN?

Have you taken at least a few moments to reflect on the situation? Have you defused your angry feelings? Are you ready to express your concern rationally? Have you counted to ten — ten times? Have you worked on the anger material in chapter 17?

Consider what happens when you're behind the wheel of your car. Driving is a challenging test of skills these days, and not just skills of handling an automobile either! The highways stretch one's patience, foresight, and ability to keep things in perspective. You'll inevitably come across others who appear less skilled than you consider yourself to be. The all-too-common impulse is to raise a protest, maybe an unheard shout to yourself and/or your passengers or a hand-and-arm movement you intend the other driver to see. Don't! This is a classic opportunity to practice the "count-to-ten" maxim. It's virtually impossible to do anything that *will* change whatever happened. Anything you do after the fact will *not* "teach the other guy a lesson." And your action may endanger yourself and others on the road. This is one to let go.

9. WOULD IT BE BETTER TO WAIT UNTIL TOMORROW?

Will you see the situation any more clearly if some time passes? Will the other person be more receptive later? Are you less likely to make a scene? Are there others around who should not see the confrontation?

Let's say your mother-in-law has been visiting for three days. This afternoon she returned from a shopping excursion with four new (and very ugly, in your opinion) throw pillows. She promptly spreads them around your living room, saying, "There! This place really needed brightening up, don't you think?" Ask yourself the questions above, and consider if this is the time to react.

10. WILL YOU KICK YOURSELF IF YOU DON'T TAKE ACTION?

Will it really matter to you tomorrow if you don't do something today? What's the worst thing that will happen if you do nothing? Will taking action help you feel better? Improve your self-concept?

You're enrolled in a college class that emphasizes student participation and class discussion. The teacher regularly mispronounces your name. You're both amused and offended by the error but would like to have your classmates know the

LIVING AN ASSERTIVE LIFE

correct pronunciation (admittedly a difficult one). Here's a good chance to practice your assertive skills! (Hint: don't make the point in front of the class — at least not the first time.)

11. HAVE YOU DONE EVERYTHING YOU CAN TO REMOVE OR REDUCE THE OBSTACLES TO YOUR DESIRED OUTCOME?

Is there anything you can do to make the change you want easier for the other person? Are you willing and able to give as much as you get? Did you ask for clarification of her intent?

Hieronymous, your neighbor's wolfhound, poops on your lawn regularly. You're tired of cleaning up after the flea-bag, but you don't want to create a neighborhood row either. What to do? How about starting by taking a few steps yourself to prevent the problem? A fence, perhaps? Or one of the many sprays that discourage unwanted pet visits? If and when you do decide to discuss the problem with your neighbor, go armed with suggestions and evidence that you're meeting him halfway rather than simply demanding action on his part.

12. WHAT ARE THE PROBABLE CONSEQUENCES AND REALISTIC RISKS FROM YOUR POSSIBLE ASSERTION?

Might you or someone else be physically or emotionally hurt? Lose a job? Lose a relationship? What is the probability that the other person may become violent? Do you *know* the other person? Would your assertion provoke a confrontation? Will your assertion encroach on him in some way? Is she a reasonable person? Is pride a factor? Money? A romantic relationship? Public face-saving (e.g., with peers)?

If you're like most parents, discovering that a neighborhood bully beats up your child on the way home from school is a recurring nightmare. When it happens, your fear turns to anger and you want to take retaliatory action. But what? Beat up the bully? Beat up the bully's father? Tell the police? Call a neighborhood meeting? Arm your child with karate lessons?

Visit with the bully's parents? Escort your child to and from school? Move? Hire a bodyguard?

Times such as this are a challenging test of judgment as well as assertive skills. Consider well your options and proceed with caution.

13. WILL ASSERTION MAKE ANY DIFFERENCE? WILL IT CHANGE THE SITUATION?

After all is said and done, how likely is it that anything will have changed? Will the change really be an improvement?

Perhaps you don't have a lot of confidence that your congressperson does a very good job of representing your views and those of your neighbors in the local district. Maybe you've written letters or called the office to express your opinions. Is it worth it to do more? Will it make a difference? Is your representative responsive to local needs, or is she or he governed by higher ambitions?

On the other hand, what about the local school board? Might you be able to make a difference there by paying attention to issues in your community and offering selected recommendations? (Chances are better if you've been involved in community or school activities.)

Choose the targets of your assertions so you get the most "bang for the buck" from your investment of time and energy. Don't be a "Look at me! I'm being assertive" zealot! Review this chapter from time to time and make sure you're being assertive when it counts.

22

When Assertiveness Doesn't Work

"I don't think there's anything wrong
with envisioning only a positive future.
The reality is that it won't happen that way . . . .
Life is a series of peaks and valleys . . ."

— A READER

THOSE WORDS OF WISDOM were contained in a letter we received from a North Carolina reader. He's right, of course. While we have encouraged you throughout this book to work at expressing yourself more effectively in order to achieve your goals in relationships, we know that it doesn't always work. Let's take a look at some of the reasons why not.

❖ Nobody's perfect.

❖ Nobody's assertive all the time.

❖ Life doesn't give us "ideal" circumstances, like the examples we've described.

❖ We — and you — can't predict the actual situations that you'll encounter or the real responses of other people.

❖ In the real world other people will often resist your assertive efforts.

❖ You'll be wrong sometimes.

❖ There are some situations you just cannot change.

244

We spoke about this in chapter 12:

> *Expect some failures. These procedures will not turn you into a*
> *100 percent success in all your relationships! There are no instant*
> *or magic answers to life's problems. The fact is assertiveness does*
> *not always work — for us either! Sometimes, your goals will be*
> *incompatible with the other person's. Two people can't be at the*
> *head of the same line. (Letting the other person go first can be an*
> *assertive act, too!) At times, others may be unreasonable or*
> *unyielding, and the best of assertions will be to no avail.*
>
> *Also, because you're human, you'll blow it sometimes — as*
> *we all do. Allow yourself to make mistakes! And allow others*
> *their right to be themselves as well. You'll be uncomfortable,*
> *disappointed, discouraged. Reassess, practice, and then try again.*

There are many obstacles in life that must be overcome to bring about change. Some of them, as we have discussed, are within you (such as your anxiety or lack of skills). Others are "out there" and may be intractable. Governments, for example, will never have the resources to do all of the things citizens would like, however effective the citizens' protests may be.

Syndicated writer Ellen Goodman tells of an incident involving a "working mother" and a cleaning "service." It seems that the family's living room rug needed cleaning. After doing the work, "The Cleaner" (as she identified the firm) refused to deliver it at a time that fit the Working Mother's schedule. Among other efforts to arrange the delivery, she "tried assertiveness training . . . delivered an ultimatum: 'Well, you can bring it on Tuesday, but I am telling you that no one will be home after 10:00 a.m.!'" The Cleaner arrived at 11:37 and left a note. Eventually, Working Mother tried "passiveness training" and stayed home for the redelivery. We've all been there, right?

IT'S ONLY FAILURE IF YOU QUIT
In the 1980s, we contributed to a book for therapists a chapter titled "Failure: Winning at the Losing Game in Assertiveness

Training." In that paper, we discussed a number of reasons assertiveness training may not be successful for some clients in some circumstances. Among the reasons we noted there were these:

❖ The difficulty defining exactly what "assertiveness" means in a given situation

❖ Inadequate assessment of what's needed in a given situation

❖ Possible contraindications to assertive action

❖ "Canned" approaches (e.g., the "one-size-fits-all" mentality)

❖ Applying the wrong technique ("But it worked with my cousin!")

❖ Severe skill deficits (maybe you're tackling something you're not prepared to handle)

❖ Anxiety

❖ The issue may be a good deal broader than it appears, requiring intervention on a number of fronts

Let's take a closer look at each of those reasons that assertiveness might not work.

Definition. It's difficult even for seasoned professionals to define exactly what "assertiveness" means in a given situation. Obviously, reaching out to another person in friendship or affection is far different from standing up to a bully. And the nuances of behavior, from the huge variety of expressions in the eyes to the subtle changes of voice tone, make it hard to pin down just what's called "assertive" when push comes to shove. We examined in more depth in chapter 4 the complexity of defining what it means to be assertive. You might want to review our discussion of the *context*, the *response*, the *intent*, and the *behavior*, as we consider further the issues in "why didn't it work?"

Inadequate assessment. You can't go around applying some "test" to every life circumstance you encounter, but it's always a good idea, when time allows, to take a step back and think through a situation. We've described in chapter 21 and elsewhere some of the criteria we suggest you adopt in considering whether a situation calls for assertiveness.

Contraindications. Here are a few of the many reasons an assertive action may be the wrong thing to do:

❖ You may be so anxious about the situation that your racing heart, sweaty palms, and stammering voice virtually assure failure.

❖ You may be so inclined to aggressive action that you're likely to get yourself (or others) into big trouble.

❖ You may be very unfamiliar with the cultural or social environment you're in, making it impossible to determine what action would be appropriate.

❖ An assertive intervention may make a bad situation worse (see "Canned approaches" below for an example).

❖ The object of your intended assertive action may be in a position to make you pay too high a price for speaking up (e.g., boss, bully, or authority figure).

Canned approaches. Our psychologist colleagues Bernard Schwartz and John Flowers, in their excellent resource for therapy professionals *How to Fail as a Therapist*, describe the "one-size-fits-all" mentality with an example:

> *Dr. Assertion ran groups and came to the belief that assertion was the cure for most if not all interpersonal problems. In one group, a young teenage boy, whose father was an alcoholic, was coached to be assertive when his father mistreated his mother and him. As the result of "standing up for himself," the boy ended up in the hospital — fortunately with no permanent damage — and the father in jail.* (Schwartz & Flowers, 2006, p. 36)

As fond as we are of assertiveness and as important as we believe it to be for good mental health, we certainly don't view it as any kind of "cure-all." As we've emphasized throughout this book, it's vital to assess yourself and each situation carefully and to respond — or avoid responding — as you consider to be in your own best interest.

Wrong technique. We've said it before, and we'll say it again: assertiveness is person-and-situation specific. The approach you use when expressing your love is different from that for disciplining your children, that for asking your boss for a raise, and that for telling a teacher you want more attention to your child's unique needs. Consider just one component: tone of voice. You surely won't speak to the boss in the same tone you use when disciplining your children!

Skill deficits. Maybe you're tackling too much too soon? We've taken pains throughout *Your Perfect Right* to describe the development of more effective assertive skills as a step-by-step process. And we've emphasized the importance of starting small and building on success. If the first situation you encounter involves your life partner, your boss, or a police officer, you may want to stifle the urge to say the first thing that comes to mind. Get the practice you need in less risky or loaded situations or with relationships that are less important to your long-term well-being. And do keep in mind the role of temperament, as we discussed in chapter 14. If you were born with a predisposition to shyness or inhibition or, contrarily, aggression, assertive self-expression will not come easy for you. It's worth the effort, however, and we encourage you to keep at it!

Anxiety. In chapter 11 we reviewed a number of considerations about the role anxiety plays in inhibiting assertive action. In this summary, suffice it to say you'll need to work at overcoming that racing heart, sweaty palms, and stammering voice before you can expect much success with your efforts to come across assertively.

An issue that may require intervention on a number of fronts. Forgive us for saying it yet once again, but *assertiveness doesn't work for everything!* And that's as true within each of us as it is for the life situations we encounter. We hope you're taking care of yourself in every realm — diet, sleep, exercise, social and economic circumstances, etc. — along with your work at becoming more assertive.

And likewise, the elements of a given life situation may require physical, social, economic, political, or other resources, as well as assertive action. Consider, for example, something as far-reaching as local citizen action to get a city ordinance passed or changed. An assertive act might be to appear before the city council at a public comment period and make your case. But that's only a small piece of what's necessary. You'll also need to do lots of "homework" in advance: research the topic, gather community support perhaps in the form of a petition, offer documentation of similar successful ordinances in other cities, prepare and submit plans and photographs, meet with city staff, etc., etc.

WHEN YOU ARE WRONG

Especially in your early assertions, you may assert yourself when you have incorrectly interpreted a situation. If this situation does occur, don't hesitate to admit that you have been wrong. There is no need to get carried away in making amends, of course; but be open enough to indicate that you know when you have been mistaken. And don't hesitate to be assertive with that person in the future when the situation calls for it.

AVOIDING FAILURES

So, how can you be sure your assertive action won't fail? You can't, of course. There are too many variables in any life situation to be able to predict with assurance. Still, there are steps you can take to make it more likely you'll succeed. First, we encourage you to review this chapter, and chapter 21 on "Deciding When to Be Assertive." Second, we urge you to be really honest with yourself in assessing each situation and your ability to handle it assertively. And third, we offer the following list of suggestions to minimize the chance that your efforts will go unrewarded:

❖ Adopt your own working definition of assertive behavior, using our ideas only as a starting point.

❖ Make sure you're choosing for yourself how you will act, not following a "formula" prepared by someone else (including the authors of this book!).

❖ Work at reducing your anxiety in social situations, in addition to developing your assertive skills. (Review chapter 11.)

❖ Avoid the "contraindications" noted above.

❖ Don't give up easily! Review our discussion of "persistence" in chapter 8.

❖ Take another look at the step-by-step process in chapter 13, and do some work on any steps you think may be weak spots for you.

❖ Choose your battles carefully. Proceed in any situation only when you're sure "it's worth it."

And finally, recognize that we all experience failure. That's part of being human. When your best efforts at assertiveness don't work, remember that you have lots of company! The good news is that, most of the time, failure gives us an opportunity to learn more about ourselves and about life.

23

Helping Others Deal with the New Assertive You

All paths lead to the same goal:
to convey to others what we are.
— PABLO NERUDA

A S YOU HAVE GROWN IN YOUR OWN ASSERTIVENESS, you have noticed changes in those around you. Your family, friends, co-workers, and others may have found it strange to notice that you have changed, and they may not be altogether happy about it.

Most folks like to be able to predict how others will act in a given situation . . .

"Mom's not going to like that!"
"You'll really get it when your father gets home!"
"The boss is going to hit the ceiling!"
"Jim will really be pleased."

. . . and usually will express surprise if their expectations are not met . . .

"Why is Mary acting so differently these days?"
"What's gotten into George?"
"It's not like you to say something like that."
"You never used to mind if I borrowed your things!"

Your growing assertiveness will have some direct effects upon those closest to you. They may be glad to see you behaving more effectively; however, they may find it uncomfortable that you have begun to talk back or to deny them full control in certain situations. You can prepare them for the changes in you; it will make a difference in how well they support you in your growth.

How Does It Look from Outside?

"What's going on with Harold recently? He's been acting very strangely. I asked him if I could borrow his car, and he actually said no!"

People will notice. They'll wonder why you are no longer a pushover or a grump. Some will applaud the changes, others will decry them — but they'll notice. It's common for students of assertiveness to overdo it at first. That makes the changes even more noticeable. Others may see you as suddenly aggressive, and you may be. If you are saying no for the first time in your life, you may get a kick out of really belting it out. "NO — and don't ask me again!"

If you overreact like that and flaunt your newfound self-expression, others will resent it. Not only are you no longer predictable, you are a royal pain in the neck! From the point of view of your friends and family, you may appear to be a pushy so-and-so — one they'd just as soon would go away.

If instead, you're too tentative about your assertions, others may notice that something is changed but not realize what you are trying to do.

It may be a good idea to let those closest to you know what you are trying to do — at least those you can trust — and perhaps even to ask them for help. Becoming assertive will involve your friends eventually if you are successful — there is no reason to hide it from those who could help you along the way. More on this later in the chapter.

BE AWARE OF YOUR IMPACT ON OTHERS

You will need to develop some sensitivity to the reactions of others to your assertion. You can teach yourself to observe the effects and to watch for the subtle clues others will give to their reactions.

Many of the same nonverbal behaviors we have stressed in assertive expression are involved. You've learned to pay attention to your own eye contact, posture, gestures, facial expression, voice, and distance. Tune in to the same characteristics in your listeners to help you know how you are coming across and how they are responding.

POTENTIAL ADVERSE REACTIONS

In our experience helping others to learn assertiveness for four decades, we have found few negative results. Certain people do, however, respond in a disagreeable manner when they face assertion. Even if the assertion is handled well, one may at times be faced with unpleasant reactions. Here are a few examples:

Backbiting. After you have asserted yourself, the other person involved may be disgruntled, though perhaps not openly. For example, if you see someone pushing her grocery cart into the line ahead of you and you respond assertively, she may go to the end of the line but grumble while passing you. You may hear such things as "Who do you think you are, anyway?" "Big deal!" We think the best solution is simply to ignore the childish behavior. If you do retort in some manner, you are likely only to complicate the situation by acknowledging that the words got to you.

Aggression. At times the other party may become outwardly hostile toward you. Yelling or screaming or physical reactions like bumping, shoving, or hitting could be involved. Again, the best approach is to avoid escalating the condition. You may choose to express regret that your actions upset her but remain steadfast in your assertion. This is especially true if you will have future contact. If you back down on your assertion, you will simply reward this negative reaction, and the next time you assert yourself with this person the probability will be high that you will receive another aggressive reaction.

Temper Tantrums. In certain situations, you may assert yourself with someone who is used to being in charge. Such a person may react to your assertion by looking hurt, claiming precarious health, saying "You don't like me!" crying, feeling sorry for himself, or otherwise attempting to control you or make you feel guilty. Again, you must choose, but it is nearly always best to ignore such behavior.

Psychosomatic Reactions. Some individuals may actually become physically ill if you thwart a long-established habit. Abdominal pains, headaches, and feeling faint are just a few of the symptoms possible. Choose to be firm in the assertion, recognizing that the other person will adjust to the new situation in a short time. Be sure to be consistent in your assertion whenever the same situation recurs with this individual. If you are inconsistent, the other person may become confused and may eventually just ignore your assertions.

Overapologizing. On rare occasions after you have asserted yourself, the other party involved will be overly apologetic or humble. Point out that such behavior is unnecessary. If, in later encounters the person seems to be afraid of you or deferent toward you, don't take advantage. In fact, you could help to develop assertiveness in that person, using the methods you've learned in this book.

Revenge. If you have a continuing relationship with someone with whom you have asserted yourself, that person may seek "revenge." At first, it might be difficult to understand what is being attempted; but as time goes on the taunts may become quite evident. Once you are certain that someone is trying to make your life miserable, take steps to squelch the actions immediately. Directly confronting the situation is often enough to get vengeful tactics to cease.

How Can You Include Others in Your Learning Process?

We suggested earlier in this chapter that you consider involving your most trusted friend(s) in your work on assertiveness. Try these steps:

❖ Tell your closest friend — be sure this is someone you can trust — that you are learning to be more assertive.

❖ Keep in mind that you will need to be careful when telling certain people about your attempts to become assertive. Those who have your best interests at heart will be supportive. Others — even some close friends and intimates — may actually undermine your efforts. Choose carefully.

❖ Tell your friend something about what it means to you to be assertive and the differences between assertion and aggression.

❖ Ask your friend to help you.

❖ If your friend agrees to help, decide together on some specific behaviors to watch for, and ask for periodic feedback on how you are doing in those specifics — particularly the nonverbal components of behavior (chapter 8).

❖ Recognize that sometimes your assertiveness will lead you to say no to your friend or otherwise say or do something against her or his preferences. Discuss that in advance and as it occurs.

❖ Avoid announcing, "I'm going to be assertive now!" — as if that excuses rudeness or other inappropriate behavior or allows you to avoid responsibility for your actions.

How a Friend Can Help

Someone has trusted you enough to ask for your help.

A friend, relative, roommate, co-worker, lover, or significant other has asked you to read this brief statement because he or she has decided to make some changes. The process your friend is pursuing is called assertiveness training (AT), and its purpose is to help folks become more capable in expressing themselves.

Assertiveness is often confused with aggressiveness, so let's clear that up right now. Learning to be more assertive does not mean learning to push other folks around in order to get your way. It does mean standing up for yourself, expressing feelings directly and firmly, and establishing equal relationships that take the needs of both people into account.

Your friend may be reading a book, taking a class, working with a counselor, or practicing alone or in a group — there are lots of ways AT can be effective. It may take a few weeks, or even a few months, but you'll begin to notice some changes. Your friend may be expressing opinions about where to go out to eat, what's wrong with the government, or how you clean up your half of the apartment; saying no when you ask a favor; taking more initiative in conversation; giving more compliments than before; or even showing anger once in a while. Not to worry. If these new actions were intended to threaten you, your friend would not have asked you to read this!

Most people find that increased assertiveness makes folks even more pleasant to be around. They are more spontaneous, are less inhibited, are more honest and direct, feel better about themselves, and maybe are even healthier!

So... how do you figure into this?

Well, your friend has asked you to read this so you'll know a little about what's going on in her or his life right now and better understand the changes you may be seeing in the coming weeks and months.

You are evidently a trusted person in your friend's life, because it can be risky to let someone know about changes one plans to make. Sort of like telling people about your dreams or your New Year's resolutions. If things don't work out, the person is vulnerable to some real hurt. Please honor the trust that has been extended to you.

Here are some ways you can help:

Find out something about how your friend hopes to change, so you'll know what to look for.

When you see the desired changes — however small — give him a pat on the back.

Be honest in your own dealings with your friend, including pointing out when she goes overboard trying to be assertive.

Read up on assertiveness yourself.

Actively coach your friend with specific behavior changes, such as improved eye contact or voice tone.

Be a good model of assertiveness yourself.

Help your friend rehearse special situations, such as job interviews and confrontations.

You'll likely find your thoughtfulness repaid manifold. You may find yourself learning a thing or two in the process!

❖ If you are developing your assertiveness as a part of some form of therapy, you need not disclose that to anyone. Simply talk about your goals, and point out that you are learning from this book.

❖ If you are working with a therapist or other trainer, you may wish to bring your friend in for an orientation/training session.

❖ If you decide to go ahead and let a friend in on your plans, you may find the statement "How a Friend Can Help" on pages 256–257 useful in orienting that person to the assertiveness training process. Feel free to copy it, as long as you include the credit line at the bottom.

24

Beyond Assertiveness

*God, give us the serenity to accept what cannot
be changed, the courage to change what should
be changed, and the wisdom to distinguish one
from the other.*
— REINHOLD NIEBUHR*

O N THE MORNING OF JANUARY 28, 1986, Allan MacDonald
said no. Tragically, as it turned out, they didn't listen
to him.

MacDonald was an engineer for the manufacturer of the
booster rockets for the US space shuttle "Challenger." He
recognized that the rockets' o-ring seals could fail in the
unusually cold Florida morning, and urged NASA officials to
scrub the launch scheduled for that day. Sadly, MacDonald's
lone voice was not enough to prevent the disaster. "There were
a dozen other engineers who supported my argument, but not
one of them spoke up," says MacDonald.

Like Allan MacDonald, *your opinion matters!* As you've
worked your way through this book, you've gained a greater
feeling of empowerment, self-confidence and skills. You know
you can choose whether and when to express your views. Allan

---

* Scholars now disagree about the origin of this prayer, but Niebuhr is generally
credited with this specific version.

MacDonald had the courage to do so; according to his report, his colleagues did not. The results were tragic.

We're not saying you should *always* speak up, of course. Our theme throughout this book has been *individual choice*. While we've consistently pointed out the value of assertive behavior, perceptive readers will have noted some of the potential shortcomings and hazards of personal assertiveness. You'll want to take into account the limitations and possible negative consequences of asserting yourself.

Assertive behavior will most often be its own reward, but the consequences on occasion may deflate its value. The young boy who assertively refuses the big bully's request to ride his new bike may find himself nursing a black eye! His assertion was perfectly legitimate, but the other guy wouldn't take no for an answer.

We don't mean to suggest that you should avoid assertiveness if it appears hazardous, but we do encourage you to consider the probable *consequences* of your assertive acts. Under certain circumstances, the value of an assertion will be outweighed by the value of avoiding the probable response!

If you *know how* to act assertively, you are free to *choose* whether or not you will. If you are *unable* to act assertively, you have no choices. *Our most important goal for this book is to enable YOU to make the choice!*

"It's Too Late Now!"

People who feel they can do nothing about a problem that happened some time ago often ask us about past situations. Frustrated by the consequences of their earlier lack of assertion, they nevertheless feel helpless to change things now.

Carlos offered us a good example of this problem. For months, his boss had been handing him projects late in the day, asking Carlos to stay late and prepare PowerPoint slides for meetings the next morning. The first time it happened, Carlos assumed that the circumstances were unique. He willingly agreed to help out. Over time, however, the "special request" had become an *expectation* and occurred often. Carlos liked his work, but it had begun to take a toll on his personal life, and he'd been thinking about looking for another job.

When Carlos somewhat tentatively brought the situation up for discussion in an assertiveness training group, he found the trainer and group members very supportive. In the group he rehearsed a scene in which he confronted his boss with his feelings. He did poorly at first, apologizing and allowing the "boss" to convince him that such "loyalty to the company" was necessary to the job. With feedback and support from the group, however, he improved his ability to express his feelings effectively and not be cowed by the executive's response.

The next day, Carlos brought it up with his boss at the office, made his point, and arranged a more reasonable schedule for such projects. In the two months that followed, "special requests" were made only twice, and only when the circumstances clearly *were* unusual. Both were pleased with the result.

The point of this discussion is that it is seldom too late for an appropriate assertion, even if a situation has grown worse over some time. Approaching the person involved — yes, even a family member, spouse, lover, boss, or employee — with an honest "I've been concerned about for some time" or "I've been wanting to talk with you about..." or "I could have mentioned this sooner, but..." can lead to a most productive effort at resolution of an uncomfortable issue. And it can encourage open and honest communication in the future.

Remember to take responsibility for your feelings when you express them: "I'm concerned..." *not* "You've made me upset..."; "I'm mad..." *not* "You make me mad..."

Another important reason to go back and take care of old business with others is that unfinished business continues to gnaw away at you. Resentment from experiences that created anger or hurt won't just go away. Such feelings result in a widening gap between people, and the resulting mistrust and potential grudge are hurtful to both persons.

Even if old issues can't be resolved, doing all you can to attempt reconciliation is worthwhile. Opening up old wounds can be painful. And there are certain risks — the outcomes could be worse than before. Despite these risks, we encourage you to do all you can to work out such problems.

One more point: As we have cautioned before, do not attempt to begin your journey toward new assertiveness with highly risky relationships — those that are very important to you. This is a rather advanced step and should come after you have mastered the basics.

THE SWING OF THE PENDULUM

"I have a friend who used to be peaceful and quiet. She took assertiveness training and now is unbearable, complaining about everything! She has really gone overboard!"

People who have considered themselves underdogs throughout life then learned to be assertive may become verbally aggressive. The message may be: "Now it's my turn, and I'll set a few people straight!" Feelings covered up for many years may come out with a "bang."

Similarly, those who have typically been aggressive may, when they first learn a more appropriate approach, pull back and become hypersensitive or withdrawn. It can be flabbergasting to have someone who was derisive and manipulative now treat you like royalty!

If this rapid change of style describes you or someone you know, don't despair. Both of these dramatic shifts in behavior are normal reactions and may be expected. It's common for people to overcompensate as they work at change. Give it some time. It's likely that the pendulum will balance after a short while, and a more appropriate assertive style will develop.

ASSERTIVENESS AND HOLISTIC HEALTH

Assertiveness, as we've discussed throughout this book, is a valuable tool for gaining self-confidence and self-control in life. Its value is even greater when it is one part of a broader plan for well-being. We encourage you to think in "holistic" terms, integrating psychological, physical, spiritual, and environmental considerations. In short, to deal with all parts of yourself.

Take a look at your current health condition, diet and sleep and exercise patterns, mental attitude, beliefs and values, living conditions, and medical history — all are important considerations in a thorough assessment of well-being. Don't assume, for example, that improved assertiveness skills alone will adequately deal with a lack of assertiveness. Lack of sleep or a physical ailment will matter, too! Examine all the possibilities, and consult professionals as well if you need help.

Interest in a holistic view of health has never been greater, stimulated by such factors as greater access to health information (e.g., online), expanded awareness of the role of fitness in overall health, increased consumer activism, and exorbitant health care and insurance costs. Despite the continuing trend toward specialization, an increasingly holistic outlook is emerging among health professionals in all fields. Dr. Andrew Weil is a leader in this field, and his works on "integrative medicine" have been a beacon. Check out his book, *Eight Weeks to Optimum Health*.

ASSERT YOUR WAY TO HEALTH

Can lack of assertive behavior make you sick?

Studies in two relatively new fields of mind-body relationships — behavioral medicine and *psychoneuroimmunology* (whew!) — suggest that deficiencies in assertiveness can play an important role in developing and treating illnesses.

Patients of cancer, heart disease, respiratory problems, gastrointestinal tract disorders, and arthritis are being studied by medical researchers to determine if stress factors related to long-term nonassertive or aggressive behavior contribute to bringing on the illness. The relationship between mind and body is complex, of course, and interpretations about the causes of illness need to be tentative. Responsible researchers observe that the cause of illness is rarely a single factor (such as assertiveness problems or smoking) but rather is a variety of factors working together.

Cardiologist Redford Williams (you met him in the anger chapter) has studied the role of hostility as a causative factor in cardiovascular disease. Numerous studies by Williams and his colleagues at Duke University point to hostile attitudes and behaviors as an important risk factor in heart attacks, right along with the key physical risk factors of smoking, elevated blood cholesterol, and high blood pressure.

Williams recommends assertiveness training as one part of his multifaceted treatment program to reduce hostility and other risk factors. He has found that the more you can deal with your feelings in an upfront, straightforward manner, the less you allow feelings to fester and come out as hostile or cynical thoughts and behaviors.

Another way to use your assertive skills to improve your health is to take charge of your own healthcare. That even means learning to be assertive when you must go to the doctor. Researchers in the mind-body field are teaching patients how to do it. Internist Sheldon Greenfield and social psychologist Sherrie Kaplan devised a twenty-minute assertiveness coaching session for patients waiting to see a physician. They rehearsed how to ask key questions in order to take an active role in the process of dealing with the doctor. Then they compared trained patients with a group of patients who had not been trained. The coached assertiveness patients were much more in control in dealing with the doctor. They directed the conversation, interrupted when necessary, and got a lot more information about their illnesses. And here's the great part...four months later those trained in assertiveness had missed less work, had fewer medical symptoms, and indicated that their overall health was better than the uncoached patients. (See Norman Cousins's fine book, *Anatomy of an Illness*.)

There are many ways to be an assertive advocate in your own healthcare program before you become ill — and after. Believing in and taking action about your ongoing healthcare is a vital application of your assertive behavior. Educate yourself about your total self: body-mind-spirit. Do ongoing preventive maintenance: a low-fat, well-balanced diet; an aerobic exercise program; and attention to psychological and spiritual well-being.

The bottom line is learning to be in charge of your own life and health. Get better at making important healthcare decisions: the doctors you select and how you deal with them; your health insurance coverage and how claims are handled; your knowledge about yourself and your illness and treatment (if any); dealing with doctor's office and hospital personnel; and decision-making about medications and alternative treatments.

Assertiveness about your health and healthcare could save your life.

ASSERTIVENESS AND COMMON SENSE

We've emphasized action in this book. When we first began to do assertiveness training back in the late 1960s, we found it an effective procedure for our clients who had difficulty expressing themselves. Most of them were shy, nonassertive, reluctant to take any action on their own behalf. For them, it seemed the most effective approach was to *activate* them, to get them going again, to teach them to "stand up, speak out, and talk back." (Full disclosure: that was the title of one of our books on the subject.) Moreover, assertiveness was a very helpful intervention for those who were inhibited by social anxiety.

Later we came to recognize that many people were using the idea of taking such action as a license to act aggressively, or at least foolishly. Some trainers were encouraging — as homework in assertiveness — that people go into restaurants and ask just for a glass of water. Or into service stations and ask just to have the windows washed (in those days service stations actually did that sort of thing!).

Let us put in a plea, then, for common sense:

❖ *Don't Manipulate.* Assertiveness goes a long way when used appropriately. But it ought not to be used as a tool for manipulation, as a means to "get your way" at the expense of others (aggressive), or as a constant style of behavior.

❖ *Don't Get into a Rut.* You need not "assert yourself" all the time. How boring — and boorish — to go about always making yourself heard, always speaking out. Make assertiveness *one tool* in your repertoire of behaviors, one way to act that you can use when it is important and needed. Nothing is good all the time! It is possible to have "too much of a good thing!"

❖ *Be Kind.* Kindness is a word that doesn't get a lot of press, but it has been our intent since the beginning of our work with assertiveness to help humans treat each other with respect, thoughtfulness, and, yes, kindness. The idea of assertiveness for those who had been "pushed around" earlier was to help them gain the respect that they had been missing from others.

Assertiveness is *not* incompatible with kindness, thoughtfulness, compassion, empathy, or politeness. Someone with a truly assertive lifestyle is very concerned for others and their rights. The term "empathic assertion" has been used to describe those forms of self-expression that are directly aimed at the needs of another person.

We're in full support of the concept of "random kindness": do acts of kindness anonymously, without possibility of recognition or reward.

❖ *Be Yourself.* Too many people have interpreted assertiveness as if there were one single definition that qualified a behavior as "assertive." We discussed this at some length in chapter 5, but we'd like to underscore it here: *recognize individual differences!*

Everybody has a unique view of the world; that is part of the joy of the human experience. Don't try to shape others into your image of them! Don't assume there is only one way to be assertive in a given circumstance! Let people choose to be nonassertive if they wish. Let there be "different strokes for different folks!"

❖ *Be Persistent — but Not a Pest.* One of the most important but often overlooked aspects of assertive behavior is *persistence*. It is rarely enough just to ask for what you want. You may need to ask again, to direct your request to someone in authority, to write a letter, to bring some pressure to bear from another source (such as a consumer advocacy group or a regulatory agency).

Is your cause important? Go back again if you don't get help the first time. See the manager. Call the president of the company. Tell your neighbor again about his noisy dog. Remind your boss about the raise.

Remember to be assertive in your persistence — nagging can be aggressive!

❖ *Practice — But Don't Get "Perfect."* Some types of so-called "assertive" responses can seem really mechanical and rehearsed. While we suggest that you rehearse while you are developing your style and skills in assertiveness, we consider it very important that you develop a personal style — integrating assertiveness with your own unique way of dealing with people. If you come off sounding like our book or like someone else's "scripts for assertive situations," you'll lose credibility, and people will not take you seriously.

❖ *Forget about Being an Amateur Shrink.* Don't try to "psychoanalyze" people! Some folks go around trying to "think psychologically," always figuring out how others are likely to react and shaping their behavior by the way they believe it will affect others. It is rare that anyone — even those of us who are trained psychologists — is able to do that successfully.

Instead, try to be yourself, be assertive, and take other's needs, rights, and respect into account.

MEMBERSHIP IN THE HUMAN COMMUNITY

In Thornton Wilder's classic play *Our Town*, a character discusses a letter that was addressed thus: "Jane Crofut, the Crofut Farm, Grover's Corners, Sutton County, New Hampshire, United States of America, Continent of North America, Western Hemisphere, the Earth, the Solar System, the Universe, the Mind of God." Wilder showed a remarkable sense of citizenship in the world; few of us have so thoughtfully considered our relationships to the entire human community. Indeed, is it even possible to deal with that virtually unreachable concept? In what sense *am* I a world citizen? I can talk with and see my neighbors in the local community. I can visit, with minimal difficulty, people in nearby states, across the country, and, if I am fortunate, even around the world. I can vote in local, state, and national elections and I share a historical and cultural heritage with other citizens of the United States. What have I in common with the people of Namibia, Lithuania, or Sri Lanka? Do I really think of them as my brothers and sisters in humankind?

No individual can exist alone. None of us has the necessary knowledge, skills, or personal resources necessary to function with total independence in the world. We are interdependent, and our assertiveness must take into account and respect our neighbors' needs as well as our own.

Even without the evidence offered by photos from space, it's easy to see the fragility of world order in any day's headlines. We note the continuing efforts by governments of many nations to maintain world peace and some balance of order on the planet. And we see how easily aggression and the quest for power disturb that balance.

So many international issues remain unresolved, awaiting assertive action by those courageous enough to transcend nationalistic limits and assume leadership in *solving problems*, rather than displaying power. These include global climate change, hunger, extreme poverty, sanitation, disposal of nuclear and other hazardous wastes, response to terrorism and religious fanaticism . . . the list goes on.

The principles of assertive action that we have discussed throughout this book apply to these concerns as well. Perhaps you have found assertiveness training helpful in your own life and relationships. We urge you to demonstrate your appreciation for that help by taking assertive action as a world citizen. Write letters supporting public officials who take courageous action. Contact your elected representatives to express your views on important issues.

Work to replace aggression with assertion wherever you can. You may choose to support tighter controls on handguns, for instance, or reduced television violence. Perhaps you support free-enterprise replacement of government bureaucracies that fail to provide necessary services or better accountability in public agencies. Some will demonstrate against environmental degradation, nuclear weapons proliferation, war, or unfair taxation. Equal justice for women or minorities may be your major cause. Support is always needed for improved access to health care, rape crisis intervention, better schools, parenting education, and child protection programs, along with dozens of other worthy causes.

The principle of assertive action is well established in Western culture and is a vital element in the U.S. Constitution. The spirit of civil disobedience, when other attempts to change intolerable situations have failed, has a proud heritage. Henry David Thoreau is the "patron saint" of civil disobedience, and one need look no further than the U.S. Declaration of Independence or such famous historic events as the Boston Tea Party for well-known and highly respected acts of assertiveness.

A vital principle of any such action, of course, is the individual's willingness to accept responsibility for the consequences of her or his behavior. Examples of such personally responsible public assertiveness from the last century are Mahatma Gandhi, Martin Luther King, Jr., Desmond Tutu, and Lech Walesa. Whatever our personal views of the substantive issues in their actions, we must stand in awe of those who have made their deepest beliefs public by living accordingly, caring more for the welfare of humankind than for their individual comfort and safety. Who will we admire a hundred years from now?

Ultimately, those acts that are in the best interest of our fellow humans are in our own best interests as well. If I act assertively to right a social wrong, I act to the benefit of all who are members of the society, including myself. Thus assertive action, in the best sense, is at once in my own self-interest *and* unselfish!

There are a thousand causes worthy of your energies. If your assertiveness ends when your steak is served the way you like it or when you get correct change, your life may be more pleasant temporarily but will not count for much.

Justice Oliver Wendell Holmes, Jr. put it in perspective (do forgive his sexist language):

> *"A man must share in the action and passion of his times, at the risk of being judged not to have lived."*

BEYOND ASSERTIVENESS
Enough. The rest is up to you. Keep in mind:

❖ *Assertiveness is learned.* You can change yourself if you wish to do so.

❖ *Change is hard work.* It usually comes slowly and in small steps. Don't try to tackle too much at once. Succeed by taking *achievable steps!*

❖ *There are no magic answers.* While assertiveness doesn't always work (for us either!), it sure beats the alternative! Don't let failures at first stop you from trying again.

❖ *Give yourself credit when you make changes* in your life. Even the smallest accomplishments deserve a pat on the back!

❖ *Don't hesitate to ask for help,* including professional help when you need it. Everyone needs help at times.

You are working with an infinitely valuable resource — yourself. Take good care. You are unique, an individual, with your own size, shape, color, age, ethnic and cultural background, gender, lifestyle, education, ideas, beliefs, values, occupation, relationships, thoughts, and behavior patterns. Since a book must speak to many, we've had to generalize a great deal. Being assertive will mean different things to different people. You must decide what is relevant for you and how to apply assertive behavior in your own unique relationships.

Remember that assertiveness is not a tool for manipulation, intimidation, or getting your way. It is a means to stand up for your own rights, build equal relationships, express your anger, reach out to others, express your affection, and be more direct. Most importantly, it is one means to becoming the person you want to be, to feel good about yourself, and to demonstrate your caring and respect for the rights of others.

APPENDIX

Assertiveness Practice Situations

THE EVERYDAY LIFE SITUATIONS THAT FOLLOW call for assertive behavior and cause difficulty for many people. Each situation is presented with alternatives from which you may choose a response. Each alternative response may be categorized in the "nonassertive-aggressive-assertive" framework we have described.

The situations are designed for your practice according to the step-by-step process described in chapter 13. Pick situations appropriate to your needs, and work slowly on one item at a time. As you read the situation description, fill in the details from your own imagination.

Follow steps 4–7 of chapter 13, utilizing the alternative responses suggested here for each situation and any others you may think of. For each situation you choose, enact the role-playing and feedback exercises described in steps 8, 9, 11, and 12; then continue with remaining steps of the step-by-step process. Remember to focus upon both *what* you say and *how* you say it!

The examples are grouped according to several characteristic types of situations: family, intimate, consumer, employment, school and community, and social. In each case, only a few situations are suggested, although the number of categories and examples is as infinite as life itself. We urge you to come up with more examples of your own to extend your practice.

FAMILY SITUATIONS

Sleepover. Your twelve-year-old daughter is having a sleepover with five other girls. You look at the clock: 2:17 a.m.; the girls should have settled down to sleep by now, but you can still hear them chattering away.

Alternative Responses:

(a) You toss and turn in bed, wishing your spouse would get up and say something to the girls. You're really angry but just lie there trying to block out the sounds.

(b) You jump out of bed and scold the girls angrily, especially your daughter, for their behavior.

(c) You get up, speak to the girls firmly (so they know you mean business), and tell them you've had enough for tonight. You point out that you need to get up early tomorrow and that everyone needs to get to sleep. You make clear that you won't tolerate any more noise.

Visiting Relative. Aunt Margaret, with whom you'd really rather not spend much time, is on the telephone telling you of her plans to arrive next week for a three-week visit with you.

Alternative Responses:

(a) You think, "Oh, no!" but say, "We'd love to have you come and stay as long as you like!"

(b) You tell her the children have just come down with bad colds, the roof is leaking, and you'll be going to Cousin Bill's weekend after next — none of which is true.

(c) You say, "We'll be glad to have you come for the weekend, but we simply can't invite you for longer. A short visit is happier for everyone, and we'll want to see each other again sooner. We have lots of school and community activities that take up most of our evenings and weekends."

Past Midnight. Your teenage son has just returned from a school party. It's 3 a.m., and you've been frantic, worried mainly if he was OK. You had expected him home before midnight.

Alternative Responses:

(a) You turn over and go to sleep.

(b) You shout, "Where the hell have you been? Do you have any idea what time it is? You've kept me up all night! You thoughtless, inconsiderate, selfish, no-good bum — I ought to make you sleep in the street!"

(c) You say, "Are you OK, Sam? I've been very upset, worrying about you! You said you'd be home before midnight, and I've been frantic for hours. I wish you'd called me! Tomorrow we'll discuss your arrangements for staying out late."

Holy Terror. The preschool teacher tells you that your three-year-old is hitting the other children. At home he pretty much does what he likes, staying up late, playing too rough with the pets, not eating properly. In the past you have thought his behavior "cute."

Alternative Responses:

(a) You talk gently to your son about not hitting the other children. He says the other kids are mean but that he is sorry. He jumps in your lap and you say, "You are such a sweet boy. I love you."

(b) You grab your son roughly and say that if he hits anyone else you'll beat his bottom till it's raw.

(c) You discuss the issue with the teacher and with your family physician. After ruling out any physical causes, you make an appointment with the nonprofit family services center for counseling help.

INTIMATE SITUATIONS

Late for Dinner. Your wife was supposed to be home for dinner right after work. Instead, she returns hours later, explaining she was out with the girls for a few drinks. She is obviously intoxicated.

Alternative Responses:

(a) You say nothing about how thoughtless she has been, but simply start preparing something for her to eat.

(b) Screaming and yelling, you tell her that she is a drunken fool, doesn't care about your feelings, and is a poor example for the children. You ask her what the neighbors will think. You demand that she get her own dinner.

(c) You calmly and firmly let her know that she should have informed you beforehand that she was going out and would likely be late. "At least you could have called me. Your cold dinner is in the kitchen. We'll discuss this more tomorrow." And you do.

Balancing the Books. Finances are tight. When you receive the credit card bill for the month, you are shocked. Your spouse has charges that seem excessive and unnecessary.

Alternative Responses:

(a) You go to the ATM, withdraw an equal amount of money, and spend it on yourself in revenge. You don't mention the credit card.

(b) You realize that you also have overspent before. You still feel upset but decide to be understanding this time.

(c) You arrange an appropriate time to discuss the finances, and tell your partner that when you opened the statement, you were shocked at the charges. Asking for an explanation, you also insist that the two of you agree on some guidelines for use of the credit card.

Sagging Sex. During the past six months, your partner has not been sexually attentive. You're having intercourse less often, and your partner is not as enthusiastic or caring. You have tried harder to motivate your partner but to no avail.

(a) You decide that two can play this game. You withdraw, complain to your friends, and criticize your partner openly in front of the children about nonrelated matters.

(b) The feelings of upset have built to a boiling point. One evening, after another dull sexual encounter, you lash out irrationally. Your partner retaliates. The verbal explosion lasts for hours. Still seething, you spend that night on the couch and the next week sulking.

(c) In a noninflammatory but firm style, you speak to your partner honestly and openly about your feelings. You suggest that you both take part in a couple's workshop or go see a counselor to work on the problem.

CONSUMER SITUATIONS

Haircut Hassle. At the barber shop, the barber has just finished cutting your hair. When he turns the chair toward the mirror so you can inspect, you notice that you'd like the sides trimmed more.

Alternative Responses:

(a) You nod your head and say, "That's fine."

(b) You shake your head and say, sarcastically, "No, man. That doesn't do it. You sure didn't take much off the sides, did you?" You loudly demand that he "finish the job."

(c) You tell the barber you would like to have the sides trimmed more.

Shortchanged. As you are leaving a store after a small purchase, you discover that you have been shortchanged by three dollars.

Alternative Responses:

(a) Pausing for a moment, you try to decide if three dollars is worth the effort. After a few moments, you decide it is not and go on your way.

(b) You hurry back into the store and loudly demand your money, making a derogatory comment about stores who "try to get you for every penny."

(c) Re-entering the store, you catch the attention of the clerk, saying that you were shortchanged by three dollars. In the process of explaining, you display the change you received back along with your receipt.

Lines, Lines, Lines. You're standing in line at a cash register waiting to pay for your purchase and have it wrapped. Others who have come after you have been waited on first. You are getting tired of waiting.

Alternative Responses:

(a) You give up and decide not to buy the article.

(b) Shouting, "Service in this store is lousy!" you slam the intended purchase down on the counter and walk out.

(c) In a voice loud enough to be heard, you tell the clerk "I'm next. I was ahead of people who have already been served. Please wait on me now."

Do Not Call. You're at home, hoping for a restful day. About 11 a.m., the phone rings, and the voice asks if you are (your name). The call sounds important. Then you hear. "This is *Rocky Road Magazine.* We're conducting a readership survey. Have you read *Rocky Road?*" You're perturbed at the intrusion.

Alternative Responses:

(a) You are polite, don't interrupt, and answer all of the caller's questions. Soon you hear a "sales pitch" instead of a "readership survey." The call lasts ten minutes.

(b) You yell, "You people are a bunch of vultures! Don't you know anything about telephone privacy? Stick it in your ear!" You slam down the phone.

(c) You state firmly, "I'm not interested." The caller replies, "I only want to ask you a few questions." You repeat firmly, "I'm not interested. Put me on your Do Not Call list, and please don't call again." You hang up the phone.

EMPLOYMENT SITUATIONS

Overtime. You and your partner are going to a party this evening; you've been looking forward to it for several weeks. You plan to leave immediately after work. Mid-afternoon, however, your supervisor asks you to stay late to work on a special assignment.

Alternative Responses:

(a) You say nothing about your important plans and simply agree to stay until the work is finished.

(b) In a nervous, abrupt voice you say, "No, I won't work late tonight! You're going to have to plan ahead!" You then turn back to your work.

(c) In a firm, pleasant voice, you explain your important plans and say you will not be able to stay this evening to work on the special assignment, but perhaps you can help find an alternative solution. (Since this is the first time you've been asked, you also volunteer to come in early in the morning to work on the project.)

Deniable Passion. One of your co-workers has been making sexual overtures toward you. You are not the least bit interested and have begun to feel harassed.

Alternative Responses:

(a) You begin wearing plainer clothing, change your hair style, and start looking away each time the person approaches.

(b) The next time the person makes an overture you exclaim loudly, "You are scum! I hate being around you! Stay away from me or I'll report you to the harassment police!"

(c) When the person next approaches you, you respond quietly but very firmly, "I have no interest in a relationship. You've been annoying me with inappropriate comments and unacceptable behavior for weeks. I've kept a written record. If you don't stop immediately, I'll file a harassment complaint with the company."

Below Par. An employee you supervise has been doing substandard work recently. You decide it is best to deal with the situation before it gets out of control.

Alternative Responses:

(a) You say very quietly, "I'm sorry to bring this up, but I know you must have a good reason why your work has seemed to slide a little lately."

(b) You shout, "What is it with you? You've really been falling down on the job lately. If you don't shape up, you'll be out of here!"

(c) You take the employee aside and say, "I'm very concerned about your work performance recently. You haven't earned a pay increase this period. Let's analyze what's been going on and see what improvements you can make for the future."

Cutting Critique. You've made a mistake on the job. Your supervisor discovers it and is coming down on you with extra-harsh criticism and a reprimand.

Alternative Responses:

(a) Groveling, you say, "I'm so sorry! It was stupid of me to be so careless. I'll never let it happen again! Please give me another chance!"

(b) You bristle and glare, saying, "Where do you get off criticizing my work like that? Since when are you perfect? Leave me alone, and don't bother me in the future. I can handle my job!"

(c) You acknowledge the mistake, saying, "I hear you, and I admit my mistake. I'll be more careful. I don't think there will be problems in the future, but if there are, I hope we can discuss them more calmly. I learn better from constructive criticism."

Late Again. One of your subordinates has been coming in late consistently for the last three or four days.

Alternative Responses:

(a) You grumble to yourself or to others about the situation but say nothing to the person, hoping he will start coming in on time.

(b) You tell the worker off loudly in front of the rest of the crew. You declare that he has no right to take advantage of you and that he'd better get to work on time or you'll see that he is fired.

(c) You speak to the worker alone, noting that you've observed him coming in late recently. You ask, "Is there an explanation I should know about? If so, you should have told me, instead of leaving me up in the air. What needs to change so you can start coming to work on time?"

SCHOOL AND COMMUNITY SITUATIONS

Hearing Aid. In a lecture with 300 students, the professor speaks very softly. You're having trouble hearing him, and you know that many others are as well.

Alternative Responses:

(a) You continue to strain to hear, eventually moving closer to the front of the room, but say nothing about his too-soft voice.

(b) You yell out, "Speak up!"

(c) You speak to the professor after class, point out the problem, and ask if he would please speak louder.

Clarification. At a Lions Club meeting, the president is discussing the procedures for the annual high school speech contest. Several of his statements puzzle you, and you believe he has incorrectly described the rules.

Alternative Responses:

(a) You say nothing but continue to mull over the question, looking up your notes from last year's contest later in the day.

(b) You interrupt, telling him he is wrong, pointing out the mistake, and correcting him. Your tone is derisive, and your choice of words obviously makes him ill-at-ease.

(c) You tactfully ask the president to further explain the procedure in question, expressing your confusion and noting the source of your conflicting information.

Morals. You are one of eleven people in a discussion group on human sexuality. The concepts three or four of the more verbal students support are contrary to your personal moral code.

Alternative Responses:

(a) You listen quietly, not disagreeing openly with the other members or describing your own views.

(b) You loudly denounce the views that have been expressed. Your defense of your own beliefs is strong, and you urge others to accept your point of view as the only correct one.

(c) You speak up in support of your own beliefs, taking an apparently unpopular position, while acknowledging the beliefs of others in the group.

Know It All. As a member of the community beautification committee, Ms. Brown's continued dominance of the group discussion dismays you. She's an opinionated member who has "the answer" to every question, and has begun another tirade, already lasting several minutes. As usual, no one has said anything about it.

Alternative Responses:

(a) Your irritation increases, but you remain silent.

(b) You explode verbally, curse Ms. Brown for "not giving anyone else a chance," and declare her ideas "out-of-date and worthless."

(c) You interrupt, saying, "Excuse me, Ms. Brown; you're making some really good points, but I want you to know that I get concerned when you monopolize the group's time." Speaking directly to her as well as the other group members, you suggest a discussion procedure that will permit all members an opportunity to take part and will minimize dominance by a single individual.

SOCIAL SITUATIONS

Breaking the Ice. At a party where you don't know anyone except the host, you want to circulate and get to know others. You walk up to three people talking.

Alternative Responses:

(a) You stand close to them and smile but say nothing, waiting for them to notice you.

(b) You listen to the subject they are talking about, then break in and disagree with someone's viewpoint.

(c) You break into the conversation immediately and introduce yourself.

(d) You wait for a pause in the conversation, then introduce yourself and ask if you may join in.

Making a Date. You'd like to ask out a person you've met and talked with three or four times recently.

Alternative Responses:

(a) You sit around the telephone going over in your mind what you'll say and how your friend will respond. Several times you lift the phone and almost finish dialing, then hang up.

(b) You phone and as soon as your friend answers, you respond by saying, "Yo, baby. We're going out together this weekend!" Taken aback, your friend asks, "Who's calling?"

(c) You call, and when your friend answers, you identify yourself and ask, "How's school going?" The reply is, "Fine, except I'm worried about an econ test on Friday." Following the lead, you talk for a few minutes about the test. Then you say, "Since the big test will be over, would you like to go to a movie on Friday evening?"

Smoke Gets in Your Lungs. You're at a public meeting in the community park. A man you don't know sits down next to you, puffing enthusiastically on a large cigar. The smoke is very offensive to you.

Alternative Responses:

(a) You suffer the offensive smoke in silence, deciding it is the right of the other person to smoke outdoors if he wishes.

(b) You're very angry, and you demand that he either move or put out the cigar. You loudly attack the evils of smoking and the health hazards of secondhand smoke.

(c) You firmly but politely ask him to refrain from smoking because it is offensive to you.

(d) You ask him to move to another seat some distance away if he wants to continue smoking, since you were there first.

SUMMARY

We've covered a wide range of assertiveness situations in this appendix. We trust you'll find them valuable:

❖ to demonstrate that assertive behavior can be utilized in many areas of our lives.

❖ to show that the nonassertive-aggressive-assertive format is more or less universal regardless of the specific situation involved.

❖ to prime your thinking about other situations in your life that need your assertive attention.

❖ to offer ideas about how to handle instances where assertive behavior is indicated.

You probably had no trouble seeing yourself in many of the examples. Chances are you recognized something of yourself in each of the responses. Remember that no one is assertive all the time. As you progress, you'll be nonassertive or aggressive less often, and you'll develop a more consistent and natural assertive style. But you won't become perfect! Even people who write books on assertiveness have trouble with nonassertive and aggressive behavior at times!

We wish you well.

References and
Further Reading

Adams, S. *The Dilbert Principle*. New York: HarperBusiness, 1997.

Alberti, R. E. and Emmons, M. L. Failure: winning at the losing game in assertiveness training. In E. B. Foa and P. M. G. Emmelkamp (Eds.). *Failures in Behavior Therapy*. New York: Wiley, 1983.

Alberti, R. E. and Emmons, M. L. *Your Perfect Right: A Guide to Assertive Living*. Atascadero, California: Impact Publishers, Inc., 1970, 1974, 1978, 1982, 1986, 1990, 1995, 2001.

Alberti, R. E. and Emmons, M. L. *Your Perfect Right* (audio edition). Mission, Kansas: Skillpath Publications, 1999.

Albrecht, K., *Social Intelligence: The New Science of Success*. New York: Wiley/Pfeiffer, 2005.

Austin, J. H. *Zen and the Brain: Toward an Understanding of Meditation and Consciousness*. Cambridge, Massachusetts: MIT Press, 1999.

Beck, A. *Love Is Never Enough*. New York: HarperCollins, 1988.

Beck, A. *Prisoners of Hate: The Cognitive Basis of Anger, Hostility, and Violence*. New York: Harper Paperbacks, 2000.

Beckfield, D. F. *Master Your Panic and Take Back Your Life: Twelve Treatment Sessions to Conquer Panic, Anxiety, and Agoraphobia* (third edition). Atascadero, California: Impact Publishers, Inc., 2004.

Benson, H. and Klipper, M. Z. *The Relaxation Response* (expanded updated edition). New York: Harper, 1972, 2000.

Bishop, S. *Sunday Times Develop Your Assertiveness*. London, UK: Kogan Page Ltd., 2006.

Bolles, R. N. *What Color Is Your Parachute?* Berkeley, California: Ten Speed Press, 2007 (annual).

Bourne, E. *The Anxiety and Phobia Workbook* (fourth edition). Oakland, California: New Harbinger, 2005.

Bower, S. A. *The Assertive Advantage.* Mission, Kansas: National Seminars Publications, 1995.

Bower, S. A. and Bower, G. H. *Asserting Yourself: A Practical Guide for Positive Change* (revised edition). Cambridge, Massachusetts: Da Capo Press, 2004.

Braiker, H. B. *The Disease to Please: Curing the People-Pleasing Syndrome* (audio compact disc). Lanham, Maryland: National Book Network, 2004.

Braiker, H. *The Disease to Please: Curing the People-Pleasing Syndrome.* New York: McGraw-Hill, 2001.

Breitman, P. and Hatch, C. *How to Say No without Feeling Guilty: And Say Yes to More Time, More Joy, and What Matters Most to You.* New York: Bantam Dell Publishing Group, 2001.

Bright, D. *Criticism in Your Life: How to Give It — How to Take It — How to Make It Work for You.* New York: Master Media, 1988.

Bryson, K. *Don't Be Nice, Be Real: Balancing Passion for Self with Compassion for Others.* East Sussex, UK: Rudolf Steiner Press, 2005.

Burley-Allen, M. *Listening: The Forgotten Skill.* New York: Wiley, 1995.

Burley-Allen, M. *Managing Assertively* (second edition). New York: Wiley, 1995.

Burns, D. *Feeling Good: The New Mood Therapy* (second edition). New York: William Morrow, 1999.

Cautela, J. and Groden, J. *Relaxation: A Comprehensive Manual for Adult Children, and Children with Special Needs.* Champaign, Illinois: Research Press, 1994.

Cheek, D. K. *Assertive Black. . . Puzzled White.* San Luis Obispo, California: Author, 1976.

Cooley, M. L. and Hollandsworth, J. G. A Strategy for teaching verbal content of assertive responses. In R. E. Alberti (Ed.). *Assertiveness: Innovations, Applications, Issues.* San Luis Obispo, California: Impact Publishers, Inc., 1977. (Now out of print, but available in many libraries).

Cousins, N. *Anatomy of an Illness.* New York: Norton, 2005 (paperback).

Crisp, S. R. and M. Lloyd (Eds.). *Developing Positive Assertiveness.* Boston: Thomson Course Technology Ptr, 2001.

Damasio, A. *Looking for Spinoza: Joy, Sorrow, and the Feeling Brain.* New York: Harcourt, 2003.

Davis, M., Eshelman, E., and McKay, M. *The Relaxation and Stress Reduction Workbook* (fifth edition). Oakland, California: New Harbinger Publications, 2003.

Donoghue, P. J. and Siegel, M. *Are You Really Listening? Keys to Successful Communication.* Notre Dame, Indiana: Sorin Books, 2005.

Ekman, P. *Emotions Revealed: Recognizing Faces and Feelings to Improve Communication and Emotional Life* (second edition). New York: Owl Books/Henry Holt, 2007.

Elgin, S. H. *More on the Gentle Art of Verbal Self-Defense.* New York: Simon and Schuster/Fireside, 2002.

Ellis, A. *Feeling Better, Getting Better, Staying Better.* Atascadero, California: Impact Publishers, Inc. 2001.

Ellis, A. *How to Make Yourself Happy and Remarkably Undisturbable.* Atascadero, California: Impact Publishers, Inc. 1999.

Ellis, A. and Lange, A. *How to Keep People from Pushing Your Buttons.* New York: Carol Publishing Group, 1994.

Emery, G. *Own Your Own Life.* New York: Signet, 1984.

Emmons, M. L. *Meditative Therapy: Facilitating Inner-Directed Healing.* Atascadero, California: Impact Publishers, Inc., 2000.

Emmons, M. L. and Alberti, R. E. *Accepting Each Other: Individuality and Intimacy in Your Loving Relationship.* Atascadero, California: Impact Publishers, Inc., 1991.

Emmons, M. L. and Richardson, D. *The Assertive Christian.* Minneapolis: Winston Press, 1981.

Fensterheim, H. and Baer, J. *Don't Say Yes When You Want to Say No.* New York: Warner Paperbacks, 1991.

Fisher, R. and Ury, W. *Getting to Yes: Negotiating Agreement without Giving In.* Boston: Houghton-Mifflin, 1992.

Friedman, M. and Rosenman, R. H. *Type A Behavior and Your Heart*. New York: Fawcett, 1982.

Fromm, E. *The Art of Loving*. New York: Harper and Row, 1956.

Goleman, D. *Social Intelligence: The New Science of Human Relationships*. New York: Bantam, 2006.

Gordon, T. *Parent Effectiveness Training*. New York: Three Rivers Press/Crown, 2000.

Greenberger, D. and Padesky, C. *Mind Over Mood: Changing the Way You Feel by Changing the Way You Think*. New York: The Guilford Press, 1995.

Grohol, J. *The Insider's Guide to Mental Health Resources Online*. New York: Guilford Press, 2003 (periodic updates).

Haney, M. and Boenisch, E. *The Stress Owner's Manual* (second edition). Atascadero, California: Impact Publishers, Inc., 2003.

Hill, N. C., Henry, C., and Barcos, K. (Eds.). *Improving Peer Relationships: Achieving Results Informally*. Boston: Thomson Course Technology, 1996.

Hunt, M. The lessons of the cliff. *Parade Magazine*. July 14, 1985.

Jacobson, E. *You Must Relax: Practical Methods for Reducing the Tensions of Modern Living*. New York: McGraw-Hill, 1962.

Kottler, J. A. *Beyond Blame: A New Way of Resolving Conflicts in Relationships*. San Francisco: Jossey-Bass Publishers, 2003.

Lager, F. *Ben & Jerry's: The Inside Scoop*. New York: Crown, 1994.

Lange, A. J. and Jakubowski, P. *The Assertive Option*. Champaign, Illinois: Research Press, 1991.

Lazarus, A. A. *Marital Myths Revisited*. Atascadero, California: Impact Publishers, Inc., 2001.

McClure, J. S. *Civilized Assertiveness for Women*. Denver, Colorado: Albion Street Press, 2007.

McKay, G. and Dinkmeyer, Sr., D. *How You Feel Is up to You* (second edition). Atascadero, California: Impact Publishers, Inc., 2002.

Meichenbaum, D. *Cognitive-Behavior Modification: An Integrative Approach*. New York: Plenum, 1977.

Meyer, J. and Lentz, P. (Narrator). *Approval Addiction: Overcoming Your Need to Please Everyone* (audio compact disc). New York: Hachette Audio USA, 2005.

Oatley, K., Keltner, D., and Jenkins, J. *Understanding Emotions* (second edition). Oxford, UK: Blackwell Publishers, 2006.

Palmer, P. and Froehner, M. *Teen Esteem: A Self-Direction Manual for Young Adults* (second edition). Atascadero, California: Impact Publishers, Inc., 2000.

Paterson, R. J. *The Assertiveness Workbook*. Oakland, California: New Harbinger, 2000.

Phelps, S. and Austin, N. *The Assertive Woman* (fourth edition). Atascadero, California: Impact Publishers, Inc., 1975, 1987, 1997, 2002.

Pogrebin, L. C. *Among Friends*. New York: McGraw-Hill, 1987.

Poor, D. D. *Peace at Any Price: How to Overcome the Please Disease*. Highland City, Florida: Rainbow Books, 2005.

Potter, S. *Three-Upmanship*. New York: Holt, Rinehart and Winston, 1962.

Rogers, C. R. *On Becoming a Person*. Boston: Houghton-Mifflin, 1961.

Rosenthal, R. *Therapy's Best: Practical Advice and Gems of Wisdom from Twenty Accomplished Counselors and Therapists*. New York: Haworth Press, 2006.

Ryan, E. B., Anas, A. P., and Friedman, D. B. Evaluations of older adult assertiveness in problematic clinical encounters. *Journal of Language and Social Psychology*, 25, 129–145, 2006.

Salter, A. *Conditioned Reflex Therapy*. New York: Farrar, Straus, and Giroux, 1949 (Capricorn Books edition, 1961; Wellness Institute edition, 2002).

Satir, V. *The New Peoplemaking*. Mountain View, California: Science and Behavior Books, 1988.

Seligman, M. E. *What You Can Change, and What You Can't*. New York: Vintage, 2007.

Serber, M. Book review of *Your Perfect Right*. *Behavior Therapy*, 2, 253–254, 1971.

Seville Statement on Violence, *American Psychologist*, 847–848, October 1990.

Shapiro, F. and Forrest, M. S. *EMDR: Eye Movement Desensitization and Reprocessing.* New York: Guilford, 2001.

Shipley, D. and Schwalbe, W. *Send: The Essential Guide to Email for Office and Home.* New York: Knopf, 2007.

Siegel, D. *The Developing Mind: How Relationships and the Brain Interact to Shape Who We Are.* New York: Guilford, 1999.

Solomon, R. *About Love.* Indianapolis, Indiana: Hackett Publishing, 2006.

Tanabe-Endsley, P. *Project Write.* El Cerrito, California: Author, 1974, 1979 (1421 Arlington, 94530).

Tannen, D. *You Just Don't Understand.* New York: Harper Paperbacks, 2001.

Tavris, C. *Anger: The Misunderstood Emotion.* New York: Simon & Schuster, 1989.

Truss, L. *Eats, Shoots and Leaves: The Zero Tolerance Approach to Punctuation.* New York: Penguin, 2006.

Weil, A. *Eating Well for Optimum Health.* New York: Knopf, 2000.

Weil, A. *Eight Weeks to Optimum Health: A Proven Program for Taking Full Advantage of Your Body's Natural Healing Power* (revised edition). New York: Knopf, 2006.

Wheeler, E. *The Time of Your Life: The Best of Genie Wheeler's Columns on Aging Issues.* Chula Vista, California: Tracks Publishing, 2005.

Whitsett, G. *Guerrilla Kindness.* San Luis Obispo, California: Impact Publishers, Inc., 1993 (now out of print, but available in many libraries).

Williams, R. and Williams, V. *Anger Kills.* New York: HarperTorch, 1998.

Wolfe, J. and Fodor, I. G. A cognitive-behavioral approach to modifying assertive behavior in women. *The Counseling Psychologist*, 5, 45–52, 1975.

Wolpe, J. *The Practice of Behavior Therapy* (fourth edition). New York: Allyn & Bacon, 1992.

Online Resources of Interest

T HERE ARE THOUSANDS OF SELF-HELP RESOURCES ONLINE, and it can be tough to sort the wheat from the chaff. The short list offered here includes sites we consider of value because they meet the following criteria: (1) they are addressed to a general audience; (2) they are produced by qualified professionals; (3) they offer helpful information directly; (4) they offer links to other potentially useful sites; (5) they are not primarily designed to sell products. Web sites change very quickly, of course, and this list may no longer be up to date by the time you are reading it. When you're seeking information or help on the Web, we urge you to use caution, and to apply these same criteria.

• *National Institute of Mental Health:* www.nimh.nih.gov NIMH is the U.S. government agency "dedicated to research focused on the understanding, treatment, and prevention of mental disorders and the promotion of mental health." The site is packed with information and links. No advertising.

• *Mental Health America:* www.mentalhealthamerica.net MHA (formerly the National Mental Health Association), with affiliate groups nationwide, is "the country's leading nonprofit dedicated to helping ALL people live mentally healthier lives." Another comprehensive site full of authoritative mental health information and links. No advertising.

• *The Infinite Mind:* www.infinitemind.com This site centers on the National Public Radio program, "The Infinite Mind," hosted by psychiatrists Dr. Fred Goodwin and Dr. Peter Kramer, and associated public television and radio programs and documentary films. Among topics of interest on recent programs: Humor, Happiness, Anxiety, Shyness, Cyberpsych, Courage . . .

• *Mental Help Net:* www.mentalhelp.net   An easy-to-use source of mental health information. Searchable by topic, such as ADHD, anxiety, depression, schizophrenia, . . . Pharmaceutical ads.

• *PsychCentral:* www.psychcentral.com   Psychologist Dr. John Grohol is a pioneer in online psychology and has put together arguably the most comprehensive collection of online mental health resources — both direct information and links available — on the Web. Pharmaceutical ads.

• *Social Anxiety Institute:* www.socialanxietyinstitute.org   The web site calls itself, "the largest compendium of information on social anxiety on the internet." SAI is Dr. Thomas Richards's treatment center in Phoenix, Arizona, specifically aimed at helping individuals who are highly fearful in social situations. No outside ads. Emphasizes attendance at SAI's therapy sessions in Phoenix.

• *The Insider's Guide to Mental Health Resources Online:* Dr. John Grohol, whose "psychcentral.com" site is noted above, has authored this comprehensive print guide to internet sites. The book has been updated frequently, and is published by Guilford Publications in New York.

• *Bibliotherapy.com:* This is a "shameless" plug for our publisher. www.bibliotherapy.com is the web site of Impact Publishers, providing information on its many publications dealing with various popular and professional psychology topics. The company slogan is "Psychology you can use, from professionals you can trust." We think that's a pretty good description.

Index

About Love, 169–70
Accepting Each Other, 168
Affection. *See* Caring feelings;
    Intimacy; Love
Affirmations, 109–10
Aggression
  anger compared to, 201
  assertiveness/nonassertiveness
      compared to, 8, 39–43, 46–47,
      52–58
  as human nature, 45–46
  impact on social change, 36
  measuring, 15
  men and, 29–30
  nonverbal put-downs as, 212
  as reaction to assertiveness, 253–54
Agoraphobia, 120
AIDS facts, 184
Among Friends, 155
Amygdala, 101–2, 194–95
Anger
  aggression compared to, 201
  buried, 187
  complexity of, 185–86, 197–98
  degrees of, 194, 195
  expressing, 198–99, 202–3, 204
  facts/theories/myths, 186–94

Anger *(cont'd.)*
  handling others' hostility, 203–4
  minimizing, 199–202, 240–41
  reasons for, 194–97
  steam kettle myth, 188
Anger: The Misunderstood Emotion, 189
Anger Kills, 193, 198, 199
Anger Management, 194, 195
Anxiety
  assessing with SUD, 115–16, 118
  as obstacle, 20, 113–14
  panic attacks, 123–24
  summary, 128–29, 248–49
  workplace examples, 216
Anxiety, techniques for overcoming
  assertiveness training, 125
  desensitization, 118–20
  diet, 120–22
  EMDR, 125–26
Anxiety, techniques for fears listed/
      grouped/labeled, 116–17, 118
  medication, 126–27
  meditation, 122, 200
  miscellaneous therapies, 127–28
  relaxation, 119, 122, 202
  stress inoculation, 107–8
The Anxiety and Phobia Workbook, 128

Apologies, 153–54, 254
The Art of Loving, 148
Assertive behavior
  aggression/nonassertiveness
    compared to, 8, 39–43, 46–47,
    52–58
  barriers to, 8–9, 33–36, 105–7
  benefits, 9–10, 39, 132–33
  definitions, 8, 38–39, 246, 250
  need for, 5–8
  qualities of, 51, 64–65
  reactions to, 48, 253–55
Assertive, Non-Assertive, Aggressive
  chart, 40–41
Assertiveness Inventory, 12–16
The Assertive Woman, 26–28, 210
Athletes, 40
Attitudes
  analyzing in journal, 19
  anger and, 196–97, 199
  behavior and, 103–5, 130–32
  as obstacles, 105–7
Austin, James, 122–23
Austin, Nancy, 26–28, 210
Automatic thoughts, 111

Backbiting, 253
Balance issues, 136, 220, 226–28
Barriers to assertion, 8–9, 33–36, 105–7
Bashfulness. *See* Shyness
Bataille, Gretchen, 214
Beck, Aaron, 78–79, 106–7
Beckfield, Denise, 123–24, 128
Behavior
  analyzing in journal, 19
  attitudes and, 103–5, 130–32
  classification of, 46–47
  examples of styles, 52–58
  modeling of, 64–65, 139, 140–41, 235
  motivation for, 174–75

See also specific behaviors
Behavioral medicine, 263–65
Behavioral Model for Personal
  Growth, 62–63
Benefits of assertiveness, 9–10, 39,
  132–33
Ben & Jerry's ice cream example, 1–2
Benson, Herbert, 122–23
Berkowitz, Bill, 37–38
Blogs, 89–90, 97, 158
Body language. *See* Nonverbal
  communication
Boenisch, Ed, 128
Bolles, Richard Nelson, 217–18
Boundaries, 43–45
Bourne, Edmund, 128
Brain, 4, 101–3, 146–48, 194–95
  See also Thinking patterns
Brainstorming, 61
Breathing training, 122
Buffett, Warren, 113–14
Bullies, 98
Burns, David, 78–79

Canned approaches, 247–48
Caring feelings
  apologies, 153–54
  compliments, 151–53
  expressions of, 148–51
  friendship and, 154–56
  importance of, 145–46
Catastrophisizing, 110–11
Categories of assertive statements, 82
Caution. *See* Risky situations
Cell phones, 90, 93, 97, 99
Challenger disaster, 259–60
Change
  extremes of, 262
  goal-setting and, 66
  reactions to, 251–55

Change *(cont'd.)*
    step-by-step process, 65–66,
        137–44, 248, 250, 270–71
Charts
    anger facts/theories/myths, 192
    Assertive, Non-Assertive,
        Aggressive chart, 40–41
    Intimacy Attitudes and Behaviors,
        171–72
    sender-receiver behaviors, 40–41
    Sexual Communication Types,
        174–75
Cheek, Donald, 83
Children, 97–99, 160–62
Choice in assertiveness
    importance of, 44–45, 68, 135, 173,
        260
    individuality of, 33–34, 260, 266–67
    questions for determining, 237–43
Churches, 35
Civil disobedience, 269–70
Classifying behaviors, 46–47
Cognitive dimensions of behavior,
    78–79
Cognitive restructuring, 219
    See also Anxiety, techniques for
        overcoming; Thinking patterns
Cole, Charles, 193–94
Common sense, 265–68
Communication
    clarification of, 95–96, 210–12, 235
    content of messages, 69–70, 81–84
    cultural diversity, 45, 83
    expressing anger, 202–3, 204
    guidelines for assertive
        expressions, 91–92
    listening skills, 77–78, 180, 200, 220
    love and, 169–70
    rephrasing, 205
    on sexual issues, 173–76

Communication *(cont'd.)*
    technology for, 89–91, 94–97, 99
    telephone messages, 93
    voice qualities, 75–76
    written messages, 93–97
    See also Nonverbal communication
Communities, 158, 268–70, 279–81
Compliments, 151–53
Components of assertive behavior
    content of messages, 69–70, 81–84
    illustrated summary of, 88
    self-assessments, 84–87
    thinking process, 78–79, 100–101
    See also Communication;
        Nonverbal communication
Compromise, 180
Confidants, 200
Conflict resolution, 205–6, 216–17,
    235–36
Consequences, consideration of,
    242–43, 260
Consumer practice situations, 276–77
Context of behaviors, 47–50
Contraindications, 247
Cooley, Myles, 82
Coping strategies, 202
Corsini, Raymond, 160
Co-worker relationships, 221–22
Criticism, 208–13
Cultural diversity
    assertive women and, 28
    assumptions about, 32
    in communications, 45, 83
    as context of behavior, 47
    growth of, 31
    importance of individuality in,
        33–34

Dangers/hazards. *See* Risky situations
Daughter-mother relationships, 163

Definitions of assertiveness, 8, 38–39, 246, 250
Dentist's chair syndrome, 232
Desensitization, 118–20
Diet and anxiety, 120–22
Difficult people
  defined, 229–30
  guidelines for dealing with, 235–36
  steps for dealing with, 231–35
Dinkmeyer, Don, 201
Direct put-downs, 209–10
Dirty looks, 211–12
Diversity. See Cultural diversity
Drugs and anger, 200
Duke hostility research, 193, 264

Eats, Shoots and Leaves, 96
Egocentricity, 106
Eight Weeks to Optimum Health, 263
Ekman, Paul, 71, 74
Elgin, Suzette Haden, 82–83
Ellis, Albert, 78–79, 110–11, 124
Email, 89–90
EMDR (eye movement desensitization and reprocessing), 125–26
Emery, Gary, 111
Emoticons, 94–95
Emotions
  acknowledging, 60, 236
  amygdala and, 101–2, 194–95
  ignoring, 234
  See also specific emotions
Emotions Revealed, 75
Empathy, 200, 266
Employment. See Workplace issues
Enthusiasm, 179
Environment and anger, 196
Equality
  boundaries and, 44–45

Equality (cont'd.)
  importance of, 112
  intimacy and, 182
  men and, 28–30
  as style, 6
  Universal Declaration of Human Rights, 24–25
  women and, 26–28
  in workplace, 225
  See also Respectfulness
Evaluation of "real world" trials, 142
Exaggeration, 106
Exercise, 120–22
Existential living, 63
Expectations, 196–97
Experiences, openness to, 62
Exposure desensitization, 119–20
Eye contact, 71–72

Facebook, 89–90
Facial expression, 74–75, 83
Fahrner, Homer, 37–38, 79–80
Failure, 135, 244–49, 249–50
Falman, Scott, 94–95
Family issues
  anger, 196, 197
  balancing priorities, 226–28
  children, 97–99, 160–62
  mother-daughter relationships, 163
  need for assertiveness, 166
  obstacles to assertiveness, 34
  practice situations, 273–75
  seesaw analogy, 159–60
  seniors, 163–65
  teens/adults, 162–63
Fears. See Anxiety
Feedback on assertiveness, 103–5, 141, 210–11
Feeling Better, Getting Better, Staying Better, 111

Feelings, taking responsibility for, 198, 201, 203, 205
Flowers, John, 247
FMRI (functional magnetic resonance imaging), 146, 151
Fodor, Iris, 163
Forgiveness, 153, 200
Friedman, Meyer, 191–93
Friedman, Thomas, 48–49
Friends and assertiveness training, 252, 255–58
Fromm, Eric, 148
Functional magnetic resonance imaging, 146, 151

Gates, Melinda, 113–14
Gender differences, 26–30, 156–58
The Gentle Art of Verbal Self-Defense, 82–83
Gestures, 73–74
Global perspectives, 158, 268–70
Goals, 59–61, 64–68, 138, 205–6
Goleman, Daniel, 102–3, 151
Goodman, Ellen, 245
Gordon, Thomas, 81–82
Gray, John, 157
Greenfield, Sheldon, 264–65
Guidelines
    for anger resolution, 197–203
    for asking questions, 221
    for dealing with difficult people, 235–36
    for twenty-first century messages, 91–93
    for workplace issues, 215–16, 220–21, 224–25

Haney, Michele, 128
Hazards/dangers, *See* Risky situations

Health and anger, 191–94, 196
Healthcare assertiveness, 264–65
Help from therapists, 134, 140
Hippocampus, 194–95
Holistic health, 263
Hollandsworth, James, 82
Holmes, Oliver Wendell Jr., 45, 48, 270
Honesty, 156
Hostility syndrome, 193, 264
How a Friend Can Help statement, 256–57
How to Fail as a Therapist, 247
How You Feel Is Up to You, 201
Human Potential Movement, 61
Humor, 234
Hunt, Morton, 65–66

Ideals, models as, 64–65
I-messages, 81, 236
Independence, 162
Indirect aggression, 42, 173, 210–11
Individuality in assertiveness, 33–34, 260, 266–67
    See also Situational aspect of assertiveness
Inhibitors of assertiveness, 8–9, 33–36, 105–7
Inner critics, 208
Insecurity, 43–44
Instant messages, 89–90, 96–97
Integrative medicine, 263
Intent of behaviors, 47
International Trainers in Communication, 76
Interviews, job, 218–20
Intimacy
    ACCEPT model, 168–69
    changing views of, 171–72
    defined, 168–69

Intimacy *(cont'd.)*
  practice situations, 275–76
  See also Sexual issues
Intimacy Attitudes and Behaviors
    chart, 171–72
Intimidation, 271
Ireland, Kathy, 153
Irrational beliefs, 78–79, 110–11, 124

Jacobson, Edmund, 122–23
James, William, 50
Jobs. *See* Workplace issues
Journals
  analyzing fears in, 116–17, 118
  goal-setting and, 61, 64
  role of, 19–22
  sample pages, 18
  tracking progress with, 138, 142

Kabat-Zinn, Jon, 123
Kaplan, Sherrie, 264–65
Kassinove, Howard, 194, 195
Kindness, 266

Laughter, 200, 234
Lazarus, Arnold, 118–19, 124, 170
Leadership guidelines, 224–25
Lifemanship, 233
Listening skills, 77–78, 180, 200, 220
Local Heroes, 37–38
Looking for Spinoza, 103
Love, 148, 169–70
  See also Caring feelings

MacDonald, Allan, 259–60
Manipulation, 266, 271
*Master Your Panic and Take Back Your
    Life*, 124, 128
McKay, Gary, 201
Measurement of assertiveness, 12–16

Medication, 126–27
Meditation, 122, 200
Meichenbaum, Donald, 78–79, 107
Memory bank of experiences, 188
Men and assertiveness, 28–30
Mental health websites, 289–90
Messages. *See* Communication
Mirror neurons, 9, 83, 139
Model for Personal Growth,
    Behavioral, 62–63
Modeling behavior, 64–65, 139,
    140–41, 235
Mother-daughter relationships,
    63
MySpace, 89–90, 97–98

Nass, Clifford, 95
Nature and nurture, 146–47
Negative thoughts
  catastrophisizing, 110–11
  irrational beliefs, 124
  strategies for stopping, 108–9,
    111–12, 124
  stress inoculation, 107–8
  See also Thinking patterns
Negotiation, 180, 206, 216–17
No-fault insurance, 234
Nonassertive behavior, 15, 39–43,
    52–58, 212
Nonverbal communication
  eye contact, 71–72
  facial expression, 74–75, 211–12
  gestures, 73–74, 211–12
  physical distance/closeness, 73
  posture, 72–73
  role-playing different styles,
    70–71
  in sexual situations, 176
  watching for, 253
Nurture and nature, 146–47

Observation of behaviors, 137–39
Obstacles to assertion, 20, 105–7, 242, 244–49
OFC (orbitofrontal cortex), 101–2, 195–96
One-size-fits-all mentality, 247–48
One-upmanship, 233
Online messages, 93–99
Online resources, 289–90
Orbitofrontal cortex, 101–2, 195–96
Our Town, 268
Overapologizing, 254
Overdone assertiveness, 252
Overstimulation, 200

Panic attacks, 123–24
Parental issues, 162
Parent Effectiveness Training, 81–82
Performance anxiety, 216
Persistence, 38, 79–81, 250, 267
Person and situation specific, 43, 49, 248
Personality and brain development, 4
Phelps, Stanlee, 26–28, 210
Phobias. *See* Anxiety
Physical closeness/distance, 73
Pogrebin, Letty Cottin, 155
Politeness, 40, 45, 153, 266
Political institutions, 35–36
Positive thoughts, 109–10, 131–33, 140
Posture, body, 72–73
Potter, Stephen, 233
Practice situations. *See* Rehearsals
Priorities, 67–68, 226–28
Project Write, 117
Psychoneuroimmunology, 263–65
Psychosomatic reactions, 254
Public assertiveness, 269–70
Put-downs, 209–11

Questions, 221, 238–43, 247

Rating scale for criticism, 209
Rational brain. *See* Orbitofrontal cortex
Rational Emotive Behavior Therapy, 124
Receiver-sender behavior chart, 40–41
Recorders, tape/digital, 75–76
Refusal skills, 28, 260
Rehearsals
  benefits, 267, 282
  importance of, 132, 140–41
  proceeding to "real world" tests, 141–42
  See also under specific situations
Reinforcement of behaviors, 134, 142, 166
Relationships and anger, 197
Relaxation training, 119, 122, 202
Repetition of new behaviors, 141, 142
Respectfulness, 23, 99, 266
Responsibility for feelings, 198, 201, 203, 205
Revenge, 254–55
Risky situations
  AIDS exposure, 184
  as consequence of assertion, 242–43, 260
  in cyberspace, 97–98
  in post-9/11 world, 48–50
  in workplace, 240
Rogers, Carl, 61
Roker, Al, 153–54
Role-playing, 70–71
Rosenman, Ray, 191–93
Rosenthal, Howard, 23
Ruts, avoiding, 266

Safer sex, 177, 183–84
Safety online, 97–99
Salter, Andrew, 233
Saying no, 67, 99, 179, 180–82, 215, 255
Schools, 34, 279–81
Schwalbe, Will, 94
Schwartz, Bernard, 247
"See-how-bad-he-is" style, 190–91
Seesaw analogy, 159–60
Self-awareness, 111, 201
Self-concepts, 43–44, 106
Self-statements
    defeatist attitude, 70, 100, 132–33,
        212–13
    irrationality in, 124
    positive thoughts, 109–10, 131–33,
        140
Send, 94
Sender-receiver behavior chart, 40–41
Senior Gleaners, 37, 79–80
Seniors, 163–65
Serber, Michael, 71, 76, 145–46
Setbacks, 134
    See also Failure
Sex education, 176
Sex roles, 26–30, 156–58
Sexual Communication Types,
    173–76
Sexual issues
    assertive women and, 27
    boundaries, 44
    communication, 173–76
    intimacy compared to, 167–69
    practice situations, 177–79, 276
    safer sex, 177, 183–84
    skills for assertiveness, 179–82
    social aspects of, 170, 176–77
    unwanted advances, 180–82
    See also Intimacy
Shapiro, Francine, 125

Shipley, David, 94
Shyness, 9, 114, 146, 248
Situational aspect of assertiveness, 7,
    15–16, 19, 49–50, 248
    See also Individuality in
        assertiveness
Situations, examples of, 52–58
    Skill deficits, 20, 248
Sleep, 121–22
Small steps, 65, 72, 120, 135, 270
Social institutions, 35–36
Social intelligence, 4
Social Intelligence, 103, 151
Social learning, 146–48
Social practice situations, 281–82
Social reinforcement, 142
Sociocultural context of behaviors, 47
Solomon, Robert, 169–70
Spontaneity, 77, 156
Step-by-step process, 65–66, 137–44,
    248, 250, 270–71
Stereotypes, 28–30, 32
Stress, 107–8, 231–32, 263–65
The Stress Owner's Manual, 128
Subjective units of discomfort,
    115–16, 118
Substance abuse, 197, 200
Success, beginning with, 133–34
SUD (subjective units of discomfort),
    115–16, 118
Supervisors, 223–24
Surgeon General, US, 184
Syntonics, 82–83, 233
Systematic desensitization, 118–19

Tafrate, Chip, 194, 195
Tanabe-Endsley, Patsy, 117
Tannen, Deborah, 157
Tantrums, 189
Tavris, Carol, 189

Technology issues, 89–91
Teens, 162–63
Telephone messages, 93
Temperament, 146–47
Temper tantrums, 254
Tests, real world, 141–42
Text messages, 91, 98
Therapy, 21–22, 134, 140, 258
Therapy's Best, 23
Thermometer model of anger, 194, 195
Thinking patterns
  changing, 107–12
  for dealing with difficult people, 230–31
  effect on behavior, 78–79, 100–101
  as obstacle to assertion, 103–7
  positive thoughts, 109–10, 131–33, 140
  See also Negative thoughts; Self-statements
Thought stopping, 108–9
The Time of Your Life, 164
Timing
  of assertive expressions, 77, 234, 241, 260–62
  of goals, 66–67
  in workplace, 223
Toastmasters, 76
Tolerance, 200
Tracking growth, 17–22, 138, 142
Truss, Lynne, 96
Trust in yourself, 63
Twenty-first century issues
  message guidelines, 91–93
  risky situations, 48–50
  technology, 89–91
  women, 26–28
Twitter, 90, 98
Type A behavior, 191–93

Understanding Emotions, 103
Unfinished business, 260–62
Universal Declaration of Human Rights, 24–25
Unwanted sexual advances, 180–82

Violence, 45–46
  See also Aggression
Viorst, Judith, 167
Visualization, 138, 139–40
Voice qualities, 75–76

War, 45–46
Web resources, 99, 289–90
Weil, Andrew, 263
What Color Is Your Parachute?, 217–18
Wheeler, Eugenie, 164
Wilder, Thornton, 268
Williams, Redford and Virginia, 193, 198, 199, 201, 264
Withdrawal, 234
Wolfe, Janet, 163
Wolpe, Joseph, 108, 115, 118–19, 124
Women, assertiveness of, 26–28
Workplace issues
  anger, 197
  assertiveness guidelines, 215–16, 220–21
  co-worker relationships, 221–22
  job searching, 217–20
  leadership guidelines, 224–25
  obstacles to assertiveness, 34–35, 214–15
  practice situations, 278–79
  supervisors, dealing with, 223–24
World citizenship, 158, 268–70
World Health Organization, 170

YouTube, 89–91, 98, 158

More Books With IMPACT

Please see the following page for more books.

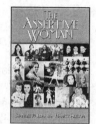